AN ENCYCLOPAEDIA OF MYSELF

Also by Jonathan Meades

Filthy English
Peter Knows What Dick Likes
Pompey
Incest and Morris Dancing
The Fowler Family Business
Museum Without Walls
Pidgin Snaps

AN ENCYCLOPAEDIA OF MYSELF

Jonathan Meades

FOURTH ESTATE • *London*

Fourth Estate
An imprint of HarperCollins*Publishers*
77–85 Fulham Palace Road,
Hammersmith, London W6 8JB
www.4thestate.co.uk

First published in Great Britain by Fourth Estate in 2014

1

Jonathan Meades asserts the moral right to
be identified as the author of this work

Parts of this book have appeared in different forms in
London: City of Disappearances, *Granta*, the *New Yorker* and *The Times*

A catalogue record for this book
is available from the British Library

ISBN 978-1-85702-849-2

Set in Sabon 11.25/15.3pt
Typeset by Palimpsest Book Production Limited, Falkirk, Stirlingshire

Printed and bound in Great Britain by
Clays Ltd, St Ives plc

MIX
Paper from
responsible sources

FSC
www.fsc.org **FSC® C007454**

For The Dead

Nothing wilfully invented.
Memory invents unbidden.

ABUSER, SEXUAL

Not applicable. I have no sexual abuser to confront.

There was no simpering, gingivitic distant cousin with crinklecut hair who beseeched me to come and play with a special mauve toy.

No wispily moustached, overfriendly, oversweaty 'friend-of-the-family' whom I was made to address as aunt, who tucked me up then, who must be hunted down now. What, anyway, was signified by that odd epithet? Could the 'friend-of-the-family' not make up its mind whom, in particular, in the family, it was a friend of? My family did not have 'friends-of-the-family'. 'Friend-of-the-family' is as much an alarm bell as 'magician and children's entertainer'.

No doddering nonagenarian former 'magician and children's entertainer' whose dirty secret was buried half a century ago and is now all but lost in the soup of dementia.

No lissom-fingered groin-pirate for me to approach as he opens his gate, all crazed-paint and rot. A ragged cotoneaster hedge flanks the gate. I can see the mange-like patches where the bungalow's render has slipped to reveal the friable bricks. The own-brand Scotch in his naugahyde bag weighs down that bad bad hand of his.

No failed oboist, foxed scores all around, listening covetously to a prodigious pupil, gazing at a soggy autumn garden and broken paling.

No, no, none of those. I was not, in the brusque cant of the day, interfered with. I didn't have what it takes. No adult wanted to love me that way. I was pretty enough, but it takes more than prettiness. It takes foolhardy insouciance, it takes uncomprehending nerve to return the stare of the not yet abuser, the tempter, and so, in his eyes, legitimise the compact and become

I

complicit, willing and an equal partner in sex crime. Only the rash venture into the unknown from which there is no chaste return. I never had that rashness, was never a daredevil. Look right look left look right again – then repeat it all.

So, now a pre-dotard, I am left bereft. I am denied the *sine qua non* of recollective bitterness, mnemonic poignancy. Denied a cause of self-pity . . . *a* cause? *The* cause. Denied, then, the chance to incite the pity of others, to milk the world's sympathy gland. I lack the paramount qualification of the auto-encyclopaedist. No abuser (I am, apparently, unique in this) – no abuser, so no life, no story.

Were I to stroll down False Memory Lane at dusk I might pick out a mac lurking in the grubby alders beside a playground: You there! You . . .

But that would to be to invoke nothing but dated cliché. Playgrounds! Macs! The predator surely wouldn't announce himself by that dun uniform: he'd have had a gift for camouflage, he'd have been in mufti, he'd have been anywhere but on the school bus.

As well as cliché it would be a lie. There are strata of mendacity best left unbroached.

Why be so fastidious? Lies are humans' desperate balms and risible solaces.

Where would we be without monotheism, fasts, judicial impartiality, the eucharist, sincerity, pork's proscription, Allah's ninety-nine names and seventy-two virgins, weather forecasts, life plans, political visions, conjugated magpies, circumcision, sacred cows, the power of prayer, insurance policies, gurus' prescriptions, the common good, astrology?

Where indeed?

But those are the big lies.

Little lies, microfibs, are different. They are insidious. They go undetected, pebbles added furtively to a cairn. Every time I write *once upon a time* I am, anyway, already exhuming the disputable, conjuring a photocopy of a faded print made from a detrited negative. I am striving to distinguish the original from its replays. So why add to the store of the provisional? The forms and shades of what used to be are already hideously mutable, every act of recall is both an erosion and an augmentation. I remember therefore I reshape.

Further, memory is susceptible to contamination by a secondary memory, of the place where I find myself when the first occurs. Thus I cannot help but picture the swaying mane of the weeping willow I was dozing beneath at East Harnham in summer 1996 when my mind was suddenly filled with a dizzy, joyful, chlorinated night more than thirty years before, the night I cut the ball of my right foot beside the swimming pool at West Park Farm (broken glass? crown cork?), didn't realise I had done so and laid a trail of blood through the loud house where teenagers clutching bottles of fruitgum-bright liqueurs shed inhibitions and just a few clothes.

The secondary location seeps into what is playing in my inner cinema just as the Gaumont's hefty 1930s-Tudorish décor would intrude on the purity of the screen's illusionism. Westerns' canyons, gulleys and hoodoos, Denver Pyle's badman grin in *The Restless Gun*, the tarred hut on the dunes in *Forbidden Cargo* where Joyce Grenfell and Nigel Patrick pretend to be ornithologists, *West of Zanzibar*'s smugglers' dhows, the shack-like Snowdonian garage that yields the clue to Jack Hawkins in *The Long Arm*: they were infuriatingly framed by beams, halberds, casques, tapestries, chandeliers. These interventions from a competing pageant exacerbated my inability to distinguish between the fictive, the factual, the fantastical.

The formula states that adults are wicked predators, children are innocent prey. In the hierarchy of abuse, paedophilia (which may be literally that, liking children) is demonised, fetishised. It has giddily attained equal status with race crime. (Stabbing an Arab in a Maida Hill launderette simply because she is an Arab is a more serious offence than stabbing her because she jumped the queue for the one functioning dryer or pocketed a garment left in the lugubrious drum by the previous user or because she is a woman. She can of course take comfort from this knowledge as she loses consciousness on a reddening moraine of fresh-baked sheets. The culprit, the gravity of whose crime is determined by motive rather than effect, will, if arraigned, plead a different cause and claim that his action was motivated by something apart from race and 'otherness'.) Homo faber. Isn't he just? Man has devised multitudinous forms of child abuse which are not sexual. Not covertly sexual, not displacedly sexual. Their immeasurable consequences may, however, be just as grave as those of sexual abuse.

Child soldier, child slave, child labourer, child miner, child skiv, child beggar, child bloody from scrounging in the shambles.

There were children before there was childhood. There have always been children. There has not always been childhood. Steam, foundries, pollution, unprecedented urban concentrations, megalopolitan sprawl, soot, canalisation, dams – the industrial revolution's manifestations were, as early as 1873, described by

Antonio Stoppani as 'a new telluric force which in power and universality may be compared to the greater forces of earth'. Since then the world's population has multiplied fivefold. Humankind propels the atmosphere. It has unwittingly created a geological age which the meteorologist and chemist Paul Crutzen named the anthropocene.

Modern western European childhood is a by-product of industrial revolutions, thus an invention of adults. It is protracted, an antechamber to longed-for adulthood, a mere waiting room before we achieve the real thing. Whilst it is hardly an abuse, it is a temporal space where communitarianism and generational apartheid are enforced. Its characteristic condition is attritional boredom, a boredom that foments the desire to escape, no matter how, and to punish the captors. Until the era of enclosures, rural diaspora and urbanisation, childhood had been the province of the lettered classes. Thereafter, throughout the nineteenth century childhood, like recreational drugs in the later twentieth century, became gradually democratised, available to all save the very poor (who needed it most). The change is readily ascribable to a succession of education acts which ordained the free provision of schooling and ever more elongated compulsory attendance. Schools occasioned a concentration of coevals: the child spends most of his time with other children.

We take for granted the existence of commercial stratagems to confine children to a specifically infantile ghetto, to prolong the age of play, to emphasise their separateness, to profit from an exclusive and imposed subculture. Yet these stratagems are of comparatively recent foundation. They devolve from the invention of childhood. They are conditional upon mass production, the separation of home and work, the statutory compulsion to submit to education after the end of physical childhood. They extend childhood, they inhibit its elision with adulthood. Not least because what follows is of course another commercially determined niche age, an even more recent created parenthesis:

when my parents were teenagers there were no such persons, they often reminded me, as teenagers. We are persistently shocked when children go straight from Lego to legover. We shouldn't be. It is as though there is a collective will to stunt them with toys, to prolong infantilism and delude ourselves about states of innocence. It is as though we creepily wish to put the pituitary gland on hold and keep them kiddies for ever. The 'us' in Toys 'Я' Us is adults who are perennially keen to keep children in stasis, to freeze them at whatever stage of development is sentimentalised as 'such a lovely age'.

When, after they had both died, I sold my parents' house, I got rid of a cupboardful of toys which had collected decades' dust, and a bookcase of *Eagle* annuals, *Tiger* annuals, *Buffalo Bill* annuals and so on. I picked through tins of broken pens and perished erasers. I wondered where my model cowboys and Indians had got to then recalled that I had lent them to Roger's younger brother when I had 'grown out' of them and had never bothered to get them back. I excitedly anticipated that the past would come rushing back. Each of these rusting tarnished pieces of metal or plastic is, surely, a potential trigger, a mnemonic of some bright day in 1959, a correlative of a particular sensation. They were however doggedly mute. A brown and cream Dinky Austin Atlantic even prompted a chronological anomaly, the recollection that when I was about twenty I had met what wouldn't have then been called an Austin Atlantic anorak who collected lifesize editions of that pseudo-American tourer. It took time in that house whose purpose was finished to realise that this was a pitiful and self-pitying exercise: I was trying to freeze myself, to transport myself back to the land of yore, to dream days which had, actually, been no such thing. I was trying to do to myself what parents do to their children.

A further persuasively significant foundation of childhood was the separation of workplace from home and the consequent separation of children from adults. Thitherto children routinely enjoyed prepubertal sex. They also endured incestuous liaisons, were bound in endogamy, or something closely related to it: life was, after all, as predatory adults realised, short.

> *Ci-gît le fils, ci-gît la mère,*
> *Ci-gît la fille avec le père,*
> *Ci-gît la soeur, ci-gît le frère,*
> *Ci-gît la femme et le mari,*
> *Et ne sont que trois corps ici.*

The Levitical taboos on incest – which don't extend to cousins – were widely ignored. Notably in remote fastnesses and the backwoods. Hence, no doubt, the plentiful supply of village idiots, victims of primal concupiscence and of a feast of recessive afflictions: respiratory problems, developmental stasis, albinism, seizures, club feet, renal and hepatic failures, tons o' snot, pallor, involuntary urination, jabbering, short life etc. Improved economic conditions, increased longevity, embourgeoisement, urban propriety and internal migration appear to have lessened the incidence in Britain of intrafamilial intercourse save among Muslims.

This prosperity and civility which encouraged sexual restraint (and moral repugnance at the absence of such restraint) were enjoyed by an ascending proportion of the populace which now lived in disgusted fear of the feral inbreds at the gates, whom they longed to hang or to transport at the first sign of a mare's slashed belly or burning rick.

Rather than rape its own children this new middle class beat them instead. There, that's a kind of progress.

The anthropocene childhood has changed. But only so much. Like education, which is, astonishingly, still symbolic of it, childhood may have become increasingly 'child-centred' rather than 'adult-centred' aka 'sadist-centred' which is the form of education still practised in preposterous faith schools with their mission to beat the biddable into superstitious submission. But 'child-centred' childhood still remains within the ghetto of adult creation. The ghetto that children yearn to escape from is now more gadget-strewn though hardly cushier. Childhood is the condition of wanting to be someone else. In play we seek to emulate the behaviour of adults, our wishfulness caused us to become grocers or soldiers, cowboys or tractor drivers. (Evidently a generationally biased list of models. Today's children long to be body-piercers, security consultants, the mutant subjects of the tattoos themselves.)

Rather, we *ought* to yearn to escape the ghetto. But when we have escaped we discover that its pull is that of the superstition that tempts the atheist, the tenderness that infects the murderer. Childhood tugs at our sleeve all our life. Look at moron executives bonding through paintballing, look at the queues in airports wearing kiddie clothes, look at them unabashedly reading J. K. Rowling. (Would an adult of my childhood have read Richmal Crompton – and in public?)

Such infantilism is a pathetic refuge. It signals a forlorn effort to be a child again, despite the bulbous evidence of the body distended by sweet comforting childish foodstuffs and the actual children who clamorously demand more, more. It's a delusory rebirth which can convince only those with a capacity for faith and credulousness. The recall of childhood from a distance – as though peering into a glass cabinet whilst wearing a sterilised mask and surgically scrubbed gloves – is different. It does not imply a denial of adulthood, it is not a soft self-abasement which sweeps us sartorially and mentally backwards. Nor does it imply that what is recalled was actual and enjoyed an existence beyond the laboratory of our imaginings.

There were projects that never, so to speak, came to fruition, never could have done. At the age of eight I began to conjure up the future, year by year. This prospective speculation was of the lowest grade, a series of acquired banalities which did not come to pass. Nonetheless it remains potently limpid. For instance, when I was ten – still a long way off – I would definitely be going on very long bike rides through a sandy terrain of broom, gorse and scattered pines (I sense the sea was close by, though it was not visible). The sun shone. I would be laughing and picnicking with healthy, Aertex-clad coevals apparently plucked from the pages of Enid Blyton though I did not then recognise that source. We would compare bicycles in amiable competition: the merits of Campagnolo and Simplex gears and their superiority to Sturmey-Archer, drinking flasks, brake systems (cable, calliper brakes were old hat), tyre makes and pressures etc. This fantasy was partly learnt from advertisements of the period, again unacknowledged. Partly from frequenting Hayball's cycle shop and scrutinising the ranks of Rudges, Hercules, Raleighs, BSAs. The fancy stuff like Dawes and Claud Butler were hung from beams. The shop's odour was that of clean oil. It was a serious place. The beefy bespectacled Hayball in a brown warehouseman's coat never smiled.

That outdoorsiness and sportiness should have informed so much of my imagined future suggests that I had only the frailest grasp of my capabilities. When I was thirteen I would be opening the batting for an eminent if undefined cricket team with my imaginary friend Andrew Parker. In fact I was a laughably incompetent cricketer. Had I dared wear glasses I might have ascended to mediocrity. But I didn't because I feared losing an eye to a shard of lens, shattered by an improbably fast schoolboy bouncer. After the age of nine when my (unfulfilled) promise as a swimmer was recognised I was seldom obliged to play cricket. Now I dreamed of emulating teenage Olympians such as the Aberdonian Ian Black and Neil McKechnie who advertised Horlicks and came from Wallasey, which I knew to be nearby the glamorous-sounding New Brighton. My photograph would appear in the *Eagle* diary with my freestyle and butterfly records listed beneath.

> *Hark hark the dogs do bark!*
> *The beggars are coming to town.*
> *Some in rags and some in tags*
> *And one in a velvet gown.*

The rhyme was hardly affecting.

The illustration, in a poster style brazenly filched from the Beggarstaff Brothers, terrified me. The leader of the motley sordids was indeed resplendent in a scraggy, ermine-trimmed ceremonial robe – a hanging judge's twin gone to the bad. He was gross, ruddy, unshaven, voracious, with obese predatory lips, a prognathous jaw and bared mustard-coloured teeth. Here was a truly aggressive beggar, a figure of abominable daymares. And my parents abandoned me to him. The very presence of the book on a shelf near my bed was discomfiting. Yet I was drawn to this beggar-king and, all affright, I would dare myself to peep at him with the pages hardly parted before I snapped them shut again lest he escape into the room. He was not the only figure I feared. Many of my earliest books had been my mother's. A child born in 1912 was routinely subjected to imaginative horrors that her son, a New Elizabethan born thirty-five years later, might easily have been spared, protected from in that golden age of euphemism and evasion which saw our young Queen crowned. But I wasn't spared: my mother still had those books, Grandma and Pop had not dumped them out the back in the steep alley behind the house in Shakespeare Avenue.

Here were Joseph Martin Kronheim's giants and child-stealers. Here was Gustave Doré's nocturnal butcher slitting the tender throats of sleeping children who had feasted on birds: poisoned birds? Here were the babes in the wood, the dark wood, the eternal wood, asleep now for evermore in each other's arms. And everywhere was Camelot, swathed in dusty crêpe, in tendrils of desiccated caul, haunted, benighted, all decay, all death. Tom the chimney sweep died, he turned into a water baby swaddled in art nouveauish clusters of weed, befriended by crustacea and sea trout. To be a child was to be close to death. How I pitied the boy sailor sprawled weeping across his mother's grave in Arthur Hughes's *Home From Sea*: but at least he had a sister to comfort him, I would have no one. I feared for the filial resolve and life of the grave little boy being interrogated in *And When Did You Last See Your Father?*

I fretted about him. What became of him? I knew all too well what became of the princes in the tower. Prescient of their fate they cowered together on a hamper in their cell or they clung to each other on a four-poster bed or they were smothered with a pillow by an armoured man whose rude companion holds a burning lamp or they were smothered by coarse mechanicals with beards and fringes or their bodies were lowered down a steep staircase by killers with the faces of angels taking them to a better place. Royal, incarcerated, innocent, prepubescent, (perhaps) pretty, defenceless, dead or about to die: the attractions of these victims to Victorian illustrators are evident. But the greatest appeal must have been that the plight of these two hapless princes of long ago would – through chromolithographs, steel prints, etchings, silk Stevengraphs – terrify countless children, incite them to tuck their head beneath an unsmothering pillow and will the image to quit their brain. Those artists manipulated my occiput which tingled in the night. Their gleefully cackling cruelty outlived them. They died knowing that children yet unborn would wake screaming from the nightmares they kindled, the nightmares that I craved: I relished oneiric abuse – the nightmares' foals would do.

I dreamed of malevolent sheep surrounding me near an isolated railway halt in a landscape of drystone walls and tufty grass. Every attempt to escape over those walls was thwarted by further flocks who penned me in, baaing at high volume till a Wolseley police car arrived to apprehend me.

I dreamed of a lugubrious, flickeringly lit gilded room, with glimmering fabrics, a chaise longue, heavy dark scarlet velvet curtains from behind which, terrified lest I make a sound and am discovered, I spy on a brooding Napoleon. (I had never witnessed a performance of *Hamlet*. But I had read it, slowly, painstakingly. More importantly I had seen stills of distant, dusty productions. Paintings of prince and arras excited me.) There was the flash of a blade, a vegetal tearing and with it a rent in the curtains. Many years later it occurred to me that some part of my brain had, in REM, conflated the names Napoleon and

Polonius and had decreed that my fate should be the latter's at the former's hand: he was, after all, still Boney. I no doubt belong to the last generation of British children to be casually warned of that spectral ogre. Mr Coleman used to caution me: 'Old Boney'll get you if you dawdle about there, Sunny Jim.'

If only! I wanted him to try to get me so I might experience the thrill of being quarry. I would of course escape. 'There' was the covered alley in the middle of the terrace on the other side of the road. It ran between the house where Roger lived with his parents and grandmother and its neighbour: the first floors had a party wall, a sliver of both ground floors had been sacrificed to this narrow passage. It was where I waited for him to come out to play. It led to the perpendicular alley between the Rose and Crown's car park and the gardens of this terrace of about twenty houses (red brick, c.1912, each with *a name* incised in stone beside the front door, as well as a mere number like ours). Mr and Mrs Coleman's house was three away from Roger's.

Mr Coleman, a grocer on his day of rest (Wednesday half-day closing excepted), would open his back gate and say testily: 'Can't you nippers keep it down!'

His tone towards me when I skulked silently was more jocular.

'Can't do better than join 'em when you're big enough, Sunny Jim,' he'd instruct me, well-meaningly, on Wednesday evenings whilst Bishop Wordsworth School's blanco-gaitered Sea Scout Troop, led by a youth twirling a baton with thrilling abandon, marched past hammering their drums and bugling their one and only tune under the martinet's eye of a naval-uniformed and atypically spruce William Golding.

'You make sure you eat them greens, Sunny Jim,' Mr Coleman instructed me, well-meaningly, whilst I queued on my mother's behalf at Mr Rose's vegetable van.

'Enjoy your pop, Sunny Jim!' he'd instruct me, well-meaningly, whilst I bought my two bottles (fluorescent lime and American cream soda) from the gleaming Corona lorry. I resented being addressed as Sunny Jim. But I didn't show it, would not have dared answer him back, for I knew that the reason the Colemans never smiled was that their son had been taken from them. Listening to the whoops and cries of their boy's living contemporaries can only have intensified their loss. There were now just the two of them. It was for only five years that there had been the three of them. It must have been grief that made Mrs Coleman pendulous-breasted, gingery-grey, myopic, musty, thin-lipped: staleness surrounded her. It must have been grief that made Mr Coleman glue hair from faraway sources to his pate. My bald father mocked these strands as *grocer's stripes*. They gleamed like oily feathers. The coarse artifice was appealing to a child who preferred plastic to leather, formica to wood, who delighted in prostheses. Every morning save Sunday the Colemans drove in an old Ford delivery van to their little shop where they whiled away their days till they too died. They left Little John Coleman in heaven and in a shaded corner of All Saints churchyard. The dead could be in two places simultaneously. At least two places: Mowbray Meades was in heaven, he was in all his family's heart, he was in a war grave at Lille, where on 9 July 1918 he had succumbed to pneumonia. Afterlife and transubstantiation, prayer, angels, hell, miracles, holy rocks, voices from above, flying horses, visitations and the very notion of the sacred, are creations of aberrant hallucination and desert fasts which might have been expressly devised to ensnare credulous children. There's no more willing religious warrior than the child ignorant of everything save what he is instructed in by his abusive imam, himself in turn a victim of doctrinal abuse – so the wheel goes round: tradition is no more meritorious than is sincerity. The flowers were fresh each week (and still are; a dwarf pine has been recently planted). The tiny headstone was scrubbed.

John Coleman
February 10th 1952
Aged 5 years and 6 months
Happiest Memories

13

I never set eyes on this valetudinarian boy, the subject of whose life was its imminent ending. He was my senior by six months. He lay dying less than fifty yards away across the road whilst I, a longer stretch before me, climbed high in plum trees and hid from marauding Comanches in a gap in between Kalu's hedge, a trunk seeping fat beads of tawny resin and a woven hurdle. He was too feeble to play. He lived in bed in a blanched room matt with sunbeams. His days were all beef tea and expectoration, plumped pillows and the doctor's hushed voice. I knew of his secret existence through murmured hearsay, through rumour's mysterious seepage. He wasn't talked about. He was hidden away. My parents never referred to him, as though infant mortality were itself infectious like polio, myxomatosis for children, the viral Boney of those years that lurked in wait to maim our bodies, to steal them forever.

Infant mortality? Any mortality. Death might go dogging everywhere but how was I to know? Intelligence of the final finality was only grudgingly vouchsafed me by my parents. For all they spoke of death, I might have believed that we live perpetually, growing ever more crooked, more and more dried up, more rasping, more fearful. (I obviously didn't know that it was death's proximity that caused the eyes of the very old to communicate unimaginable terror.) Did my parents talk of it in camera where the renchild could not hear? I doubt it. It hurt my father too much to consider it. Death was denied by near-silence: what was not spoken of did not exist. So it was not addressed, nor were dying and the invisible invaders which honeycomb this internal organ and make leather of that one. The names of the dead were dropped from conversation, as one might drop that of a disloyal friend. Death seemed to be a kind of disgrace. The dead were somehow culpable. They brought it upon themselves. The rare times they were remembered, it was with irked brusqueness. This quasi-muteness might have been designed to protect me from a truth that was evidently considered just about unspeakable. It more likely derived from the near-paralysis that any thought of his father's death caused my father.

George Meades had died at the age of forty-one in 1920 when his third child and second son was eleven years old. John Meades, who twenty-seven years later would become my father (twenty-six, if measured by the Seathwaite Conception), considered, so far as I could ascertain, that this premature departure was a gross betrayal, like that of a star batsman who has too easily surrendered his wicket to his team's cost. (This *must* be an exceptional matter: I have never before used a cricketing simile.) Apprised by life's whispering campaign that all this ends for all of us, I asked my father about his father's death. He regarded me with astonished hurt that turned into a defensive flinch I had not seen before, it was an expression of vulnerability that a more malign (or less timid) son might have exploited. I had neither the nous nor the will.

'How did he die?'

Perhaps he pretended to himself that his father had never existed. He had no photo of him. I had furtively pocketed one that I found buried among piles of *Picture Post* and tobacco tins filled with screws and wingnuts in the shed behind my grandmother's house in Northwick Road where, equally, he wasn't on display. It was obvious whom the photo showed – he was the double of his eldest son Harry, my uncle Hank, save that the ambit of his eyes was sooty with disease or fatigue.

'Died in the night. Been ill. Grandma told us in the morning.'

My father glared a furious and wounded warning. I knew I must never again ask about, never again even mention my grandfather. And I didn't.

Was George Meades, as my father had it, a solicitor and Evesham's part-time town clerk? In Hank's version he was a solicitor who contributed law notes to the Harmsworth press. I suspect that they had both promoted him out of filial pride. Or out of social shame: they wanted to elevate themselves just as their father, son of a joiner, had wanted to elevate himself by membership of a profession, cynosure of the unimaginatively aspirant. The house in Northwick Road – mean, terraced, dark, no bathroom, outside toilet – was improbably the home of a middle-aged solicitor. And Kitty recalled riding with him across the hills in a dog cart to Chipping Camden where he collected rents, a task more likely undertaken by a solicitor's *clerk* rather than a solicitor. In the year of his death he had passed the Law Society's examinations in trusts, accounting and bookkeeping. Did those successes complete a tardy qualification or was there further struggle and exhausting lucubration to come? With bitchy glee Kitty observed to my then wife that Meades men don't live long lives. My father once pointed to a double-fronted stucco villa around the corner from Northwick Road near St Peter's church and ruefully observed: 'That was where we were just about to move to.'

Further wishfulness? Or was this true? And, if so, was his resentment then worldly, a festering regret about a property denied him, about status unattained? It wasn't a matter that my father did much to rectify. He had no aptitude for making money, a resigned contempt for those, like Smoothie Derek, who had, and would not own a house till he was fifty-three.

Death was, then, off limits with my father. He told me in a matter-of-fact way that my maternal grandmother had died the previous night as we passed the church at Fugglestone late one Sunday afternoon: I had been sent to the Lush family for the weekend, presumably in anticipation of her death, of whose imminence I had of course not been foretold. 'Mummy's upset.'

Charles Wallis, brother of Barnes, married Christine Benn – his first and only, her third (first widowed, second divorced). She cooked Anglo-Indian curries which my father scorned as inauthentic. I was thus obliged to pretend to him that I did not enjoy them. She lived with her two sons in a flat at the top of an Edwardian house overlooking Chafyn Grove School's lopsided playing fields. The flat below was occupied by a couple with the fine name of Saxon-Harold. Charles was a gentle decent man who rarely shed his crisp white mac. He was amused by my fondness for The Platters' 'Smoke Gets In Your Eyes', a song he recalled from the version in a film of the 1930s. He drowned on his honeymoon trying to save a child in difficulty in a Cornish bay. He was mourned by my father: 'Christine isn't taking it too well.'

Anthony, the infant son of my parents' bent solicitor Eric Broad, had also drowned, early in the war, a few hundred yards upstream from our house. There was little sympathy for his negligent parents who had left him in the garden.

Both the great horn player Denis Brain and the heir to the Sun-Pat peanut butter fortune died at the wheel of sports cars. That was the way to go.

My mother taught Mary N——, the daughter of an army family. In her early twenties, after a brief failed marriage, she took to prostitution in Bristol. She was strangled by a john. My mother, reading a newspaper report, shrugged as though there was an inevitability to that end and that surprise was misplaced although sympathy wasn't.

Although my mother's instinct might have been to speak to me about death with qualified candour she acceded to my father's will. Together they were conjoined in reticence. When alone with me she was slightly more open though hardly voluble. So I developed (or inherited by mimesis) a guardedness in public whilst cultivating a clandestine obsession with the forbidden: if the living reckoned it was *that* terrible there must be something to it. Like winklepickers, illegitimacy, tinned salmon, canals, hair cream and gross nipples it was a secret vice to be shamefully indulged, guiltily pored over and obviously not admitted. I kept deaths to myself.

Jolyon Spiller. Late August 1957. Richard Griffiths sat down beside me at the Cathedral School swimming pool and told me his father had just been phoned: a fatal bicycle accident in Sherborne. Two years later his father Laurence Griffiths, head-master of the Cathedral School, was giving me daily lessons during the holiday to remedy my innumeracy. I arrived at his house beside the school at 9.30 sharp. The door was opened by his elder daughter Lilian. She told me that her father was unwell. I learned a few hours later that he had died in the night. Her calm stoicism was extraordinary.

David Hayden. September 1958. It was said that his parents, coach tour operators, never got over the loss of their beefy son whose brother had already died. Alan Moss, elder brother of my contemporary Melodie, was injured and hospitalised. Car crash near Tilshead on Salisbury Plain.

Richard Sturdy. April 1959. He and his father, a Wareham vet, were drowned when their skiff capsized in Poole Harbour. I heard from a friend whom I had run into outside Beach's bookshop, my de facto alma mater; most of the staff had been taught by my mother and were happy to let me sit on the floor reading for hours on end without pressing me to buy anything.

Seven years earlier, in February 1952, I had been on the very same spot with my mother when she noticed the lowered flag above the Close Gate and realised that King George VI had died. We were on our way to The House of Steps a few yards away. My first act as a New Elizabethan was to eat hot buttered crum-pets in that most sinisterly named tea-rooms from whose owner my parents bought my first bicycle when his son Peter Rothwell had outgrown it: a maroon BSA with a curved crossbar, an American design made under licence.

Spiller and Sturdy were my fellow pupils though I hardly knew them. David Hayden was seven years my senior. I have no idea how I met him. But at the age of eleven my aptitude for indiscriminate acquaintanceship was already coming along hummingly.

Since my parents had improbably heard of any one of them during their life I didn't bother to familiarise them with them now dead. My silence, in these instances, was guiltless.

It was not always so.

A. Hand & Son (groceries, provisions, post office) stood on the corner of Ayleswade Road, Harnham Road and St Nicholas Road, at whose southern end two bridges cross branches of the Avon: the houses between the bridges were often flooded and A. Hand was not immune. As the handle of a high-geared Berkel bacon slicer was turned ponderously the blade rotated at twenty times the speed in an enticingly lethal blur which prompted me to tuck my scrotum between my legs. A spiral staircase rose to a storeroom, and a wooden ladder, smooth as a shove-ha'penny coin, to the highest shelves whose glass-fronted compartments held cotton reels, Kirby grips, pins, needles, decorative combs, Germolene and lint. A wire-mesh screen signified the post office area.

Period product inventory. Hairy cardboard boxes; hairy Izal toilet paper; Weston's Wagon Wheels; Nestlé's segmental chocolate bars with green mint filling and green wrappers, Fry's segmental chocolate bars with white mint filling and navy wrappers; Fry's Turkish Delight; Crosse & Blackwell Russian Salad; Trex; Robinsons Lemon Barley Water; Kia-Ora (which meant good health – it was everyone's single word of Maori); Walls' disgusting pork sausages; Millers' even more disgusting pork pies; Smiths Crisps (which often weren't); parlously balanced displays of Daz, Omo, Persil; Weetabix, Grape-Nuts (for the cleaner colon), Welgar Shredded Wheat from Welwyn Garden City (the name suggested a corner of paradise); Keillers butterscotch; individual fruit pies; Lyle's Golden Syrup (Out of the strong came forth sweetness); packet soups; tinned soups, fruit salad and cling peaches; bottled sauces – A.1., HP, OK, Daddies, Heinz Salad Cream and ketchup; cut flowers in dank water according to season; glass jars of Black Jacks, bullseyes, aniseed balls, licorice allsorts and shrill boiled sweets; scrubbing brushes; Oxo and Bovril; Rowntree's Fruit Gums (which caused mouth ulcers) and Fruit Pastilles (which didn't); baskets of wasp-bored apples and blighted vegetables; towers of biscuits; Camp Coffee; Shipham's Paste; Sandwich Spread; Sun-Pat peanut butter (smooth – crunchy was still far in the future); Energen rolls and Dutch rusks; red Edam, mousetrap henges, St Ivel lactic cheese and Dairylea; Nestlé condensed milk (sweetened for instant sick), Ideal Milk (evaporated); Spangles and Refreshers; stacks of the *Salisbury Journal*, the *Salisbury Times, Harnham Parish Magazine*.

Dun split peas in burlap sacks seemed hopelessly old-fashioned among the gaudily packaged products of the first age of food colouring.

By the summer of 1956 an up-to-the-minute freezer had been wedged into a corner beside the slicer and window display to store ice cream, Koola Frutas, Mivvis, Birds Eye fish fingers, Findus fish cakes, Ross peeled prawns and fish and chips in a box designed to resemble crumpled newspaper – a Mudd Pack by H. Mudd & Sons of Grimsby. All this and much more was contained in a shop hardly larger than the combined front and dining rooms of the houses in the adjacent terrace. Mr Hand (cleaner-shaven than his wife, wirewool hair en brosse) had two assistants: the severe, bespectacled Mr Weston (grocer's stripes) and the chummy one (grocer's stripes). They wore long tan warehouse coats. They edged nimbly through canyons of boxes. They clambered daintily over teetering crates. Customers were less practised in negotiating the multiple obstacles. When more than eight people were in the store things went tumbling because of the squash. Everyone was so close you smelled your ripe neighbour. No gossipy whisper went unheard.

Midday, early September 1956. I was waiting in the bunched

queue to be served from the freezer when a woman in a pacamac squeezed into the shop, causing the bell on a spring to ring. There was the usual murmur of 'Good morning or [polite laughter] is it afternoon already?' The pacamac took her place at the back of the queue. And that would have been that had she not espied the fat-arsed woman in front of me. She busied through. She spoke in hush-voice to her friend's ear.

'Did you hear . . . terrible . . . Dr Laing's little boy . . . they don't know if he was thrown off . . . fell he could have fell . . . he fell on his head . . . his own pony . . . brand-new . . . he had one of those hats on cap things but . . . in the field behind their house . . . where the barn is . . . the ambulance took him up Odstock . . . too late they said . . . nothing they could do to save the little mite nothing . . . didn't regain you know . . . died in the theatre . . .'[1]

She wasn't as hugger-mugger as she believed.

The shop fell silent.

Thus I learnt that Jeremy Laing had been killed. He was my first friend to die. I thought of his nice wise face and his thick round glasses and his quizzical earnestness and the strain of mockery he got from his father. I dawdled home with my lolly – now somehow shameful, undeserved.

There were, as usual, the gusts of stinging sourness from Hawk Bowns's dairy, of scorched horn from Curtis's smithy. I loitered outside Sid the Butcher's shop: unburdened by horrible knowledge he was, as usual, sawing and gabbing. Sid the Butcher's bicycle's rear wheel's translucent plastic veil to protect his mac from spray that escaped the mudguard was, as usual, crazed and engrimed. Mr Thick the Drowner grunted, as usual, through his abundantly encrusted moustache. The wicket fence that supported his arthritic bones was, as usual, rotten and miraculously vertical. Ian Horn's parents' front garden was, as usual, full of axles, tarpaulins and

1 Jim Laing believed that he could have saved Jeremy, but Hippocratic ethics of the day forbade doctors operating on their kin. He subsequently rued not risking being struck off. He knew the limitations of the surgeon who did operate.

buckets. The Lovely Queenie's rouge was, as usual, like a scary clown's. The russet fur round the collar of her peplum'd serge jacket was, as usual, thick as a bush. Iridescent feathers glinted, as usual, in her hat. She greeted me, as usual, with her blowsy cackle and her former-barmaid-trying-but-failing-to-make-come-back leer. Even though it was a minute further from her house than the R & C, The Lovely Queenie was, as usual, off to The Swan for her lunchtime noggin. Old Street's ragged metalled surface was succeeded, as usual, by muddy gravel, cinders and puddles. The alley off it that was also a drain flowed with foul leucous liquid, as usual. In the small square of reeking rookeries it led to the pye-dogs howled, as usual.

This was all wrong.

Someone had ceased to exist in the form he had enjoyed till earlier that morning, had stopped being a person, had made a monumental shift into a state that wasn't a state.

Yet this routine itinerary's stages, scents and personae had not changed. Nor had the way I perceived them changed. There was no revealed acknowledgment that he was dead. What did I expect? Wilting flowers? The collapse of Mr Thick's fence? A shocking fact was hidden in my head. That it had no effect on the exterior world signified that world's heartlessness. I tried to calculate where Jeremy was now, what he was now. Was he a void? And was a void like a vacuum? Probably. Where he had been there was nothing – but where was this freshly created nothingness to be found? How did lack and emptiness manifest? Did a hole appear in the sky with nothing beyond it? Was he going to heaven? If so, had he already got there? How long did the journey take? Did it begin immediately after death?

Jeremy won't be round to play again, to go out in the boat again, to row upstream to Alligator Island again. I went through the high gate between the brick sheds into the garden. Crazy-paved path, two fruit trees, hurdle fences, cotoneaster hedge, wallflowers and currants, sandpit I'd grown out of just as I would grow out of short trousers, cowboys, water pistols, Jokari, sport,

War Picture Library, sleeping with a night light. All of which Jeremy would never grow out of. He was condemned to be forever frozen in Aertex and Startrite.

My father was already home. So I remained mute. Over lunch I volunteered nothing of what I knew. It was too embarrassing a subject to broach. Even had I wanted to blurt out the news I wouldn't have known how to. I lacked the moral means to contravene the etiquette of silence he decreed. And, besides, the start of each academic year brought into my mother's class new pupils, a catalogue of whose foibles and quirks she treated us to. My father and I ate, she picked at her food and talked. After lunch she returned to the C of E primary school a couple of minutes' walk away.

My father went to his den to do his 'writing'. On a 1930s Remington he typed, in multiplicate, the orders he had written down by hand in the shops he had called on that morning. Later in the afternoon one copy of the orders would be posted to Southampton, a second to Bristol, a third to Liverpool, the headquarters of William Crawford and Sons, where Brigadier Sir Douglas Crawford DSO (1904–1981), Lord Lieutenant of Merseyside (1974–1979), presided over the great baking empire. He lived, surrounded by imperial Chinese gewgaws, at Fernlea, an Edwardian barrack between Sefton Park and Mossley Hill. He shared it and a house in Marbella, Costa Lotta, with his widowed sister, Jessie. He never found the right girl.

It was counted a privilege to shake the white hand of this powdery, childless paternalist and collector. I was twice honoured, at the Royal Hotel in Bristol, which merely reinforced the weird perception that I was being introduced to royalty. He seemed to demand deference as though his blood were blue or blueish, a baron of biscuits receiving forelock from his vassals and their children, his dependents: Chas Perry, Mr Berrett, Mr Uren, Mr Tyson etc. I hated to see my father demeaned, blusteringly pretending that he was the old snob's fellow officer.

That these painful encounters took place in Bristol was

particularly inappropriate, for this was a city that, more than any other, I associated with unmitigated pleasure. This was partly due to a friend of my mother's charming lodger, Dick Lalonde. His route to the estate agents where he was doing his articles was the same as mine to school. He was a voluble propagandist for Bristol: he had been brought up there, had gone to Clifton College and returned when he qualified. Because I admired him I wanted to share his enthusiasm. That wasn't difficult. The zoo, unlike London Zoo, didn't reek of animals with hygiene deficiencies. There were deep-fried egg and chips at the Marine Café on the Triangle. Across the road, I ate my first 'Chinese' meal, and, in a barrel-vaulted cellar, my first pizza. At Daniel Neale on Park Street I bought a yellow and black dogtooth shirt and a French navy Windac windcheater. I gazed longingly at the chisel-toe slip-ons in a shop window on College Green. My father returned the old Morris Eight (reg JFM 897) which had been defeated by Hardknott to William Crawford and Son's car fleet and collected a brand-new Morris Minor in which I took proprietorial pride. The words 'floating harbour' were enchanting.

Later I would bunk off school trips to the Old Vic – Dürrenmatt's *The Physicists* was the most memorably dire play imaginable – and head with John Rosser and Jonathan Goddard to The Rummer, the very first Berni Inn, to drink 'schooners' of sherry. An exception was Harry H. Corbett's *Macbeth*. His performance, immediately pre-Steptoe, was so dourly captivating that I did not accompany my friends to the bar. Three years later I saw Richard Pasco's *Hamlet* (in gratuitous Napoleonic garb, which accorded with my childhood nightmare, but can have made little sense to anyone else). I had left school by then and had, I told myself, grown out of schooners.

And by then I had begun to appreciate the city's manifold peculiarities. The jazz modern Smiths Crisps factory at Brislington; the literality of Totterdown's name; the deep flights of outdoor steps; the sudden exhilarating glimpses of verdant hills outside the city; the sheer might of the tobacco warehouses; the streets of red sandstone Gothic villas; the terraced gardens of Clifton; the thrill of the gorge and the heartstopping suspension bridge and beyond them Leigh Woods where Mary N——'s body had been found.

ACCESS TO THE UNKNOWN

There was a class divide whose boundary was the two almost conjoined mediaeval bridges across the Avon at East Harnham. South of the river stood modest dwellings of many eras. Over the bridges at the northern end of St Nicholas Road the Liberty of the Cathedral Close culminates at De Vaux House on the corner of De Vaux Place. Liberty means, here, outside the Close but within the ecclesiastical jurisdiction of the Dean and Chapter whose stewardship of their sublime architectural charges was habitually as crass as their faith: Salisbury's clergy were not afflicted by aesthetic probity or by doubt. These pious snobbish moralistic desiccated philistine bigots, unusually in their era, actually believed in their sanctioned mumbo-jumbo and its cruel rules.

Dr Harold Burt-White, the owner of De Vaux House, was probably not the sort of person they looked on with sympathy or wished to have live within the Liberty of the Close. He was a gynaecologist, an expert in puerperal infections and formerly senior house surgeon at Barts. Jim Laing's atypically bar-room characterisation of another gynaecologist is perhaps appropriate: 'He couldn't think of anywhere better to play than where he worked.' Burt-White was struck off the medical register in 1932 for having conducted *an improper relationship with a patient* and was cited as co-respondent in a messy divorce (is there any other sort?) which was also public. Dallas Burt-White, his sister, a mainstay of that decade's society columns, accused the petitioner Harold Bevir of blackmailing her brother. She was duly sued for slander. Harold Burt-White countered by bringing a libel action against Bevir who had described him as a cad. And so it went on: appeals, rapprochements, paltry reputations worth fortunes.

He was reinstated by the GMC after five years. A campaign had been waged by three hundred of his patients. He served in the RAMC in Ulster and took up a post at Salisbury Infirmary soon after the war. He was dark, sleek, saturnine, urbanely suited. He was said to drink heavily.

Outside De Vaux House, in the lee of a slightly raised pavement, stood his drophead Lagonda LG6, bulbously streamlined in the fashion of the late Thirties. It was liver-brown and fetish-black. I was mesmerised by it. The wheels were unperforated, solid-state and stately. There were spats over the rear ones. Such spats and wheels were unsporty, against nature, they spoke of worldliness, of arcane urban depravities. Until my mother or The German Girl tugged me away I followed my reflection in the bodywork's millpool-deep enamel. That Lagonda was a sinister sleeping animal. And then it was gone. It was the car's sudden absence, the very fact that it was no longer there, which would fix it for ever in my nervous system.

Mrs Bacon cleaned every morning at St Nicholas Hospital, the almshouses close by De Vaux House. Two afternoons a week she cleaned for my parents. I sat at the dining-room table toying with the tea she had made me, a glass of squash and a crumbling slice of bread glued with a slab of butter. She was in the kitchen with my mother, garrulously confidential, talking in a deafening whisper which meant that I wasn't supposed to hear.

'Suicide. Stst ohf . . . Old-fashioned cut-throat it were he used . . . That poor woman . . . Stst ohf I don't know 'ow 'e could . . . Pool of blood, pool of blood . . .' Her tuts were salacious and prurient. She was a *News of the World* reader, as moralistic, then, as the Dean and Chapter though more humane. 'Stst ohf – that lovely 'ouse . . . Such a gentleman . . . Always raises 'is 'at. Stst ohf . . . Don't 'old with suicide . . . And a doctor too . . .'

I heard the new word again. Suicide.

A pool of blood was as big as the garden pond at the bungalow in Britford Lane where Uncle Ken and Auntie Jessica lived. She had seen an adder swimming in it. Eavesdropping on Mrs Bacon I saw the water in the pond turn crimson.

It was autumn. Late the previous afternoon, Harold Burt-White had severed the radial artery of his left wrist and the anterior artery of his right leg. He could have had no better training in the procedures of suicide. His wife found him prone and unconscious on a tiled floor. To attempt suicide was still, in 1952, illegal in Britain. Rather than call the emergency services and risk his suffering prosecution should he survive, she contacted a colleague of his, an anaesthetist called Simpson. Not the obvious choice in the circumstances, but he lived nearby with his alarmingly flat-footed son. In defiance of his specialisation he succeeded in getting Burt-White to come round, only to be told: 'Don't bother. If I live I'll kill myself.' He didn't live, he had already killed himself.

Lagonda. Lagonda is unfathomably complicit. It is not a necessarily rare sighting of a vehicle of that marque but the name, the very word, that triggers a swooning dream of release by the barber's blade that was a physician's, of the snake – evidently an adder – on the barber's pole, of Roman death, of laurels, of the physician in a toga weighted with viscous blood, of noble disgrace and scorn for Christian obsequies. Where was he buried?

Once I discovered its defining property, which took some time, suicide became a secret within a secret. I kept my knowledge of it from the world. This was before the prepubertal investigation of sex and the dangerous vocabulary attached to it had to be cached deepest in my brain. Suicide was the most special death because it was chosen, as one might choose a Lagonda over an Allard. It was a peculiar luxury.

The propositions that the suicide may have no choice and that the act is one of necessity were inconceivable. Before we have heard of, witnessed or experienced irreparable despair, betrayal, persecution, boredom, depression, obloquy, self-disgust, guilt etc., suicide is a causeless, strangely glamorous occurrence apparently undertaken with free will (as we do not yet know to call it).

Like all the manifold mysteries of infancy self-inflicted death is a magnet for the curious. Its contemplation is tonic. Puzzling about this way of death made me feel so alive despite the frustration of having to rely on scraps of information and not being able to ask any question more direct than 'Where has the Lagonda gone?'

ANAL PENETRATION

Courtesy demands that the object of this intervention should be made aware of the intent before the act is prosecuted. It is merely good manners.

Were such good manners exhibited towards Jonathan Venus and Jeremy Leveret?

May 1957. Early one Wednesday evening my parents made me attend a choral recital in the gardens of Wilton House. Every stratum of South Wiltshire's bourgeoisie was represented along with a few grandees: landowners, wiry soldiers of high rank, gentleman garagists, arty nobs. There was the bemusing buzz of chitchat: what do people say to each other, what is it that takes so much time? How long can an expression of deferential greeting be extended? Everyone spoke proper English or aspired to speak it: open 'o's and stretched diphthongs peculiar to the area were inadequately disguised by doilies of refinement. Everyone dressed and behaved with all the decorum due to an Earl's demesne. We enjoyed the privilege of standing on ground granted to his ancestors four centuries previously by Henry VIII as a reward for their loyal services to the royal rectum. It had rained for the first time in a couple of weeks. The grassless ground around beeches' pachydermal feet shone. There was the elemental odour of damp earth. The returning sun picked out beads of moisture on the Earl's noble lawns. His ancient trees' limbs dripped.

A loudspeaker announcement was made. The recital would begin later than intended.

There was an unspecified problem. The makeshift stage, no doubt: it was merely a series of turfed terraces in front of a roofless exedra. Perhaps the singers were in danger of losing their footing in the wet.

England was fecund, inviting. I left my parents and walked alone to the Palladian bridge across the Nadder. A roofed bridge, a fancy which had long drawn me, had fascinated me since earliest childhood. Its lichenous stones glistened. My hand tried the water's temperature to check whether it was fit for swimming. It was warm enough, but lack of trunks and nervy propriety stopped me even in this place where I was out of sight: until a couple of years previously I'd have had no such inhibition. Then I swam naked in rivers without self-consciousness.

I squatted on the bank so that my grey school shorts wouldn't get wet. The waterweed danced and wriggled to the stream's beat. I adored this river and those it conjoined. They were my playgrounds, my familiars, my companions, my solaces. To have remained there gazing at the taut green glassy surface was a greater enticement than a concert. Many of my teachers and certain of my fellow pupils who would be singing tonight comprised Salisbury Cathedral's choir. They were specialists in the multiple idioms of Anglican joylessness. Music was a trial I endured at school. An extra dose out of school was cause for resentment. I had, apparently, regressed. My infantile appreciation of Britten's folk settings and Handel's operas – an appreciation born of subjection to little else – had been quashed by the sensational barbarities of early rock and roll: Elvis Presley, Charlie Gracie, Little Richard. Most of all by Tommy Steele. I longed for his cantilevered quiff and for drainpipes with a sequinned stripe down the outer seam. My taste was for crass trash, mindlessness: I knew because I was told so most days of my life at a school where every room had a flimsy music stand. Teachers who otherwise treated me fondly, even indulgently, remonstrated with me, mocked me, told me I would come to no good if I listened to such 'music'.

I walked back along the river past reeds and willows, between cedars and follies, to rejoin my parents. There was an agitation in the audience, a more vital din, a more intense clamour than earlier. Many people had abandoned their crude folding chairs, exemplars of the ergonomic discomfort of those years, and were knitted in preoccupied groups. My mother and father were seeing off midges with their stiff white programme sheets. They exchanged glances which I was slow to read.

My father said: 'They're rearranging things. Mr Blythe isn't going to be singing tonight.'

Mr Blythe was one of the less proscriptive among the musicians on the school staff. But I couldn't have cared less whether or not he was going to be singing a load of lieder. A few rows away I saw Chris for whom, to my father's irritation, I had spent prep transcribing the lyrics of 'Singing the Blues' earlier in the year: he had remonstrated with me in his car whilst waiting for a gap in the traffic to turn from Exeter Street into St Nicholas Road, at a T-junction where I used always to think of the Duke of Edinburgh.

I pushed through the chairs towards Chris. Their crescentic ranks were now disrupted. His mother and one of his sisters were with him. Of all my friends' mothers Beryl Lush was the most impressive: cinched waist; black hair; dramatic clothes – gypsy skirts, tailored blouses with an upturned collar; ill-planned house where Brack the labrador snoozed by the Rayburn and game grew high in a larder and *The Times* was read – a marker of social superiority.

Beryl, whom I would never have addressed thus, made delicious rusks, soaking stale bread in milk and cooking them in the bottom oven overnight. She was vaguely haughty, handsome. She wasn't cosy. She was often exasperated. Like my parents she often seemed to forget I was thirty-five years her junior, forgot to treat me as a child, sometimes addressed me as though I were an unusually doltish *adult* – which I persuaded myself was a form of flattery. She had been an only child. She pitied me for that state. As Beryl Gray she had studied ballet – even if only in Salisbury. She liked theatre and performance. She tried to infect me with her tastes, Chris being resistant to them. Four years later she would take me, whilst on holiday at Thurlestone, to the Drake Cinema in the newly rebuilt city of Plymouth, to see *South Pacific*. Result: a lifelong antipathy to humourless Hollywood musicals and to anyone called Mitzi, a name fit for a poodle. But that evening, as I extricated my clumsy feet from a chair's crossrung, she glanced at me discomfitingly, looked away as though she had more pressing matters to deal with. Chris was brother to three elder sisters, hence practised in a gamut of sophisticated gestures I was a stranger to. He somehow made it clear that he had not seen me and that, even had he seen me, he was otherwise occupied. So, a yard away from Beryl, two from Chris, I did what I did through so much of my childhood. I pretended not to be there. I turned invisible. I beat it. Without showing I was beating it. Oh, there are Poth's parents – father from Swanage, mother pining for Braintree in far-distant Essex which I had never seen but knew to be all golden wheat and white clapboard mills. But Poth wasn't with them. And they too were determined not to catch my eye. I turned again as though I had forgotten something I had to do and went on pretending till I felt all eyes – what eyes? – were off me.

I was skulking alongside, almost inside, a yew bush. I took comfort from yews, from their gloom, their peeling red bark, their alluringly treacherous berries, their dust, and from their shed needles' incapacity to absorb water so that drops rested like mercury on their surface beside twisted trunks and writhing roots.

Michael Lea whose middle name was Simcott – the son of the vicar of Miserden in the Cotswolds, a scrumcap-wearer, a future Rugbeian and orchestral player, a chorister due to sing treble that night – sidled up to me, smugly excited, his breath, as ever, scented with Meloids. His catchphrase was 'mitts off'. I suspected that he would claim ownership of the yew as he did of stray pens, rubber bands, Wrigley pellets.

But: 'D'you know what? D'you know what! Mr Blythe has been sacked. He kissed Venus One. Sacked!'

At Salisbury Cathedral School the convention of major, minor, minimus did not apply.

Jonathan Venus was Venus One, his younger brother David

was Venus Two. Terry Lovell remained Lovell Two although his brother had left. The accretion of unrelated Youngs was such that there existed a small ginger creature called Young Five.

Mr Blythe had kissed Venus One? I was mystified. For many reasons. The long e and terminal sibilant meant that Jonathan Venus and Jonathan Meades were near homophones to the latter, whose hearing had been permanently damaged at the age of five. Thus when the name of either Venus brother was called I would sometimes respond. On the occasions – very rare – that convention was suppressed and our shared Christian name was used I would *always* respond. I confused myself with Jonathan Venus. Had Mr Blythe suffered a similar confusion? Was I not the boy he wanted to kiss?

Kissing was of course sissy.

In the Cathedral School's swimming pool changing hut, a riot of asbestos, degraded concrete and REEMA panels, just-prepubescent boys boxed with their penises in a spirit of friendly companionability and competitive violence: he who drew blood won. They aptly dignify this as cockfighting, insouciantly associating covert pugilism with the hedgerow gamblers' sport conducted between roofless brick cowsheds where flames from pyres of palettes relieve the ruined farmyard's midden chill and lend ceremony to the bucolic rite.

On Harnham Hill where the chalky paths down the steep slope were diagonal and polished there were hidden places among the blackthorns and barrows which became familiar in late childhood summers. Exploratory sex – I never actually articulated that word to myself – with two girls, my mother's former pupils, was no more or less than a form of play, innocent and delighted discovery and, not that we considered it, an ancient rite in an ancient Jutish place. Deep beneath the grass which we recreated ourselves on were buried the skeletons and flint tools of our distant forebears who had been at it too, in their time. That's why we were here. We nuzzled, we felt each other's genitals, we laughed and giggled and never kissed – that was for adolescence and *going out with* and love, which was also sissy. The hillside was littered with knotted frenchies, rubber-wrapped seed. They were as common as crisp packets. We knew what they were for. They used to tease me: 'About time you was able to fill one of them up.'

Prepubescent sex with both boys and girls provoked no guilt though we knew that it should. It was 'mucky behaviour'. It was wicked. But it didn't involve anyone who wasn't our age. What occurs between coevals is not necessarily willing – but with us it was, it was all enthusiastically consensual, we taught each other as children always have. It was fun, it was living well at a tender age. It was illicit, another intimation that pleasure derived from pain – smoking hurt and was dizzying, stolen sweet liqueurs burnt my mouth. It would obviously have been different had an adult been involved, even if that adult had not been coercive. That adult might have been enjoined by us or, yet better, persuaded by me alone. If only . . .

Maybe, after all, I just wasn't pretty enough. How I longed to be loved by a handsome master with the looks of a fighter ace.

When boys lie sated they do not consider kissing each other. Like the Spanish girls (or town prozzies) with nits in their mile-high beehives they never kiss. When Dave told me he had felt his one-year-old sister's nappy'd vagina whilst she was in the pram at the plum orchard end of the garden I was less shocked than I would have been had he told me that he kissed her. (What actually interested me was Dave's mother's negligence in parking her in a place that teemed with wasps gorging on fallen fruit. In my moral hierarchy exposing a baby to the possibility of a wasp sting was a graver offence than casual fraternal violation.)

What was Mr Blythe thinking of? Kissing!

It evidently didn't occur to me that Michael Lea had merely repeated the euphemism used by whoever had told him the reason for the sacking. It didn't occur to me that the informant might have been an adult to whom *cockfighting* was but an ancient memory or even a matter of ignorance and that *bugger* was a word never to be spoken save as an oath and, even then, not in front of the renchild.

That night they sung without Mr Blythe. The programme was, evidently, amended. I didn't notice. I didn't know or care how Mr Blythe's special bits of lieder were taken care of. I was bereft and puzzled. Why had I not been favoured with his attentions? He liked me. Douglas Blythe was young and charming. His smile was shy and inviting, too inviting maybe. He smelled of lavender cologne. His hair was rakishly long for the era, if rather crinkly; it was stepped and staggered. He wore a British Warm, canary-yellow pullovers and tan suede shoes: someone said 'he smooths around at suede miles per hour'. He had some pet guinea pigs in the garden of his digs in Salisbury Cathedral Close. His hand-writing, which I sought to emulate, was exquisite, derived from italic, as crisply orthogonal as the terraces of his hair.

His expulsion was swift. He vanished, he was not spoken of. What had become of him and his guinea pigs? Any question about his fate was met with a frosty churchy silence that warned not to ask again. I feared for him. My father had spoken in a regretful, uncharacteristically couched way of a Chafyn Grove schoolmaster named Mills who had been a squash partner of his when I was a baby. Mills had committed suicide. He was queer. Very good sort, had a really killing drop shot, just on the cusp of the tin, but queer. And queers committed suicide. Out of shame, guilt, dishonour, self-disgust. That was the received wisdom of the era. Not that it was much discussed. Cruel crim-inalisation and persecution were unconsidered, never spoken of. For a few days I longed to be assured that Douglas Blythe had not followed the same route as Mills and as Nancy's bachelor brother Jack Misselbrook who worked at the Admiralty in Bath and slit his wrist. Was Dr Burt-White queer?

Then of course, I forgot Douglas Blythe.

Six months after his banishment from Salisbury I was honoured to be deputed to sort the school's morning post in a mediaeval vestibule coarsely partitioned with painted plywood. I repaid the faith shown in me, arranging the letters with taxonomical diligence in trays according to boarding pupils' houses, masters' common room, bursar's office, domestic staff etc. Among them were several to the headmaster E. Laurence Griffiths. One caused me to gasp: a small, square, cream envelope addressed to him in what was, unmistakably, Mr Blythe's writing. It was postmarked Wolverhampton. The junior detective within me, a Blytonian nosy parker, scrutinised the envelope. When I was sure no one was approaching from either the direction of the changing rooms or that of the undercroft I held it to the window. But the paper was frustratingly thick and disagreeably rough: handmade paper was hopelessly old hat. What did the letter say? I toyed with stealing it, pretended to toy with stealing it, knew I was deluding myself. Unlike Stammler, a persistent and boastful shoplifter, I didn't have the nerve. Its very existence bemused me. It suggested a lack of finality in the affairs of the world: a sacking was not, evidently, a complete rupture. Why was Mr Blythe in Wolverhampton of all places? He spoke with an amused drawl (which I coveted and failed to imitate). What connection could he have with a sooty factory town whose primitive inhabitants' accent I knew from Uncle Hank's misanthropic take-off to be a matter of ridicule? Worse: Wolves, in those days a force in English football under Stan Cullis, wore 'old gold' shirts which offended my eyes; I hurried past the colour plates of them in *Charles Buchan's Football Monthly* and the countless annuals I acquired. Moreover Wolves had had the temerity not to recognise Duncan Edwards's brilliance. No one went willingly to Wolverhampton. Then it occurred to me: there must be a gaol there to which Mr Blythe had been confined for kissing. How could I confirm this suspicion which would, through the course of the morning, turn into a certainty? It was a terrible secret between the headmaster, Mr Blythe and me. Had I asked any of my teachers about penal institutions in south-west Staffordshire I would have been bound to reveal it. So, tense, I waited till I got home.

But: 'Go and look it up,' said my mother.

'Where, Mummy?'

'In . . . Oh, Jonty darling, go and ask Daddy.'

My father, in his den oiling a reel, merely said that it was the kind of thing that Uncle Hank – Deputy Town Clerk of the north-east Staffordshire town of Burton-on-Trent and soon to ascend to the very Town Clerkship itself – would know. But, no, I'd have to write to him. I couldn't phone Hank because it was too expensive – a trunk call. And it could prove especially expensive if answered by his voluble landladies who might be at home when he, wigged and robed, was attending an important mayoral event. My father went on getting on with the one thing that really engrossed him.

That was the problem with curiosity. When something big came up it was reckoned to be small. But I had to feign casualness in order that no one guess at the overwhelming importance of the matter to me. And I was too embarrassed to disclose my reason for seeking this recondite knowledge. I was too embarrassed or shamed by everything out of the ordinary ever to mention it – as I was when Jeremy Laing died.

Six months previously, and four months after Jeremy's death, during the Christmas holiday, I had been walking with my father and Posty one Sunday afternoon. We had just descended the chalky flight of steps, booby-trapped by beech roots, from the heights of Bouverie Avenue to Old Blandford Road. There, ruddy-faced from the chill and beating their gloved hands together against it, we encountered Douglas Blythe and Peter Northam who had been walking on the Hill. The latter's eau-de-Nil Biro, with which he marked my work, so persistently fascinated me that he had given it to me at the end of one term. An act of generosity that seemed to trespass into the conspiratorial, for pupils were forbidden to write with ballpoints, always called Biros and deprecated as non-U: this was a secret between us, I hid it from my parents. Here were my favourite teachers, young, glamorous, shivering – and out of school and out of term time, which somehow made me their equal. Though my father knew them by sight and reputation I introduced them with due formality, as though they were my friends: friends who bore the title Mister. It was getting on in the afternoon. The orange street lights near the entrance to Government House were already on. Winter leaves were crisp beneath cold feet. A frail sun was disappearing over the triangular pines beyond the tennis club. My father had read my mind, he had noted my pride in my friends – or maybe he was indulging his appetite for gregariousness and acquaintance: 'Why don't you chaps come back for a warmer?' I was thrilled. Mr Blythe and Mr Northam were coming as guests to my home. Warmers were drunk at home, noggins in the pub. And because it was a Sunday evening, almost, I would be allowed whisky with sugar and water. That would impress them. I could talk to them man to man about, say, cars – even though Mr Blythe didn't have one and Mr Northam's bottom-of-the-range baby-blue Austin A30 hardly suggested an overriding interest in the subject. Or about, say, the red-shirted Busby Babes, still with a year and a bit to live – even though neither master oversaw games and, besides, as future gentlemen we played rugby at school. Football was as common as Biros, haircream and ITV (which we did not yet receive in the south).

We squeezed into the tiny sitting room crammed with furniture intended for a house not a cottage, for a home for married life that should surely have been led in more expansive spaces, free of scraping and renting. Two hefty wingbacked neo-Georgian armchairs, another streamlined armchair, a gross veneered radiogram with a mesh speaker, a perished leather pouffe, an unsteady wrought-metal standard lamp (its shade was crisp, cracked parchment), the television set on the 'corner unit' carpentered for it and for outsize books by Mr Smith in his workshop three doors away and painted chipolata pink, a William IV davenport with hidden, spring-released compartments. This miscellany – only the last was of anything other than familiar value (£40, Woolley and Wallis auction, April '56) – had to be negotiated like a chicane with added pratfalls in the form of threadbare Persian carpets ruched by a chairleg's faintest movement and Posty who snored, dreaming of food, and more food. Kalu merely glared. And though I hardly participated in the tentative conversation – little more than an inventory of shared Close acquaintances and courteous anecdotes – I was mutely proud that I had effected so special an hour in that tightly fitting room.

AYLESWADE ROAD

John Morton's microbiological research was into the viability and infection rates of airborne microorganisms and radioactive spores. Many of his trials were necessarily conducted at sea in the approved gung-ho manner of the day. Like many other middle-aged Porton Down scientists of the Fifties facing an impoverished future he joined what would, in the next decade, become known as the brain drain to the United States, land of plenty, land of handsomely rewarded weapons technologists, land of modernity, streamlining, dams, freeways, cars with fins, cars with gurning radiator grilles, square watches, observation cars, air conditioning, Kodaslide Highlux projectors, teen camps (Adirondack Woodcraft, Western Caravan and Ranch, Gay Valley). But also, puzzlingly, land of the Wild West. How could that be?

He prospered, eventually took American citizenship. His wife Peggy didn't. After their divorce she returned to England with their son and their pretty twins, dizygotic girls who were readily distinguishable and who I was convinced were not real twins but impostors, perpetrators of an incomprehensible deception.

The Goddard twins, monozygotic boys, were real twins. I couldn't tell which was which. Identification was exacerbated by their usually being dressed in identical clothes. They relished the confusion they caused. Further, they were so confusingly akin to Freddie and Ferdie Fox in *Rupert Bear* that I cannot now picture one set without the other. They lived within a few yards of Beaton's Garage in Ayleswade Road. The Beaton brothers, only a year apart in age, might have been twins. A few minutes' walk away in one of the Royal Artillery houses there lived, temporarily, Aubrey, Arnold and Ann Sessions. Biscuit-skinned twins? Triplets? Mere siblings?

41

Ayleswade Road was a street of, mostly, banal Edwardian terraces which concealed multiple births, interchangeable identities and puzzling doubles. It must have been its intricate genealogies which caused a momentous thought to occur to me. I was standing outside The Swan, raised on a bank across the road from the Goddards' house and Beaton's Garage. The people coming out of Hands's shop with their uniform wicker baskets, the people getting off the 55 bus and hurrying home for lunch, the group of people heading for The Rose and Crown – all these people and all the other people I couldn't see all across the world over were men or women, girls or boys. Why? Why were people restricted to membership of one sex or the other? Perhaps they weren't. There must, I decided, be a third sex. And that third sex was gypsies, swarthy, leather-faced clothes-peg folk with horses, wild dogs and plentiful scrap metal who were mistrusted precisely because being of the third sex they were given to different behaviour.

For many years after I learnt that gypsies were, according to taste, self-pitying, special-pleading minor criminals or persecuted rovers clinging to an ancient, threatened way of life, I'd still gape at The Swan's gravel car park and allow the notion of the third sex to capture me.

BARNETT, MISS

The far-distant end of Britford Lane where the rutted, puddled, cindered road ended. From there on the route to the watery village of Britford was a narrow footpath bordered by a thorny hedge and, on its other side, a barbed wire fence. Beyond the field that way, unseen, signalled by a suspended mist strip, ran Navigation Straight. A gilded copperplate signboard on legs in its garden announced that Britford Lane's penultimate building, a pebbledash chalet-bungalow, was a school, a sort of dame school, my first school. The single classroom occupied most of the ground floor. Its ceiling was impressively high; all ceilings were impressively high in comparison with my home's. I had never seen such a bright room, I had never seen such light before. The end onto the back garden was entirely glazed. Late in the morning it admitted stout rods of sunlight dense with churning motes which vanished when I went to stroke them. Where did they go? To the garden where stooped the vestiges of an orchard, withered plum trees that no longer bore fruit? To the lane behind where wooden sheds and ad hoc garages teetered and rotted? On the third day of term we were instructed to paint these barren trees with our watercolours. I made some sploshes on a sheet of paper then drank the muddy water from the jar in which we cleaned our brushes. It tasted interesting. I drank more. A fellow pupil grassed me up to Miss Barnett, a spinster in pince-nez which caught the sun. They heliographed a virgin's hatred of life. She marched to my desk and hissed. She told me that I was not just stupid to have drunk the water, she said that I would die, that I deserved to die. But that I was not to die at school. Her assistant teacher, a young woman in plaid, drove me home in her van so that I might die in my own bed. The alarmed

German Girl ran up the road to my mother's classroom to fetch her. I waited anxiously. I hoped to see my mother before I died. Until the moment when I had to retire to my deathbed I waited for her on the dining-room window seat. The assistant teacher paced between the van and the front door, smoking. I wondered how to check for symptoms. How would I know when I was dead? Was transport to heaven immediate? What form did it take? If handsomely liveried tourist coaches were used I prayed that the vehicle would not be a wheezy Bedford which might fail to climb the slopes but a sleek Guy with a cast-metal Red Indian's head above the radiator: I prided myself on being able to distinguish lorries by the sound of their engine. I could tell a handsome Foden (those crazy radiator grilles!) from a Dennis (locally tested, in skeletal form, no cab, no bonnet, all working parts revealed as though the driver was driving an exploded drawing). I craned my neck for a sight of my mother. Had I been a good son? Then my mother was hugging me, telling me I wasn't going to die, wiping the tears I had thitherto been too numb to shed, getting The German Girl to make me cocoa. She comforted me so long that my fear abated. Then she went outside, out of my hearing, to talk to the assistant teacher. I had never seen her gesture before, never seen her shake her head that way. She was berating the young woman whose expression was increasingly sheepish. Whatever was said was presumably mild beside what was said to Miss Barnett herself later that day. That was the end of that school. I did not enquire whether I was expelled or withdrawn.

BLUE SPOT

When my father carried me high on his shoulders grasping my ankles in his giant's hands I would caress a circular blemish on the top of his head, a birthmark made visible by baldness. (He had already lost most of his hair by the time he married at the age of thirty.) This fascinating spot, the circumference of a cigarette, was approximately the colour of the penicillium mould in blue cheese. Prying in some long-lost book I had been frightened by a Medusa's head in what I could not then identify as the brothelish style of Rops or Moreau, whose paintings, like all others, I accepted with a dogged literality. My father called Gorgonzola 'gorgon', thus conflating in my mind the worms that were rumoured to seethe through the all too living lactate with a Gorgon's venomously vermicular hairdo. It was this homophone which made me shun the stuff. Besides, I preferred the saltier, less rich Danish Blue, which my father took a dim view of because it didn't taste of cow. At Christmas there would appear a stoneware crock of Stilton festering in grocer's port, a sludge as repulsively pungent as an adult's stool. Mercifully this cheese which, macerated or not, I have never appreciated, was in those days a seasonal 'treat' and so unglimpsed and unsmelled throughout the rest of the year. That was not the case with Cheddar, always called 'mousetrap'. Salisbury's best grocery, the coffee-and-bacon-scented Robert Stokes, stocked wheels of farm Cheddar, a rarity, for the majority of prewar producers now sold their milk to factory-dairies such as Cow & Gate in Wincanton or Horlicks in Ilminster which processed it into lumps of generic cheese-style product. That was the future: industrial food, rational food, soon to be plastic-wrapped food. It was a future which my parents scornfully opposed whilst I succumbed, shamefully,

45

to Primula, Dairylea triangles, citric Philadelphia, Huntley and Palmers cheese footballs which tickled mucous membrane, Roka cheese crispies in their recyclable blue and yellow tin (pencils, dividers, erasers etc.). I knew I shouldn't enjoy such foods: I was so advised often enough. I longed to leave childhood taste behind me but it wouldn't leave me. Even at the age of seventeen I would be excited by Golden Wonder cheese and onion crisps, the first flavoured crisps manufactured, the first flavoured crisps I ate, in that sweetest of all summers, 1964.

At least this litany of vintage lactic colour did not include Kraft cheese slices, tan leatherette rectangles whose textural bounce and astonishing flavour were *tours de force* of chemical engineering. However, they did not appeal to me. Nor does it include Cracker Barrel 'Cheddar' – oblong, granular, fudge-like, a stinging palatal assault which my father would probably have dismissed had it not been advertised on telly by James Robertson Justice, who like Jimmy Edwards and Stinker Murdoch, was generally (and maybe erroneously) accepted to be a jolly good chap rather than a mere actor; bluff, beery, down to earth. He was occasionally to be seen in Salisbury hauling his big-boned beardie bulk from a gull-wing Mercedes.

The Cracker Barrel commercials were directed by Lindsay Anderson. Another cause, then, of his gnawing self-despisal.

BOBIE

Long O. My parents' affectionate nickname for each other. Only used vocatively. Derivation unknown. Its infantilism embarrassed me. It belonged, like much else, to an era, close but quite ungraspable, when they had yet to make me, when they had been a world of two, unintruded upon, carefree and yet to be separated for almost half a decade: I was no doubt the glue designed to reunite them, to transport them back to the Thirties, to the coming enormity whose germ was there to be ignored by all, to collective amnesia about a future bereft of treasure hunts and roadhouses.

Not yet Bobie and Bobie, they meet in Southampton, at the Banister Park ice rink, in 1937. My future father falls at my future mother's feet. He is a tyro skater, she is practised. She literally picks him up. Is it a deliberate fall? What the morons of the football industry now term simulation? Probably. He was, though, a clumsy dancer and an awkward swimmer. The likelihood of his being able to remain upright on skates was slight. Still, the matter of predetermination was never discussed. Maybe romance's integrity was better served by ascribing it to chance. And maybe they were loath to admit to each other, let alone to me, that they frequented somewhere so proletarian as a glacial meat market. Between that encounter and their marriage three months before the outbreak of war their life was one of heedless enjoyment recorded in crinkle-bordered monochrome.

Here is a sailing holiday on the Broads aboard *Perfect Lady* with Ken and Jessica Southwell: Ken wears a short-sleeved Aertex shirt with a lace-up front. Post-war they would be addressed as Uncle Ken and Auntie Jessica though I knew they weren't. They came and went according to Ken's RAF postings. He lost his temper, often; subcutaneous ropes swelled in his forehead. He had also lost control of his hair which refused to be tamed by brilliantine and rose in Mayan strip lynchets. They found me a tiresome child. I found them frightening adults. I was occasionally foisted on them at wherever they were currently calling home – a bookless cottage at Boscombe, a bookless bungalow along Britford Lane with an adder in the pond, subsequently rented by the Braithwaites. The last time I saw the Southwells was near Barnstaple in the summer of 1964. Now they found me more than tiresome, an insolent, sneering teenage know-all with, as Jessica said, a tongue in his head. They were inordinately proud that their lame daughter was engaged to be married to a member of the family descended from Henry Curry, founder of the fridge and digital goods retailers. This was their social triumph. Their son had joined the Merchant Navy, that may have been a social triumph too. Ken was by then employed as a golf club secretary, which is how choleric passed-over officers nostalgic for mess life often ended up: a house came with the job. Through its picture window, there across blanched fields, shimmered the distant sea. It was no solace to Ken. The country was going to the dogs. And if that man Wilson gets in . . . That man Wilson did get in.

Here is my father fishing, always fishing: casting a fly in a chalkstream, displaying his catch, up to his wadered thighs in white water, crouching on rocks beneath contorted pines, seated on a dead trunk adjusting a reel with a jeweller's screwdriver, netting a trout from a rowing boat's stern with the rod parabola'd by the struggling fish. He often wears a Norfolk jacket with two buttoning breast pockets and a belt. The material is Donegal tweed. The photographer was my mother. There are fewer snaps of her, a towny acclimatising to willowy, watery places with the eagerness of new love. Here she's standing beside the ford through the Blackwater at West Wellow. My father made lifelong friends of the Gradidge family. He fished their stream, a feeder of the Test, and he shot on their three farms. At the party in the village hall for Mr and Mrs Walter Gradidge's golden wedding anniversary Mrs Gradidge indicated my girlfriend and asked my mother: 'Where did Jonathan find her then? I wish Clifford could find himself one . . . he could buy her a Jag straight off.' Clifford, then pushing fifty, did find one not long after, a multiple divorcée from Bournemouth who got a Jag straight off and who cost the family one of their farms when she offloaded her latest husband after only three years.

Here are my parents in a country pub's garden with friends. Young men looked older then. They wanted to look older. Hence the ubiquitous moustache and the absence of a specifically youthful form of dress. But the faces are older too. Diet? Physical endeavour? It is certainly the case that today the only young men who look older than their years are professional sportsmen who sell their bodies for sums that other prostitutes can only envy. That sleek-haired (and moustachioed) fellow raising his glass to the camera is Wagstaff. He is familiar from their wedding photos. The war was a divider on another scale too. When he returned from service he had two prosthetic legs but seldom moved from a wheelchair. Although his wife had been one of my mother's bridesmaids they soon lost contact. I never met him. Was he called Ray? Or was that her name?

BUCKHORN WESTON

We travelled to a rugby match by stopping train. I loved that journey. Trying to calculate the very point where, above the deep cutting after Wilton South station, the Lush family's house was. The Nadder valley's reduced palette – grey woodsmoke, black skeletal trees, brown hillocks, hints of hidden combes. After Semley the landscape changed, shed all intimacy. Big fields; heavy west country plough; Buckhorn Weston, up a slope to the north of the track. (When I returned home that evening I pored over the map till I'd identified its name.) It appeared to be a village of stone houses the memory of whose prettiness I all but destroyed for a time thirty-five years later when I was meant to be doing something else but noticed a signpost and negligently diverted to it. I found a group of galvanised byres and garaged tractors. I cursed myself for having gone back. *Never go back*. Truism or true? But I had never gone in the first place. I willed the early memory to re-establish its primacy. Gradually it did so, and my Buckhorn Weston today is that of over half a century ago: a snapshot through a third-class window. A modest mnemonic triumph, the victory of the distant past over the recent. We steamed through Templecombe, close to Posty's birthplace. Milborne Port is not a port, can never have been a port. There's no river. It was a cloth town and glove town. Some cottages have almost entirely glazed upper storeys to admit light so that weavers might see to weave. (Not enough, they still went blind.) We walked from Sherborne station past the Victorian–Jacobean Digby Hotel, an impressively grand establishment for a small town, then entered the Middle Ages, all ironstone cloisters and pointed arches. It was only by proximity that Sherborne Preparatory School was attached to the public school which, given the former's moral squalor, would have doubtless preferred to detach itself: for the moment it turned a blind eye. The premises were barrack-like, of no merit. The school's distinction derived from its being the fiefdom of the Lindsay family whose motto was *Dieu et Mon Droit du Seigneur*. The ownership and, with it, the headmastership passed from one churchy generation to the next. The then headmaster's son, Robin Lindsay, was, in the century's late fifties, in his early thirties. He cannot have believed his luck in being born into such a dynasty, into such a milieu, into such a plenty of prepubescent flesh: a carnivore's paradise, temptation was just a wet towel's flick away. He was evidently sated by the sight of 'his' naked boys in the showers, fed up with the sameness of his diet. Christopherson, Webster, Sheriff, Barry, Rose . . . even had they been masked he would have been capable of identifying them by their genitalia, which were on the very point of making the big leap. Visiting school teams offered variety. As a special feast for himself he organised an annual seven-a-side tournament for sixteen schools. Postmatch he processed slowly beside the communal showers and cast the expert, appreciative eye of the true professional over the fresh flesh: a beauty contest of unwitting participants staged in water that was now freezing, now scalding. In 2006 a notice inside the door of Sherborne Abbey announced that 'Choirboys are available for £10'. Tradition in action.

CLOSE THE DOOR THEY'RE COMING IN THE WINDOW

My uncles were Uncle Hank and Uncle Wangle. There was also Uncle Eric but Uncle Eric wasn't blood, merely marriage. And then there were uncles who were not even uncles by that familial fluke, whose title was honorific in accordance with the lower-middle-class practice of the Fifties, uncles whom I'd never have considered addressing without that title. Uncle Ken, Auntie Jessica. Uncle Norman, Boscombe Down boffin, was my godfather. He was an atheist. Wife: Auntie Nancy.

Uncle Cecil, pharmacist. Wife: Auntie Rae.

Uncle Edgar, dislikable optician. Wife: Auntie Cath.

Uncle Edgar, bearded boho restaurateur / potter / antiques dealer / debt welsher whose raggedy truant children, at least a decade and a half my senior, I envied for their licence to call my parents by their Christian name without prefix. Wife: Auntie Grace.

Uncle Os lived far away beyond the Severn; he owned a pub surrounded by orchards and hopyards. Wife: Auntie Margot.

Uncle Jerry, soldier, had been among the first British infantry officers into Belsen. He drank. He killed himself with sleepers and Scotch when I was eleven, thirteen haunted years after he had witnessed the unimaginable: he suffered the guilt of not having had to endure it. No wife, no widow, no auntie.

Uncle Eric might not have been blood, might not have been officer class – he had no rank to attach to his name in Civvy Street in the days when such a device was supposed to prompt respect. He did have a metal leg, the replacement of the original lost when the Cunliffe Owen Swaythling factory (which manufactured components of the Supermarine Spitfire) was bombed in the Southampton Blitz of November 1940. This loss caused him to postpone his marriage by more than a year. He owned a garage called Gibson's Motors, a subscription to *Glass's Guide to Secondhand Car Prices*, an entire set of Giles annuals, a season ticket to watch Third Division South Southampton at the Dell where the sheer numbers excited me and the ancient cantilevered stands frightened me – I had read in *Charles Buchan's Football Monthly* that such a stand had once collapsed at Stoke or Bradford or somewhere. I regarded my presence in Southampton's as a death-defying, as an exhilarating rite to be suffered in the progress towards teenage, which had just been invented and which was associable with crowds, groups, mobs and the crush of cities. I was necessarily familiar with the crush, for Uncle Eric was slow, gimping up the stairs to our seats whence he'd bark barrack-room calumnies: shirker, NBG, fairy.

Until I was six or seven Uncle Eric, his wife my Auntie Mary, my only cousin Wendy and their corgi dog Jinx lived with my maternal grandparents in Shakespeare Avenue, Portswood. This

was the house my mother had grown up in. There were two storeys at the front, four at the back: this part of Southampton swoops precipitously. It was, thus, a house of steep stairs, unsuited to Jinx's tiny legs. The placid, massively overfed dog developed a stentorian wheeze, adapting himself to a family of chronic hawkers and career coughers. My grandmother could really cough. She smoked three packets of Kensitas per day. Kensitas was not merely a brand of fag, it was an efficacious expectorant. Uncle Eric, no mean smoker himself but a Player's man, used to confide to me in no one else's hearing that she needed them for the coupons. Seventy-five coupons brought a Turkish Face Towel from Robinson & Cleaver, 150 a Lady's Morocco Purse. The coupons carried the warning: 'If you do smoke cigarettes leave a long stub. Remove from mouth between puffs . . .' My grandmother had clearly not got as far as that last bit.

It was a house of brute tables, heavily incised wood, samplers, lardy antimacassars and fussy beading, ornately framed birds (a Redwing Blackbird and a Jay) which my great grandfather John Baird bought in New York, where he had briefly emigrated as a young man in the early 1880s: he returned to Scotland in the middle of that decade to marry his sweetheart Agnes McInnes. The walls were hung with prints and photographs of Bridge of Allan, Stirling, stags and the Wallace Monument, of which my grandmother's grandfather had been the first keeper, a post no doubt coveted by the central belt's entire janitocracy.

John Baird and Agnes McInnes were both born in 1861 in the Stirling suburb of St Ninian's. He was a steamship engineer. His bettering himself took him through a world of horse trams, coal gas, hurdy-gurdies and temperance halls, from grimy port to reeking port. As well as New York he worked in Glasgow, Hull, Liverpool (my grandmother, also Agnes, was born in Bootle in 1888).

When Agnes Baird junior was in early infancy he moved his family to Southampton where he would prosper and live the rest of his life. Agnes Baird junior married Edwin Percy Felix Hogg (b. So'ton 1885). His Scottish forebears had moved south, initially to Niton on the Isle of Wight in the 1840s. They were tenant farmers, market gardeners and lighthouse keepers. Edwin Percy Felix's father, also Edwin, was a carpenter. Despite the pressure of Scotland weighing on her, my mother (b. So'ton 1912) never considered herself anything other than English.

There was always a catheter attached to my grandfather after my grandmother died of lung cancer. He lived on for five years, Pop did, treating me to *frites* and ice cream on trips to St Malo where he had old friends from his lifetime with Southern Railways, which ran the cross-Channel ferries, old friends who had stashes of wine from before the fall of France, in cellars that had been concreted to hide them from the Germans – or so it

was claimed. They all knew the words of 'It's A Long Way To Tipperary', a place I confused with Timbuktu.

We got cheap fares and trophy wines. Pop gave me prewar Sauternes from a tooth mug in a room we shared in the Hôtel du Louvre in St Malo, just six weeks into his widowhood, the day after he'd bought me the Swiss Army knife I still have. The wine was a colour I got to know well, the colour of the contents of the catheter bag that I'd pour away in the morning. Some days he'd take a bus to Dol de Bretagne, where he had a lady friend of long standing. Some nights he'd miss the bus back. By day he would accompany me on walks around the rebuilt ramparts and at low tide to l'Ile du Grand Bé, where lies the unmarked tomb of Chateaubriand whom he encouraged me to read, thus introducing me to the first of the two Breton fantasists who have marked my life.

He sold the house in Shakespeare Avenue and moved a mile away to Uncle Eric's and Auntie Mary's new house, one of two that my mother designed. That's two too many. Pop moved with a modicum of souvenirs. What happened to the furniture? Did it end up outside a totter's premises in Bevois Valley? What happened to the souvenir biscuit tins and the souvenir biscuit tin catalogues? It occurred to me many years later that these were items that my father had given his future parents-in-law to butter them up, to let them consent to a life with their elder daughter who would bear me after she'd given up wearing the coat of aborted lambs' fleeces captured in a *Southern Evening Echo* photo a few days before they met in collision on the ice rink. When the house in Shakespeare Avenue was taken from me so was the thrilling walk from the alley behind it by way of roads named Thackeray and Tennyson all the way to the front door. This was a treeless labyrinth, all industrial brick and terracotta of 1910–11. My grandparents were its first tenants. I suspect that a Baird held a shotgun to a Hogg head. My mother was born eight months after they married. They eventually bought the house with a windfall between the wars. But they never changed the way it looked. It was for ever 1911. I lived little more than twenty miles away but in a different world. Salisbury is a church city, an army city. In Southampton there were the red and black funnels of great liners, there were predatory cranes, there were vast hangars on the Itchen where boats were built and where flying boats put down in furrows of silver spume. The river was crossed by the 'floating bridge', a chain ferry which landed you in Woolston, where there were streets with names like Vespasian and more houses. Southampton was a city of relentless houses. Yellow brick, red brick. Faced in stucco with bulbous bays in a coarse pastiche of Brighton. There were houses with gables, houses with diapering, houses with overblown capitals and crudely cast mouldings. There were houses where Lascars lodged – that epithet which signified Indian and Malayan seamen was still current. There were the houses where Ken Russell and Benny Hill had grown up. They might have been twins sired by Donald McGill. There wasn't a house in Southampton that didn't rock with bawdy laughter. Fat bottoms, bloated bosoms, big jobs, the barmaid's knickers, all the nice girls love a candle, all the nice girls love a wick. I didn't know whether to block her passage or toss meself off . . . The city lacked decorum. Its police lacked decorum. At a public lavatory on the Common, officers, curled in foetal discomfort, spied from the eaves on sailors perpetuating sailors' mores. Every house I knew had about it the whiff of the public house, of a particular public house, one whose guv'nor was Archie Rice, whose punters' tipple was navy gin. There was indeed a pub by the old town walls that was licensed to distil its own. The Juniper Berry, of course. Uncle Eric kept a boat moored on the Netley shore. It was a Royal Navy cast-off, a sometime lifeboat. Uses of: drinking bottled beer and gin on Sundays, and navigating under the influence. Apart from Spanish holidays which prompted postcards saying 'The beach is lovely. Eric can take off his leg and slide down into the water' and rare visits to relatives in his native Manchester, Eric seldom ventured further than his boat. He didn't see much point in the country though he was happy enough provided he didn't have to get out of the car. Like all my mother's family he belonged to the city, the smoke, the bevelled-glass gin palace rather than the mellow country inn.

Uncle Wangle, né Reginald, Evesham, 1913, lived, when I first remember him, in a flat overlooking the sea at Southbourne, where Bournemouth straggles towards Hengistbury Head. He was determinedly hypochondriacal: migraine, neuralgia, lumbago, cold, heartburn, grogginess, tummy ache. His wife Auntie Ann was frail, freckled, valetudinarian. She was to be pitied because she was an orphan rather than because she was married to Uncle Wangle. Her maiden name was Pope. That is all I know of her life pre-Wangle. It surely cannot have been as hermetic, frugal and loopy as that which she led during the twenty or so years of her marriage (she was a war bride). Wangle had enjoyed failed careers as a mechanical engineer, a policeman, a conscientious objector, an ambulance driver. Now he wrote technical manuals for the De Havilland Aircraft Company and swam in the sea every day of the year. But mere immersion and a view were evidently not enough for him – or indeed for frail freckled valetudinarian Auntie Ann, whose health, he decided, would improve were she subjected to a more fulsome marine contact. So they bought a caravan which they named 'Bredon' and parked it a couple of miles east at Sandhills beside Mudeford Quay. There were pines, dunes, shifting lagoons, crumbling cliffs and other caravans. Theirs was no ordinary lot. The caravan was parked on the very shore. Waves broke over it, they battered the sheet-metal walls of the pioneering home, they caused tympanic mayhem, they promised natural disaster, their potency was amplified so a squall seemed like a gale, a gale like a typhoon. An agency of the local authority threatened action to remove the caravan from the shore before Auntie Ann's health had had a chance to improve. The congress with the elements would be continued a couple of miles inland in a regrettably less exposed

position. The caravan site at Walkford Woods was close by a railway line. The brown and cream Bournemouth Belle raced past hauled by the Southern Region's green Merchant Navy-class locomotives (designed by Oliver Bulleid, second only to Nigel Gresley in the Steam Pantheon).

I was forced to spend part of every summer holiday with them and the shared Elsan and the neighbour's girl Shirley whose favourite record was The Stargazers' 'Close The Door They're Coming In The Window', which I believed had something to do with a plague of locusts. It terrified me. I prissily told Shirley that my favourite record was Handel's *Water Music*. Uncle Wangle's favourite record was anything depressing by a dead Scandinavian or anything gloomy by a dead Finn. When Auntie Ann's health once again failed to improve they moved a further couple of miles to Hinton Admiral where they bought the lodge of a decrepit, unoccupied William IV house whose grounds were being covered in bungalows. The sitting room was octagonal. Its floor was marked with Ls of white sticky tape which indicated precisely where to position a chair for maximum auditory efficacy when listening to the new hi-fi which played Grieg, Grieg, Grieg and occasionally Sibelius. Cruder music, the music which excited me, was not welcome. My taste for Elvis Presley was again incredulously mocked. I bought 'All Shook Up' and got bollocked for it. I put on a pullover one chill September evening and was told how soft I was – the implication was that I was a mummy's boy who had inherited his mummy's sissy city ways. When I admitted to having gone in to Christchurch to see a film called *Light Up the Sky*, a feeble ack-ack comedy with Benny Hill and Tommy Steele, Uncle Wangle rolled his eyes. He abhorred the cinema, never owned a television, listened only to the Home Service and the Third Programme, read the *Listener* and the *Manchester Guardian* (it arrived a day late, by post. The organist, composer and English teacher Richard Lloyd also subscribed to it by post: with sober fury he passed round our class the edition which reported the Sharpeville massacre). Wangle didn't eat meat;

rather, he didn't buy meat. He was a practised scrounger. He ate Grape-Nuts, a cereal as dentally unforgiving as pebbledash. Auntie Ann made equally challenging nutroasts. Bread and sugar were brown. Pipe and tobacco were brown. Clothes were brown or brownish. Auntie Ann wore oatmeal hopsack and had a diarrhoea-colour pea jacket for best: she was oblivious to style. Uncle Wangle wore Aertex the whole year through, a hairy tweed jacket, a knitted tie, khaki drill trousers, sandals or canvas sailing shoes called bumpers. It goes without saying that the house was virtually unheated, that his Morris Minor was a convertible (it was called 'Janet'), that Auntie Ann wore no make-up, that he was dismissive of the grandest house in the locality, the ruinous Highcliffe Castle, which he reckoned bogus and ugly – this would, of course, have been the reaction of most of his coevals to Victorian mediaevalism. It was not its retrospection that he deplored but the theatricality of its expression, and the pomp.

The stratum of old England he sentimentally connected with was that of down-to-earth yeomanry rather than nobility: stout not flash, worthy not chivalric. Uncle Wangle's and Uncle Hank's idealisation of a certain England contained some dilute element of blood and soil. This hodgepodge of pernicious anthropomorphic sentimentality which dignified itself as a doctrine was not, incidentally, a Nazi creation. It was merely hijacked by that regime's ideologues. The identification of a particular people with a particular place and a particular past was a parochial goal whose paradox was that in the years when Uncle Hank and Uncle Wangle (and my father) grew up it was a pan-European commonplace proselytized by Barrès, Maurras, Hamsun etc. Walther Darré's programme was merely an extreme manifestation of that commonplace. In England it went no further than the primitivist chapter of the Arts and Crafts, the Boy Scouts, the Order of Woodcraft Chivalry, the Kibbo Kift, the English Mistery (get that 'i'), the English Array, Social Credit, Distributism, H. J. Massingham, Henry Williamson, Rolf Gardiner, John Hargrave, Jorian Jenks, Captain Pitt-Rivers and a few other eco-fascist fruitcakes, some of whom were detained under Regulation 18B. It was peripheral. And so too was England's proud host of land colonies, repetitive essays in failed communality and spiritual root crops (which also failed). Not that Uncle Wangle ever went back to the land. He was merely a fellow traveller of bucolicism who discerned moral worth in camping. He revelled in discomfort. He was a man who loved a Primus stove and who insisted in defiance of all evidence to the contrary that a half-raw potato half-baked in the embers of a campfire was a peerless treat.

When I was thirteen I put my foot down. I told my parents that I was no longer willing to be farmed out to Uncle Wangle and Auntie Ann during holidays. I'd had enough of being sent to kennels. Two years later Auntie Ann's health was declining. On the second day of a holiday in Devon she had been hospitalised in Bideford where she would remain for a month. Uncle Wangle visited her twice a week, driving through the night. According to my father her frailty was more conspicuous than ever. Her freckled skin was papery, yellow. She appeared severely jaundiced. But it wasn't her liver that was the problem. It was her heart. When she at last returned from Bideford she had open-heart surgery, a procedure that was then in its infancy. The operation was performed at the Royal South Hants Hospital in Southampton. It was apparently successful. When she was discharged she spent her days dozing. Her face was drawn and she was junky-thin. But she was in good spirits. As soon as he judged her fit Uncle Wangle took her away to convalesce. They went camping in the Cairngorms. They were accompanied by their arty and – it follows – entirely artless friends Heather and Bertie. A photo, taken by Heather, shows her and Bertie's Series III MG Magnette, Uncle Wangle's new half-timbered Morris Traveller, two tents, a boulder-strewn stream, a mountainside, Uncle Wangle beside an upturned plastic bucket, Bertie on a folding chair, Auntie Ann on a second folding chair shrouded in blankets and car rugs, wearing a bobble hat. Soon after they returned home she suffered complications resulting from pneumonia. She died on 25 July 1963. Uncle Wangle wrote in his diary 'Black Thursday'.

Despite my protests three years previously my parents, on the point of departing for Germany for the first time since 1938, insisted that I go to stay with him. Keep him company! Cheer him up! I failed. After a couple of days, worn down by his litany of complaints (car tyres, drains, workmen, weather, anything) and his deferred self-justification, oblique exculpation and sly self-pity, I packed my grip and went to crash with some friends who had rented a caravan at Sandhills, only a few yards from where in better times he had parked 'Bredon' on the shore. One night he turned up on the pretext of checking I was OK. There were girls from another van with us (one of them subsequently married a bigamous car dealer in Swindon). There was pop music. There were bottles of beer, cigarettes. I had never seen an adult look so woundedly bewildered. Outside his own milieu, which was halved by Auntie Ann's death, he was at a loss.

He was the loneliest man in the world. His wife was dead. Heather and Bertie had returned to Canada. In his widowhood he was virtually friendless. He absented himself from work. He drove aimlessly round rural England and Wales, sleeping alone in a tent made for two, bathing in brooks. He occasionally sailed with our near-namesake Brian Mead, editor of the *Christchurch Times*, but this was an exclusively marine acquaintanceship. His obstinacy and pride and self-delusion were such that he very likely never admitted to himself that it was his determination to adhere to his code of faith (or whatever it was) that had ruptured his world. When he died five years later, at the age of fifty-five, it was not so much from a broken heart as from an unconquerable isolation, from incomprehension of another world, one that her death had forced him to frequent if not quite inhabit. He was displaced. He was also temporally adrift: for my twenty-first birthday, a few months before he died, he gave me a model railway engine, a Hornby .00 shunter. It wasn't a joke either.

Uncle Hank, né Harry in Evesham, 1907, also wore Aertex, hairy tweed and khaki drill trousers. He smelt of tobacco and of a sandalwood cologne and of coal-tar soap. He never married. Uncle Hank had been engaged before the war to a woman called Vera, who eventually married someone else.

Uncle Hank lived in digs. He lived in digs while at Birmingham University and he lived in digs when he went to work in that city's town clerk's office upon graduating. In 1934 he moved to Burton-on-Trent as deputy town clerk. In 1957 he was promoted and was appointed town clerk, which position he held till he retired in 1972. All those years in Burton he lived in digs with two spinster sisters. There was a hectic week in 1949 when they moved from one suburb of Burton to another, and he moved with them. They addressed each other as mister and miss. At weekends and for holidays he drove to Evesham. Evesham was always home for him. He'd never escaped from his mother – my grandmother. Nor from his sister – my maiden, literally maiden – Aunt Kitty, the Virgin Witch. And when he retired he of course returned to that house to live with Auntie Kitty. It is a life out of Larkin – the carefully delineated confines, the eschewal of the exotic, the Midlands topographies, the walk through the foggy streets back to the digs. But we know now that Larkin's life was not quite Larkinesque. Both my mother, who was only too happy to entertain such ideas, and the woman with whom I lived throughout the Seventies used to wonder at the precise nature of the sibling relationship between Uncle Hank and Auntie Kitty. Whatever it was, they, like Uncle Wangle, were both childless. Uncle Os, who owned the pub surrounded by orchards and who became the owner of a string of hotels, once said of the three of them that 'they lived life in fear of life'.

Uncle Hank had a molar extracted when it was poisoned by a strand of pipe tobacco that was caught between it and the gum. That might suggest a cavalier attitude to personal hygiene, but Uncle Hank was a keen washer even in the days when the house had no bathroom, and a tin tub was filled in the kitchen.

He was a wet shaver, a cold showerer. When he was eleven he swallowed a watch-chain and never knowingly passed it. It was presumably still there, lurking in his duodenum, when his corpse entered the fire at Cheltenham crematorium on a fine brisk day in February 1978. Auntie Kitty cried more than sisters are wont to cry.

Evesham is where two landscapes conjoin in collision rather than elision, the Cotswolds and the Vale. The Cotswolds and their satellite Bredon Hill are all oolitic limestone. Their buildings are geologically determined, now golden, now silver, now grey – but despite chromatic variation they are essentially homogeneous. All quarried stone. All out of the immediately proximate ground, supra-local. From Stow on the Wold, the road to Evesham descends the Cotswold escarpment through Broadway, the show village of all England, the perfect place – immemorial cottages, weathered stone mottled with lichen, greenswards ancient as time itself. The landscape of drystone walls and limestone cottages is of course atypical of England – but it is so persistently photographed, so persistently held to represent some sort of ideal, that it becomes familiar, a norm.

This mendacious fantasy, this dream of olde Englande ends, harshly and suddenly, at the point where a bridge of the old Cheltenham–Birmingham railway crosses the Evesham road. Beyond the bridge a sort of normality was resumed: 1930s houses in their abundant forms lined the road. There was better to come. An entirely different country, geologically apart too. It might have been designed to offend the sensibility which responds favourably to the homogeneous good taste of Cotswolds.

The Vale of Evesham is a vital, scrappy delight, an accretion of intimate details, dense with incident. It is an *unofficial* landscape that is, so to speak, habitually swept beneath the carpet. Best place for it, too, was Uncle Hank's conviction. Badsey, Willersey, Wickhamford, Childswickham: village upon village of fruitholdings, smallholdings, blinding greenhouses, rich earth, wheelbarrows, hurdles, wickets, glinting cloches, orchards, narrow paths between beanpoles, rusty rolls of wire, stacks of pallets, wooden warehouses, rotavators, crates, raised beds, palings, fences made of doors, unscared crows perched on scarecrows, punnets, hoes, corrugated iron, rudimentary dwellings in vegetable plots, shacks, sheds and roadside stalls selling pears and asparagus according to season, a landscape bright with the red industrial brick houses of market gardeners and with the caravans of itinerant pickers. Ordered lines of cabbages and kale stretched to the horizon. The light falling on furrows made them iridescent. It was an open-air factory. Polythene, stretched across fields, shone like an inland sea. It was a bodgerscape, knotted with twine, secured by Birmingham screwdrivers, roughly improvised. Everything was reused, a vehicle chassis here, a mattress there, damp burlap and mould-bloomed tarpaulin, prams, a jerry can. Uncle Hank's despisal of it was prompted by its crudeness, by what he considered the ugliness of the structures. Many of the market gardeners were Italians. They had no sentimental bond with the land. They had rendered the Vale of Evesham an industrial site. The earth was, for them, merely a resource. It was unholy, commercial, material. If you grow greengages or cauliflowers for a living you are very likely disinclined to seek spiritual succour from the earth – unless you have been instructed in such practices by an animistic townie. Uncle Hank wanted everywhere to be like the Malverns or Bredon Hill, places that were sacred to him, places of which he had taken solipsistic possession, places that spoke to him, places that were repositories of mysteries, places that had been invested with the most morbid magic by Housman, who came from the Birmingham satellite town of Bromsgrove. Uncle Hank's conception of these places was a sort of religiose affliction.

Piety demands that we respect other people's faith, but what is there to respect in the delusion that a transcendental bond exists between people and place? Awe in the face of geological phenomena or overwhelming natural beauty is one thing. It is quite another to grant landscape powers other than affective ones. It is aberrant to conceive of the inanimate as though it possesses feelings or thoughts or human capabilities. It is daft enough to attribute these qualities to animals, but to hills and dales . . .

In Evesham, the exotic was represented by a singular trophy which captivated me when I was tiny, a Gothic arch formed by a whale's jawbone, brought back to the town by some long-dead lad who'd signed up as a whaler in the 1870s. Uncle Hank never went whaling. So far as I know he never left England in his seventy-one years. To have done so might have cracked the shell built of layers of habit which protected him from, say, the Brummie blue-collars who used to picnic in the park where the whale's jawbone stands, who used to ride in the pedalos on the Avon. He enjoyed eavesdropping on them and mimicking their twanging inanities, a task he prosecuted with unmistakable despisal for the subjects of these parodic monologues. He had no fondness for them whatsoever. City dwellers were targets; townies were targets (he excused himself); towns themselves were targets, especially towns that had been built after the advent of canals and railways and which were not thus reliant on local materials for their buildings, e.g., Burton-on-Trent. Under his stewardship Burton destroyed itself. The mega-brewers, whom Uncle Hank sucked up to and who plied him with cases of limited-edition beers each Christmas, were men whose all too English mores he admired. They were given carte blanche to demolish the great brick warehouses that defined Burton, the brewery of the Empire. The oast houses, the maltings, the cooperages – they all went. They were expendable (and Victorian). Cities are temporary things. Only the country, the specially sanctioned parts of the country, are eternal.

Uncle Hank's and Uncle Wangle's bucolicism may have been a state of mind – they were not, after all, farriers or farmers or hedgers – but they certainly practised the sort of thrift associable with the rural indigent. Uncle Wangle, who much preferred to be called Reg, owed his name to a supposedly charming childhood capacity to persuade people to give him things. Uncle Scrounger would not have had the same ring to it but would better have summoned his oblivious, unembarrassed tendency to 'borrow' and never to return. He was happy to abandon his vegetarianism if someone else had bought the meat. Uncle Hank was even more costive. My father, who earned less than him and had a family to support, was serially swindled by him over family wills – small sums certainly, but that's not the point – and over what turned out to be an interest-free loan for the Aston Martin. Uncle Hank persistently tried to touch my parents on behalf of Auntie Kitty, who had never worked. And when Uncle Wangle, who was over six feet tall, died, Uncle Hank, who was barely five foot eight, had all of Wangle's meagre wardrobe shortened to fit him so that had my father, also six foot, been inclined to claim a share in it, it would have been no use.

Uncle Hank and Uncle Wangle never met Uncle Eric. They belonged to the country. Or so they deluded themselves. And they never made much effort to dissemble their contemptuous bemusement that their brother, my father, should have married a city girl. They wouldn't have thought much of Uncle Eric. I was apprised from an early age of their footling snobbery, of the hierarchy of places they believed in, of their explicit conviction that an affinity with England's grebe and pheasant was aesthetically and – more importantly – morally superior to a fondness, a weakness, for the fleshpots of the city.

Some fleshpot, Southampton: the Port Said of the Solent.

A poor whore has only to sit in a window in Derby Road, and a major police operation will be launched. All the coppers who've been on Cottage Patrol squeeze out from beneath the rafters to race a mile east from the Common. Their route takes them past Great Aunt Doll's chaotic bungalow where there were peals of dirty laughter and sweet sherry and sweet Marsala, and a room heated to eighty degrees and fish and chips for a dozen in an enamel bowl, and gossip and ribbing and silly stories, and gaspers, and will someone let the dog out else he's going to wee on the couch, and Jonathan you better go with him if you want a widdle 'cos Eric's been and done a big one and you won't be able to get in the karzy there for half an hour – ooh the whiff! And there was chortling wheezing and the feeling that you might be alive.

COMANCHE

The lithe back of the brave in the foreground; the petroleum sheen of his black hair; the headband; the unoxidised tomahawk (Made In Birmingham); the wigwam; the Winchester '73; the smoke signals like freak cloud formations; the heliographic bottle shard . . .

All these could be staged through a compact between my brain and the back garden – more or less, give or take. What couldn't be staged were: depth of field; Monument Valley; canyons' cliffs; Technicolor's peculiarities; squaws.

At the age of seven it occurred to me that there was a squaw-shaped void in my life. This coincided with my leaving Holmwood School. My parents had been asked to remove me: they pleaded on my behalf, to no avail. They were inured to my misbehaviour: Mrs Douglas Guest, wife of the cathedral organist, and Mrs Morgan, a vicar's wife, were among those who sent me home from their daughters' parties for infractions of pass-the-parcel's rules or spitting out disgusting food. The school too had had enough of my unwitting disruptiveness. I hadn't meant to projectile-vomit melted butter in class: I had requested half a pound for breakfast and The Third German Girl had obliged me. I hadn't meant to yelp every time I was pinched by Janet Wheelwright who lived in a house with its own squash court. I hadn't meant to step in dog shit and trail it through the school. But I had. I was castigated too for my persistent lateness, and my reveries. It was at Holmwood that I first suffered the intermittent hallucinations which have visited me all my life.[2]

2 Late one afternoon in the summer of 1984, three and a half years after he had died, I saw my father at Lewes railway station. He was standing at the end of a platform close to where the track enters a tunnel. As I ran along the platform towards him he vanished. He disliked train travel and had probably never been to Lewes in his life. So why there?

Then, like my dreams, they often involved loutishly aggressive sheep. I was sitting on a bench outside the windowless room where we hung our coats. A flock ascended the staircase towards me. I gasped with delight. This was a secret world which, instinctively, I knew not to tell my parents about. Rather, then, like masturbation, but without RSI.

Because I was too young yet to enter the Cathedral School I was sent for two terms to the Swan School, founded in 1931 by the redoubtable Miss Swanton whom I feared and adored. I craved her approbation. She was a burly gust of tweed out of Margaret Rutherford by Nancy Spain. The school occupied a timber-framed house of *c.* 1500 which would be destroyed in 1970 when Rackham, the vandal employed as City Engineer, built an inner relief with a spur on stilts that led nowhere and was inevitably known as the ski jump. I had to wear a uniform: navy blue blazer with white swan on the breast pocket, navy blue and grey quartered cap with a second white swan. This was a novelty which I enjoyed. My parents didn't. All that expense for just two terms; hence, no doubt, their pleading with Mrs Mears at Holmwood.

The beginning of Easter term 1954 was exciting. I got to walk to and from the Swan School with Roger, who had attended it since he was four. He introduced me to parts of Salisbury's mediaeval grid that I didn't know, intersecting streets which allowed us to take a variety of routes, to explore alleys and courtyards safe in each other's company. But after a few weeks he left for Brazil, where his father had been seconded by the Royal Mail to assist in the planning of São Paulo's telephone network.

I was alone among unknown antagonists who were bigger and rougher and maler than Janet Wheelwright. Many had three years' start on me during which they had formed gangs and alliances. This first experience of a single-sex environment was a shock. Janet Wheelwright apart, I missed the girls: Liz, Elizabeth, Jenny, Sue, Clare, the two further Janets, Penny, even the haughty Caroline, who seldom deigned to speak to me and who was chauffeured in a tudorbethan lodge on wheels by her mother, a headscarf rumoured to know the Queen. No girls meant no calm solicitude, no sweet fragrance of talc and cleanliness, but, rather, the soilpipe smell of almost a hundred shrieking, blubbing, blundering, chucking, grubby, boisterous, energetic, savage, merciless small boys.

And there was another smell, a far worse smell. One of the permutations of route that Roger and I could follow through the grid took us up Trinity Street. It's no doubt fitting that a city whose major industries were god and war should have in its centre a dozen almshouses for Christ's brides, old soldiers, pious widows of the fallen etc. Trinity Hospital was crumbly red brick and worn stone quoins. It has been grotesquely restored when it should have been allowed to perish like the generations within it. A Wrennish chapel stands on one side of a courtyard which we investigated unnoticed. It was too ordered to appeal to us. Nonetheless some time later I did creep in again, alone this time, daring myself to trespass. A parchment woman was upright and immobile on a chair by the chapel's door. She was unconscionably old, older than my paternal grandmother, older even than my father's nanny Mrs Hopkins, who could remember reading the news of General Custer's death at the battle of the Little Bighorn during the smallpox summer of 1876, older than anyone I had ever seen. She appeared not to notice me. And as I left, silently, a man shuffled out of his set towards her. He was, incredibly, as old as she was. These people must belong to the third sex, which I had thitherto believed was the domain of gypsies. They were all matt, all dried up. They bore the complexion of split cement sacks, which caused me to shiver. Trinity Hospital was heaven's (or hell's) antechamber where the pallid waited for judgment. In late winter they emitted no odour. You could not smell them. You could not smell their mortal fear. You could not smell their food. Initially the reek was faint and fleeting. By the time my nostrils had got a message to my brain it had disappeared, an olfactory vanishing act. Such instances of evanescence did not last. As the weather grew warmer so did the odour increase. Even though there were days when I detected nothing it was becoming ever more assertive, more frequent, more protracted. It was putrid, clammy, vegetal *and* carnal. It prompted disgust, then dread, then confused compassion. This was the smell of old people as they relinquished life. This was the stink of death, as rank as that of the long-hung pheasants Padre inflicted on my parents. That route past Trinity Hospital was far from the only choice. I could have taken St Ann Street and Love Lane, or Payne's Hill where the German spy who worked at a tannery had lived, or grey Rampart Road's raised pavement, or Dolphin Street and Culver Street. But these were the ways I did not go, for I was drawn to putrefaction, I took shameful pleasure in whatever disgusted me. Were the old living corpses who began to rot before they died? Did maggots seethe beneath their skin? Did they flap helplessly to repel the rodents that gnawed their limbs? The rats in the nearby Friary slums were said to be as large as cats.

Mine was not a case of *nostalgie de la boue*. That would imply a yearning *to return* to brute sordor. I had never left it. It had merely been shepherded into abeyance by the everyday presence of girls who even in prepuberty insouciantly inflict couth on the rough puppies that will grow into the dogs called men. My mother had wanted a girl. And I wanted a sister among whose contemporaries I would find a squaw. Boys with sisters had girls on tap. It was easy for them. Everyone knew that.

My gregarious parents had a quick turnaround in new acquaintances. Not because a mutual animus was struck, though that did inevitably sometimes occur. It was, rather, due to the transitory nature of Salisbury's population. Service postings were often less than two years. People came and went. Their children came and went throughout my schooldays. At the Swan School there were menacing charts on the wall with our names listed down the left. Along the line from each name, performance in class and obedience were marked by shiny triangular stickers. Blue and green indicated achievement and good manners,

73

shit-brown and Satan-black were the signs of academic failure and moral impoverishment. At the end of my first term I had an averagely polychrome horizontal mix. Now that Roger had gone I considered my best friend to be a boy called Richard Hallmark, whose chestnut hair was beautiful. We never spoke. But he didn't hit me. In all likelihood he did not wish to add to the log of his offences. He had acquired nothing but browns and blacks. He was the only boy in the school to have done so. Advised by Miss Swanton that he was a disgrace he burst into tears. I wanted to comfort him. When we resumed for the summer term he wasn't there. Perhaps he felt himself unworthy of the school. Perhaps he had been asked to go elsewhere. Some weeks later I learned that he had moved. His father had been posted from CDE Porton Down to Cornwall. A far-off wild sea county which I knew of as the home of my father's late uncle, the Revd John Tarpley, vicar of Roche, and of his daughter Molly, who had enjoyed the privilege of sitting – inapt word – for no less a coyly erotic painter than Russell Flint. A far-off wild sea county where production of Sarin and VX had begun at CDE Nancekuke.

Diana Colombine's skin was deliciously fawn like a doe's, like a high-baked biscuit. Precisely, like a Huntley and Palmers Breakfast Biscuit – a smooth 10-mm-deep rectangle whose corners were curved, whose centre was marginally concave and which I longed for because it was forbidden (rival manufacturer). I longed for her too and her sweet smooth limbs, her sun-streaked bobbed hair whose bangs she was coltishly learning to throw. She didn't know that she was going to be my squaw even though her qualifications were impeccable: she was the only girl of my age whom I now saw regularly. She had arrived in Wiltshire from Colombo with her parents Harry and Beryl, who had quickly become great friends of my parents. Colombo was in Ceylon. I knew that. And knew too that Ceylon was nearly India. She bore a name that derived from that city and whilst nearly Indians and Red Indians were from different continents they were clearly kin for otherwise they would not be so called. A further link: a lifesize painted statue of a Sioux warrior stood above the entrance of the Indianerhof, a prodigy of Viennese social housing designed by Karl Dirnhuber, father of one of Harry's co-authors of microbiological and bacteriological papers. That proved something.

The interior of their thatched cottage at Winterbourne Gunner was dark. The sitting room was all files and bookshelves. The ceilings were unusually high. He would sit at a staunch table placed against the back of a high-back pub settle to whose planks he drawing-pinned notes. He wrote on foolscap notepads unfazed by any activity around him, lit as though by an annunciatory beam. The house was set back from the road beyond a lush paddock which a pony cropped. I confidently impressed Diana with assurances of my equestrian prowess though I had never ridden a horse. I confidently impressed her with my Apache outfit one day when she and her parents came for lunch.

I greeted her naked save for a Lone Ranger mask over my eyes, a paisley handkerchief round my head with a rook feather stuck in it, bolts of warpaint lipsticked on my cheeks, a leather belt round my waist and an improvised breechcloth – a length of fabric secured by the belt to cover my genitals and my bottom. This ensemble was completed by an air rifle *and* a bow and arrow, more mature choices of weapon than a plastic tomahawk. Beryl was startled by my appearance. She was a tense woman forever on the point of breaking into tears. She looked at me with a look my parents wouldn't see, a look which I knew I could not mention. She must have wondered what they were thinking of in allowing me to dress thus. Harry was balding, saturnine, dark-eyed, restless, energetic. He had skin as smooth as his daughter's, well-cut clothes and what I supposed to be the mien of a brahmin.

He joined my fantasy with the amused bonhomie he displayed towards both children and adults. I liked the way he could turn on life-and-soul joviality. And I was grateful that an Indian of a sort – even an Indian who, unlike me, did not look the part, but

75

who like me did not speak with an Indian accent – was apprised of the Apache's homelands. He was familiar, too, with Cochise, the Chiricahua chief I favoured over the publicity hog Geronimo who had the face of an ancient charlady. I knew that the Apache used poisoned arrows. Harry explained how they were poisoned: with the pounded liver of an animal (often a deer) which had been bitten by a rattlesnake, or with that snake's venom glands. Such arrowheads were used against enemies but not for hunting. Did I know why? Because they might contaminate the meat of beasts so taken. This was information that grown-ups seldom imparted, were seldom interested in. He did not, however, share my preoccupation with the homicidal (and probably *right*-handed) Henry McCarty aka William Bonney aka Billy the Kid. This oversight was a disappointment to me. No matter. Apaches ate plants which made them dance and reel for hours, which made them courageous in battle, which made them see things they had never seen before. Visions? Precisely! Holes in the sky, Old Chap. Mountains changing shape as much in a minute as they had done in a million years. Cacti smiling at them. They stared at the sun till it blinded their eyes. Were they mad? Harry clapped me on my naked Apache back, congratulated me on my perception – and how delighted I was to be so patronised!

He asked me how I was enjoying the Swan School, he hoped I appreciated the historic building. I described the smell of the old people waiting to die in Trinity Hospital. He made a caricaturally quizzical face. A few moments later as we were sitting down to lunch he laughed at whatever aperçu his brain had conveyed. He was also laughing at me. I had learnt early that I prompted laughter without intending to, a characteristic I rued. He suggested that what I thought was the smell of old people was the smell of the mash in Gibbs Mew brewery just along the street from Trinity Hospital. I had surely noticed the building with the hoists, the cranes, the barrels? He explained how beer is made and why the process smells the way it does. He explained in detail I could not understand. He was suddenly oblivious to his audience's shortcomings, making no allowance for children or indeed non-scientists. I was taken by Harry's enthusiasm. But I still thought that was the way old people smelled.

After lunch Diana and I crept under the plum tree into the cheap plastic and canvas conical tent that I called my wigwam. She agreed to be my squaw. I gave her a headdress of plastic feathers that just about fitted. I stroked her skin.

The next day:

Diana and I returned as pupils to our respective schools.

My mother walked 200 yards up the road to the school where she taught. My father rose early to go off on his rounds.

Beryl probably congratulated herself on not pouring her first drink before noon.

Dr Harry Cullumbine (not Colombine, not that I realised for years) drove five minutes from the cottage at Winterbourne Gunner to CDE Porton Down, where he monitored marmosets on atropine, observed rats breathing kerosene fumes and pigs hooked to ethanol drips, fed *Datura stramonium* to monkeys and ketamine to lambs. Having attended to his zoo of junky primates and barbiturate-dependent quadrupeds he dosed human volunteers with LSD. This perpetually tanned Yorkshireman (who occasionally failed to suppress the ghost of that accent), sometime Professor of Physiology and Pharmacology at the University of Colombo, was now head of the Physiology Section at Porton. The volunteers were national servicemen. In this context volunteers is today habitually written 'volunteers'. A little less than a year before, Leading Aircraftman Ronald Maddison[3] had died in Salisbury Infirmary four hours after participating in a Porton experiment which exposed him to 200 mg of Sarin. The Coroner came under pressure from the Home Office, from the Intelligence

3 Ronald Maddison died 06/05/1953. Tony Blair was born the same day. His mother, unhappily, hadn't enjoyed the right to choose. Maddison came from County Durham, where Blair would live from the age of eight. The Ceauşescus of Connaught Square died, hideously, on 23/09/2016.

Services, from the Minister of Supply, Duncan Sandys. Nonetheless, it is conceivable that the verdict of death by misadventure might have been returned even without those illegitimate influences: *autres temps, autres moeurs*.

Exceptionally, a second inquest was held fifty-one years later in 2004. To the doubtless smug delight of Attorney General Goldsmith and DPP Calvert-Smith, brown-nosed cretins of the New Labour establishment, it returned the altogether predictable verdict of unlawful killing. Like the quotes round 'volunteers' this verdict was the presumptuous judgment of the present on the past. Here was the Age of Apology or Rights or Compensation or Complaint castigating the Age of – what? Duty? Exploitation? Service? Mortal Quackery? Such retrospective perdition is cooked up in a whiggish void. With confidently 20/20 hindsight it over-looks the threats of nuclear devastation, Soviet aggression and world war which were omnipresent at Porton half a century previously. A society which deludes itself that risk can be elim-inated is unlikely to understand one which accepted privation and danger with stoic fatalism, with forelock-tugging resignation. The volunteers' choric plea that they believed they were assisting in the researches of the Common Cold Unit at Harvard Hospital eight miles from Porton on the other side of Salisbury would be plausible were it not for the fact that experiments had been conducted over two years before Maddison's death and would continue subsequently.

Only a handful of men were used in a single day. After the experiment each would return to his base. It defies credibility that there was no mess talk, no tap-room gossip, no barracks rumour about what happened in the chambers. Potential volunteers of the future would thus have known to expect something other than Harvard Hospital. Five hundred and sixty-two men had been involved in the Sarin experiments before an adverse reaction was suffered. At which point the dose was reduced from 300 mg to 200 mg. Maddison was volunteer no. 745. For the volunteers it must have seemed like light prostitution. In exchange for a meagre sum and a day free of the boredom of conscripted life they surrendered their body to a chemical rather than a human intrusion. The liberal judiciary's discernment of a moral equivalence between Porton's experiments and those conducted by SS doctors is an instance of the usual grotesque *trahison des clercs gauchistes*. Of course we all know that the camp doctors loved their children, hearth and Bach. The many Porton doctors and boffins whom I met exhibited similarly congenial traits. This does not make them wicked. Nor do their experiments, although age and ethical climate weather a scientist. I was twelve when I first met Ken James.[4] He was forty-three and had bought the plot of land next to my parents'. His opinions were no doubt different then from those he held fifty years later.

He was an organic chemist, an expert in chemical warfare and defence against it, a jazz trumpeter, a pioneer of operational research, an inventor, a craftsman, an entrepreneur, a writer. He was a man of formidable learning, exceptional energy and limitless curiosity.

4 Ken James was a signatory of the Official Secrets Act.

He was born at Shepherd's Bush. His father, then serving as a soldier, never really recovered from the First World War. When he was demobbed he became a groom in Neasden, then still more or less a village. It was in such places on the periphery of west and north-west London that Ken grew up as his father moved from job to job and his family moved from one rented flat to the next. Alcoholism, indigence and bailiffs followed them.

His mother walked out – she would live to a great age on the north Kent coast. He left Latymer Upper at the age of sixteen after taking the School Certificate and sought work in order to provide for his increasingly unemployable father. By night he played trumpet in a jazz band with, inter alia, Les Hitchcock, nephew of Alfred, and Cliff Townshend, future father of Pete. At Number One Rhythm Club, off Haymarket, they were joined on stage one night by Louis Armstrong.

By day he was a laboratory chemist. At C. A. Vandervell he was employed by the father of Tony Vandervell, who in the late 1950s manufactured the Vanwall F1 car. At British Drug Houses he was precociously involved in the development of an early commercial thyroxine used to stimulate underactive thyroid glands. It was made clear to him that an autodidact, no matter how talented, would always suffer a competitive disadvantage to a graduate, no matter how dull. He cut down on jazz and enrolled in evening classes at the Northern Polytechnic in Holloway to take a London external degree. He had yet to complete it when, just before the outbreak of war, he was offered a job at the Chemical Defence Establishment at Porton Down.

Salisbury had not then, and still has not, a seat of tertiary education. Its intelligentsia was mainly composed of Porton Down scientists. They were clever people and, incidentally, my ad hoc teachers. Ken said that Porton had 'the atmosphere of a university . . . there were scientists of every discipline – there was even an archaeologist who had dug round Stonehenge.' Having received his degree and several promotions, he was, after little more than a year devoted to the design of chemical weapons, appointed head of the Munitions

Section of the Australian Field Experimental Station. 'Assessing bomb performance . . . What that actually meant was laying waste to a considerable area of the Queensland jungle.'

Post-war he was seconded from there to BAOR, and then to Washington DC, Utah and Alberta, where he encountered the practices of operational research.

The house next to my parents' that Edward Fielden's firm had torpidly built for Ken and Peggy was hardly finished when Ken was appointed Director, Chemical Defence Research and Development at the War Office. They let the house and moved to Twickenham. The first tenants sublet the granny annex to a girl who played host to Salisbury's folkies, among them the future actor Brian Protheroe (né Jones), then a lab assistant at Porton. Ken sat on various NATO committees, went on to become Director of the Operational Research Establishment at Byfleet. In 1968 he was given the post of Scientific Adviser to the Treasury with a brief to apply operational research methods to large-scale government projects including the funding of the Channel Tunnel and the Thames Barrier, the NHS's expansion and the introduction of decimalisation. He was instrumental in bringing computers into government. A move which was widely, though ultimately unsuccessfully, resisted. When he retired he was Chief Scientific Officer. He had come to admire William Armstrong, Denis Healey and Harold Wilson. He had foreseen, correctly, that Victor Rothschild's CPRS – which he reckoned to be a club-like vanity project – presaged the advent of partial 'special advisers' and battalions of consultants. He was astonished by Tony Benn's 'silliness'. His reaction to any mention of our eventual Salisbury neighbour Edward Heath was to suppress a laugh.

Although he was an ambulatory encyclopaedia he was reluctant to foist his knowledge on the unwilling. He was a measured optimist who believed in the values of the Enlightenment and in the beneficence of science. He was, equally, bewildered by the intellectual baselessness and fatuity of religious 'faith' and contemptuous of the tribalism that accompanies it.

'I suppose we did do some pretty terrible things [at Porton] . . . In the chambers. The chambers . . . Even thinking about those chambers is, ah . . . Putting on masks to go in them . . . We did some pretty terrible things to ourselves too. It's amazing there weren't more like Bacon[5] – no one followed the safety drill. Pretty reckless, but that was how it was in those days. Thankless task Darlow[6] had – no one took any notice . . . The thing is, we didn't think of what we were doing as terrible . . . It wasn't terrible then . . . Defence of the realm – not too fashionable nowadays. Being one step ahead – that was the deterrent . . . *Letting them know* we were one step ahead. No one wanted to go to war again . . . Anything but that. Anything. Not like this . . . *bunch*.'

He considered that to judge the seldom injurious experiments conducted at the height of the Cold War by the standards of the rights-obsessed early twenty-first century was morally, judicially and philosophically flawed. He was inured to the sensationalism that attaches to experiments that go wrong. Such experiments were, he argued, the very rare exceptions that proved the rule of Porton's probity. They provided, and still provide, a straw for the enemies of science to clutch at.

That God's Own Bomber – the most religious thus most delu-sional British prime minister since Gladstone and the most belli-cose since Palmerston – should have presided over a government that sanctimoniously damned a predecessor's chemical warriors is risible. Of the 30,000 men who underwent experiments at Porton less than 2 per cent, about 500, claim to have suffered ill effects. Because the suits brought against the MoD have mainly rested on the question of whether informed consent was obtained, the plaintiffs' representatives have not concerned themselves with

5 Dr Geoffrey Bacon died on 01/08/1962 after infecting himself in a laboratory accident with *Yersinia pestis*, the organism responsible for bubonic plague.
6 Dr H. M. Darlow, author of *An Introduction to Safety in the Microbiological Laboratory* (1960) and *Safety in the Animal House* (1967), was Porton's Safety Officer.

differentiating between nerve gases and psychomimetics. Anyone else would differentiate. The recreational use of nerve gases is a masochistic specialism. That of psychomimetics is not.

The SIS (Secret Intelligence Service, precursor of MI6), on whose behalf the experiments with LSD were conducted, concluded, peremptorily and wrongly, that its uses in both conflict and interrogation were few because its effects were unpredictable. But it does not follow that they are uncontrollable. Reactions are almost wholly determined by the subject's surroundings and companions. Amend these and you amend the experience. Harry Cullumbine understood this. He persisted in the belief that such a trigger might possess protean psychotherapeutic properties. And because Porton was not monolithic he managed to grant himself permission to continue to test it: he held a senior post, he was known as 'the Chief'.

Further, LSD was still more than a decade away from proscription. He used it in non-clinical circumstances. He took his work home with him. He dosed himself. He discovered its capacity to promote wonder, to make *him* see mountains change shape, to show *him* holes in the sky. He shared its powers (aesthetic, oneiric, chromatic, comic, moral, hedonistic) with a close coterie. Did they witness cosmic phenomena as they dosed themselves in tweeds and Bedford cords, in twinsets and circle skirts? Did downland junipers mutate into pyrites? Did hares boast of being jackals? Did they know that the leathery crones' faces at Great Yews were really bole knots? Did they forget that the berries were poison? Did they read the chalky scrawl inscribed in turf as rabbit runes? Did they believe they were hallucinating when they saw myxomatotic faces grinning from warrens?

Given LSD's availability, its legality and the level of intellectual and pharmacological curiosity it is hardly surprising that it was used clandestinely. In the period 1953–55, when Harry Cullumbine was experimenting with it, the suggestive linkage of LSD to religious or animistic experience had yet to be made. There was no reason to suspect that this crystal-clear chemical would foment a sloppy goofy subculture. Cullumbine's tests had ceased by the time that Aldous Huxley first dosed himself on Christmas Eve 1955. Huxley had a long history of mystical enquiry. His bias towards such revelations, propagated in *Heaven and Hell*, would have a determining effect on the millions of people who took LSD over the next quarter-century. If you expect to suffer transcendence or expect to find god you are more likely to do so than if you dose yourself without such preconceptions. The drug does not take complete control of the brain. It is susceptible to guidance, it can be nudged in a particular direction both by intellectual preparation and by exterior stimuli – place, people, climate. The effect of the experience can be purely material. That is what Porton scientists would probably have expected, thus would probably have got.

Ken James, who once mentioned that he had coined the Porton nickname for LSD – 'sparkle' – told me casually that: 'In our generation it was only the gullible who took to religion . . . the semi-educated . . . the Irish of course. You know – we thought we were through with all that.' That was the generation which defeated Nazism, a genocidal theocracy which led the easily led to the abyss. That generation was immediately obliged to prepare for war against another genocidal theocracy, the Soviet Union. It witnessed religion raising its beardie halitotic head throughout the Middle East, font of all of monotheistic lunacy. It suffered the indignity of seeing LSD hijacked by DIY animists, headbanded transcendentalists, camper-van mystics, campus shamans, epiphany tourists, vision diggers, the credulous armies of kaftans seeking The Simple Answer to The Big Question. LSD became a shortcut to the states achieved by fasting. And only the credulous ever fasted (or dervish-whirled or flagellated themselves or perched on desert pillars).

Albert Hofmann's delightful key to the fairground within every skull was reduced to soma, ambrosia. He himself was enjoined by R. Gordon Wasson, the New York banker who styled himself an *ethnomycologist*, to participate in Mexican field-experiments

– all shamans and fungus, peyote and gods. Wasson was doctrinaire: any use of psychomimetic plants and drugs to ends which were not specifically religious was frivolous. He thus dismissed their purely aesthetic capacities. Hofmann's collaboration with Wasson was an implicit admission that LSD, the mighty force he had synthesised, was nothing more than an *entheogen*:[7] but, then, maybe Stradivari was not much of a fiddler. It seems indisputable that religions, their supernatural mythologies (ascensions, miracles, mutations) and the very notion of divinity owe their existence to ancient hallucinogens.

In their wonder our ancestors believed that their marvellous visions owned a reality that was external. They misunderstood the mechanics of *Amanita muscaria* and mandrake. They understandably failed to acknowledge the enchantments of secular solipsism. But that was no reason for the transcendental vanguard of the New Age to do so too. In a gross abnegation of science the most advanced of psychoactive agents came to serve backwardness, to be employed in pursuit of threadbare superstitions, in validation of inexcusable ignorance, in confirmation of hackneyed nostrums. Such mystical decadence was not inevitable. Harry Cullumbine's work with LSD was eventually curtailed.

In the summer of 1956 he left England for ever, taking his wife and my squaw with him. The following year my mother bought an insanitary cottage in the village of Boscombe for a few hundred pounds. Builder Rigiani did it up. My father refused to move there so to my mother's and my chagrin it was sold. Every time we drove there we passed the Cullumbines' house, *former* house. I pined for Diana. Her father no doubt quadrupled his Scientific Civil Service salary as Professor of Pharmacology at Toronto University. Some years later we heard that Beryl had died: I imagined that, shortly before, her hair had turned white

7 Like *ethnomycologist*, *entheogen* was Wasson's coinage. It was intended to distinguish between a drug taken in search of god and the same drug taken for pleasure, a mere psychedelic.

overnight. Later still Harry wrote to say that he had remarried. In the mid-Sixties he went into commercial pharmaceuticals in Pennsylvania. He joined a country club between Philadelphia and Trenton, somewhere round about there. He was elected its president in 1969. How much did his fellow members know of his past as a germ warrior and of his psychotropic progress though the world's laboratories?

By the pool, in the sexually active prepubescent summer holidays of 1957, in an access of that most childish of delusions, identification, I would suppose that Paul Anka's perky, mawkish song of pre-teen angst, 'Diana', was my song of my lost squaw. And then I forgot her. Until twelve summers later. 1969.

In his steep-ceilinged garret on the top floor of a house opposite Holloway Gaol David Sadgrove put on *Happy Trails*. Quicksilver Messenger Service. The record was no more or less wearisomely tuneless than any other by San Franciscan longhairs of that era. But its cover! It comprised a retina-fixing painting of a cowboy on a galloping pony waving his hat in farewell to his sweetheart. The subject matter is that of Charles Russell or Frederic Remington, pictorial mythologists of the Chisholm Trail, Abilene, Wichita – the place names Roger and I knew so well. The style is almost Maxfield Parrish's. Was this the work of some neglected master of their era? It turned out to be an accomplished psychedelic pastiche. The rocky landscape is drowsy and saturated. It's lit by the last of the sun, at the golden hour. The Old West had never seemed so intense, so distilled. The scene appears to be atomising. The painter George Hunter's eyes had been cleaned to a sparkle by LSD.

I thought of Diana Cullumbine for the first time in over a decade. I imagined my full-grown squaw in the fringed chamois dress which the buxom Dale Steinberger, the Jewish Cowgirl of R. Crumb's priapic imagination, burst out of. I wondered idly if, three thousand miles away, she had seen *Happy Trails* and, if she had, whether it reminded her of her childhood brave.

Probably not. No, definitely not. I then forgot her for a further decade and a half till one summer night on Oslofjord, fishing for cod from a skiff, I watched a carmine sky bleed behind pines' silhouettes on the western shore. It was the décor of *Hiawatha*. I was infected for a moment with a longing for my dreamy-eyed Minnehaha, the daughter of the ancient arrow-maker, a figure from so long ago that she was as graspable as quicksilver, as mnemonically substantial as the ghost of an imaginary friend. The past won't sit still for a moment.

EARLIEST MEMORY

My earliest memory is churning white water and an Alsatian dog. The sluice's deafening roar must have shut out the snarling creature's barking, but there is no escape from its restless sinewy prowl, its bared teeth, its milky saliva. The place is the Old Mill at West Harnham which in my infancy I called 'Dog West Harnham', a better effort than Soming (Homington) or Trimet (Triumph).

When I see an Alsatian approaching I cross the street.

My earliest memory is being pushed in my pram along Exeter Street by Nanny Barham. Another pram approaches us from the direction of town. As it passes I throw my rag doll and a cup into it. This merits a scolding. Above us looms the crenellated Close wall. Across the street are a monkey puzzle tree and the convent of the Sisters of Charity of St Vincent de Paul, dry-skinned wimple-people who belong, like gypsies, to a third sex.

My earliest memory is of the half-timbered state-owned shop in Exeter Street's continuation, St John Street. This shop sold, or exchanged for ration coupons, thick orange juice which might have been cooked, Virol, rusks, cod liver oil, rosehip syrup, Energen rolls.

My earliest memory is of lying supine, watching swaying poplars stretch to the sky. I suppose this must be in Riverside Gardens, close by the sewage works in what used to be called Bugmore.

My earliest memory is a swooping, undulating road. The distant sea beckons. It would be indistinguishable from the blue sky if it did not sparkle with such promise. Then, as the car hurtles downhill, it disappears. Now the horizon comprises merely the hill's tarmac brow and dusty green downland. I am cheated by landscape's vagaries.

My earliest memory is a sloping street of uniform grey stone houses and regular pollards with leaves like tutus, bracelets, necklaces. A lorry – just a cab with an unladen rectangle behind it – is parked beside the spreading boughs of a churchyard yew.

Years later, when I am six, I will identify the yew as being beside the flat square in the centre of Wilton.

The same day I will identify the street as the high street of Hindon, ten miles west of Wilton, where there is no such churchyard but there are a marked slope, pollards, stone cottages.

My earliest memory is loitering in False Memory Lane, idling in blissful suspension on amniotic briny, constriction without fear, muffled voices, gradations of temperature, quotidian rhythms: perpetual dusk with interludes of static red darkness and agitated red light, hurdy-gurdy gurgling, groaning machine parts that are separate from me, up and down, big dipping.

This is an invention, probably.

What is sure is that when we're in utero:

a) we don't know the definite article;
b) the state of total dependence we enjoy is a preparation for addiction. Instead of the womb, over which we exercise no choice, we can select whom we relinquish our body to: Bogota gangsters; Seagrams; rogue chemists in a Minsk suburb; heavy-gutted microbrewers; pharmaceutically inclined utopians; Glaxo; overconfident mycophiles; Medocain patricians; Old Tozer with his pot-still he believes no one knows about in the asbestos and tarpaulin shed you can see from the alley between the gardens through a gap in the rotting pales.

EDWARDS, MRS

Harnham is the southernmost part of Salisbury. It stretches along the valley of the Nadder upstream of that river's confluence with the Avon. To its south is an escarpment of the downs which was hardly built on till the 1920s. Much of Harnham was owned by the Longford Castle estate, seat of the Earls of Radnor: hence such road names as Bouverie and Folkestone. Until the mid-Thirties when New Bridge was built (to the design of Owen Williams) East Harnham was joined to the city only by a narrow bipartite bridge of the same era as the cathedral, and West Harnham by a pedestrian causeway across the water meadows, the floated meadows.

In the 1950s the pre-c20 vestiges were these.

At East Harnham:

The half-timbered Rose and Crown (boxing, cockfighting).

A meekly neo-Gothic church where I was baptised (and whose only congenial incumbent would be done for cottaging in Bournemouth).

The neighbouring school where my mother taught.

Three brief terraces of cottages.

Government House, an officer's mess – formerly owned by the Radnors; then it was known as The Cliff, the name Mrs Dear still used. It was sited in a bowl between precipitous beech-covered slopes and was comically lugubrious.

A whiting works' owner's blowsy mid-Victorian villa, again on former Longford Castle land. Its overgrown riverside spoil tip might have been a 'natural' feature.

Further lavishly tile-hung villas of the 1880s and 90s in park-like gardens of cedars and wellingtonias.

*

On the hill above East Harnham:

A sanatorium built as a private house by Bishop Wordsworth but never occupied by him: his wife considered its proximity to a chalk pit dangerous for children.

A workhouse of the 1870s, the Alderbury Union's Tower House Poor Law Institution, in a style by then thirty years out of date.

At West Harnham:

A dull Norman church (chequer walls: Chilmark limestone, knapped flint).

A dull Victorian chapel.

A horizontal mediaeval mill (chequer walls, again); beside it an austere, vertical, latest-Georgian brick warehouse.

A pub and houses of the same time by the same hand no doubt.

An incongruously wealden former vicarage.

Some uniform, so perhaps tied, cottages; stylistically similar to those built by the Wilton Estate at Netherhampton.

All subsequent accretions conformed to Salisbury's twentieth-century architectural norm.

West Harnham: low-rise council housing of the immediate post-war; Wellworthy's piston ring factory and its modesty fringe of see-through poplars; a sprawling chalk pit, the latest in a line of such quarries – the green hill gnawed as though it were a giant apple, leaving a trail of half-eaten grubby white precipices, ramparts, slipped cliffs, coves. Matt powdery dust lay on every surface – nothing glistered.

East Harnham, where I lived, had expanded in the 1910s and 20s: drab red-brick ribbon development, jerry-built terraces of varying degrees of meanness.

Yet this was the décor of my everyday existence, adored and mysterious and ever-expanding – the more I looked the more I saw. I revelled in minutiae's minutiae, in the gamut of sensations provoked by different sights and smells a mere few steps from each other – a patterned fanlight, the manhole cover outside the Horns' gate, the reeking gust from Bowns's dairy, the grooved rails attached to door jambs to accommodate slates against floods, a house name incised in stone in a pompous font, the flashing flames and scorched bone stench and doomy hammering in Mr Curtis's smithy, a tarred fence stake, the shambles reek of the cold store which Sid the Butcher leant his bike against, Mr Thick's hollyhocks and foxgloves which marked him as old, as much as his arthritic drowner's limbs did.

I did not then discern the unfailing banality and offensive timidity of the buildings which had caused two former villages to coalesce into one inchoate suburb. And even though, when I go back, the all too English dreariness is inescapable, it is *my* dreariness, the dreariness I was born to and longed to escape but which is so indelibly imprinted in my memory, so much within me whether I like it or not, so wholly appropriated by me, that the paramountcy of old familiarity is entire: it extinguishes the dismissive indifference that I might feel in any similar site of such architectural paucity.

Nostalgia is not simply a yearning for a lost home, a yearning which can never be satisfied by revisiting that home, which could only be satisfied by becoming once more the child who inhabited that home, at that time. It is also primitive, pre-rational, pre-learning. It quashes developed taste, aesthetic preference, learnt refinements. It insists that the chance associations of infancy are more obstinately enduring than the chosen positions of our subsequent sentience. It tells us that we are lifers in a mnemonic prison from which there is no reprieve.

53–59 Harnham Road is a white-rendered terrace of four double-fronted cottages. Thatched terraces are uncommon, even in this part of England where thatched roofs abound. Thatched porches on tree trunk pillars are rarer still. The pillars, if they are contemporary with the rest of the terrace, indicate that it was built around 1800. The terrace otherwise displays none of the fancy associable with the *cottage orné*. Even if not expressly intended for that purpose, for many years the cottages housed the staff of The Rose and Crown, then a staging post on the road from London to Exeter. An incident in *The Woodlanders* derives from a coach accident at the junction of Harnham Road and (what was not then Old) Blandford Road, less than two hundred yards west of The Rose and Crown. Thomas Hardy, truffling in the *Dorset County Chronicle*'s archives, read a report of it in the edition of 20/07/1826, fourteen years before he was born.

My parents were married in the early summer of 1939. They rented 55 Harnham Road for six months whilst they searched for a house to buy. They would remain there for twenty-three years. In those last months before the war the house was still owned by The Rose and Crown, which had just been bought by a retired Malayan rubber planter, Stiffy Edwards, and his second wife. They lived at number 59, which possesses an extra bay.

Stiffy was doubly badered – he suffered alcohol-induced Tourette's and amputations of both legs. He propelled his wheelchair from house to inn down the middle of Harnham Road swearing and cursing at whoever was available to be sworn and cursed at. He left two children by his first wife who had died in the early Thirties and his gentle shy reclusive widow who retained ownership of the cottages whilst selling The Rose and Crown to Ushers, a Trowbridge brewery. She had no job so presumably lived off capital and the meagre rents she received. The elder of those children was Jane, whom I confuse with Jane Robertson who lived at no. 57 and owned the first Posty: they were both dark-haired. The younger child, Glynn, would become a ubiquitous television actor, whose heavy features' increasing resemblance to his father's my parents never failed to remark on.

As a boy Glynn seems to have spent a lot of time with my parents. He was boisterous, noisy, outdoorsy, outgoing. This was the sort of son my father had hoped for. He was amused rather than angry when Glynn and John Jacobs were violently sick after smoking tea leaves in a roll-up. It was, after all, just the sort of thing that my hedgehog-eating, trout-tickling, clay-pipe-smoking, hare-bone-whittling, Stalky-imitating father would have got up to when he was a boy.

This most staunchly down-to-earth actor – who would play Dave, proprietor of the Winchester Club, in *Minder* – is no one's idea of a romantic lead: a Badel, a Delon, a Stamp. Yet he was a distant figure of romance to a small boy.

Glynn is learning to be a sugar planter in the West Indies – the West Indies!

Glynn runs a nightclub in Trinidad – a nightclub!

Glynn has a girlfriend! A girlfriend! How I wanted to be old enough to have one of those, a real one beside me in my sports car, hair streaming in the wind. My prepubertal approaches failed to secure me a girlfriend rather than girls to muck about with.

Glynn abandons colonial commerce to become an actor: I wasn't quite sure what an actor was but if Glynn was going to be one . . . Later I would be grateful that he had chosen to successfully pursue what I could never bring myself to call *The Profession.*

I was a baby when he left Clayesmore School, left home, left the country. Maybe because he was so often spoken of I carried an idea of his lithe largeness from then, though my first accredited memory of him is from 1953, when he returned to England. He was twenty-two, I was six. I was beginning to figure that there were people who were a) not children, b) not of my parents' distant age but c) somewhere in between. Of course there were teachers such as Miss McFarlaine and the delicious Miss Bundy in her tight cherry cardigan and tight grey skirt. There were my nannies, Nanny Mary, Nanny Barham and Nanny Chant with buck teeth who came from Shrewton, close to where the last bustard had been shot. There were the serial German Girls: Christine, Lotte, Ruth. There was the hulking Brigitte, Edwina's Breton au pair, who had *big bones* and a totalitarian attitude towards the composition of a vinaigrette. But they suffered the handicap of being female. And boys look up to men. The hideous construction *role model* – favoured by, inter alia, football pundits, asinine politicians, conformist chief constables and moron journalists – had not yet been coined, nor its arithmetical progression *role supermodel*. There is nothing a prepubescent boy wants more than to be a young man, to be over toys, to be doing *real* things – cars, drinks, smoking, girls – in a young man's world.

The gallery of Government House's squash court in Romer Road off Wavell Road. Both roads named after GOCs of Southern Command whose residence it was in the decade between the Longford Estate selling it and the outbreak of war in 1939 when it became a mess. For the first time I watched the only ball game (table tennis excepted) that I'd be any good at: and I wasn't *that* good at either. The windowless brick shed was clammy and cold. The walls streaked with black rubber. An archive of ancient sweat as rank as market cattle. The ball's scorched reek. The ball's repertoire of screams, squeaks, dulls thuds, the ailing yelp when it struck the tin. Squash seemed sordid. But I wanted to play because this was what men did. They panted, they grunted, they cursed. They joshed: chulaka, jammy bugger, well played sir! My father lost. I was hardly proud that Glynn beat a man who was exactly twice his age, for that would have been disloyal, even traitorous. But I was mysteriously excited. For this was a triumph of a young man. I would be a young man in the unimaginably far future and I would no longer have to take the rent folded inside the rentbook next door but one to Glynn's stepmother Mrs Edwards to whom no Christian name was attached in either the second or the third person. Always thus: *Mrs Edwards*.

Such a form was common enough in the nominative regulations and vocative rules that the 1950s inherited from a far distant century, and which were to be mastered like declensions from yet further distant.

Thus:

Mrs Sadd. Often in the construction *Mrs Sadd and her Bedlington*. She dressed exclusively in suits as pallid as her beigeish rinsed hair, as her massively powdered face, as her lamb-like terrier whose feebly sloping lower back lent it the unresolved silhouette of a Jowett Jupiter or Westland Healey. Did my parents know her Christian name? What had become of Mr Sadd? Had such a person existed?

Miss Spottiswoode, who lived in The Friary, and *Mrs Manning* played bridge with my mother. They were, like Mrs Sadd, a generation older than my parents. Perhaps it was that gulf that occasioned the form of address. But the Viennese Mrs Lambert was *Lammi*: her son had risen enviably high in Hilton Hotels, further proof that to succeed you had to leave Salisbury. And Mrs Hill, another bridge player, was so old she was ancient yet she was always *Babs*. When I was eleven she gave me a fresh Fontana edition of a book called *The Rare Adventure* by her monocled nephew Sir Bernard Fergusson, Baron Ballantrae, Chindit, Arabist, black-ops specialist in Palestine, Black Watch Brigadier, Governor General of New Zealand et al. I haven't quite got round to it yet. Nor have I got round to *Born Free*, a gift from a bossy Scot called Belle who was *Mrs Hiddlestone* to me and a cousin of George Adamson, guardian of the celebrity lioness.

My parents referred to Bowns the toothy farmer and dairyman as *Hawk Bowns* and to his headscarfed, down-in-the-mouth, lightly moustachioed, bicycle-pushing, milkbottle-carrying wife as *Rene* (pron. *Reen*) – no surname required. For all I knew they addressed them as *Hawk* and *Rene*. I didn't address him with anything other than a nod in reply to his grunts, which he punctuated with lavish expectorations that landed at my feet.

One autumnal dusk in 2003 I was walking with a couple of friends down Cow Lane near Pritchett's old brick abattoir when an elderly woman and a man whom I took to be her son appeared from the orchard and told us, courteously enough, that we were on private property. I explained that I was revisiting a site of my childhood. We got talking. Mrs Meades! Oh yes. She had taught one of her other children, his sister. Her best friend had been *Rene Bowns*, now departed. I said that of course I remembered *Rene* and *Hawk*.

'Who?'

'*Hawk. Rene*'s husband. *Hawk.*'

'Eh? Who? No. No, *Rene*'s husband was *Bill.*'

It was then, half a century late, that it dawned on me that *Hawk* was my father's covert name for him, a sobriquet which honoured the shining orbs of sputum and paraboloid trails of mucus that Mr Bowns launched from the crevices of his respiratory tract. I managed to keep a straight face. We walked with them across the wooden bridge towards Harnham Road. It occurred to me too that maybe this single-track, unmade lane was *Cow Lane* to no one save my father. I realised that I never heard anyone else refer to it thus.

Barbara Marks was *Miss Marks* to me, *Barbara* to my parents. She was the only one of my mother's fellow teachers with whom that degree of intimacy was broached, though they hardly met out of school. Her sister Betty who worked at the pungently leather-scented Tills, the saddlers, was *Miss Marks* to me and to my parents.

The other teachers were *Miss Ellaby*, the terrifying headmistress on a sit-up-and-beg who was succeeded by *Mr Wood*, known to be Arthur but not so addressed; to my mother's amusement he was referred to in the third person by certain pupils as *Sir* and she was unable to persuade them of their solecism.

Mrs Webber-Taylor was married to *Inspector Webber-Taylor* (notable for the exemplary cleanliness of his shoes: I lived in dread of meeting him and never did).

Mrs Ponting's husband was *Jim*, not Mr Ponting; this for reasons possibly connected to his being perpetually homesick for the north-east which marked him as a queer fish to be pitied.

Tom and Mildred Nicholas were known as *The Must-We?* He was a short-tempered martinet. She was his embittered victim. They had recently moved from Salisbury to a gaunt house in a forested Carmarthenshire valley. It had been built for an early nineteenth-century ironmaster the ruins of whose forge stood nearby. My father was not entirely oblivious to the couple's aggressive dreariness but their property was bordered by a fast-flowing river (giggling, gurgling), a tributary of the Towy notable for sewin. And they had invited him to fish whilst we were en route to *Padre*'s cottage on the Teifi. An invitation which he had neglected to inform my mother of. It was not until we had reached the Brecon Beacons that he mentioned that we were going to drop in on them, as though it were some sort of treat. My mother was incredulous. 'Must we?' She repeated this question with increasing irritation. 'Must we?'

The Pigdens rented Ken James's house. They had the ill manners to take his phone number when their tenancy ended. He was a smugly ambitious young bank manager whose looks were appropriately porcine. *The Pigbins*.

Major-General (retd) Arthur Austin of the Royal Army Dental

Corps was *Gen* to my father and the Friday night regulars over their ale at the *White Jam Tart*. In all other company he was *Arthur*. Smoking killed him having first stained his teeth mahogany. His wife was jocularly referred to as *Mrs Gen* but answered to *Gladys*. Poor Gladys. The spinach incident put me off that vegetable till adulthood: a pressure cooker exploded; boiling green leaves clung to her face; plastic surgery (which showed, how it showed). Their younger daughter was Bunty and their ad-man son-in-law *Smoothie Derek*, Smoothie being omitted when he was present, smoothly mixing drinks, smoothly smoking du Maurier, smoothly drawling.

The formidable founder, owner and headmistress of the Swan School was never anything other than *Miss Swanton*. Her long-term companion whom she had married in secret was, however, never anything other than *Teddy Bear*, a hearty stout mousta-chioed retired Gunners colonel almost as tweedy, almost as masculine, almost as baritone as she was. It is improbable that these two delightful people had a sexual relationship. But one never knows.

The Reverend Ronald Leigh-Jones, widower, had no sexual relationship with his timid spinsterish second wife. He was a rambunctious Welshman who often fished with my father. I first met him when I was eight. I returned home late one Saturday afternoon to find him naked, clutching a whisky bottle in front of the sitting-room fire with skeins of soaked longjohns, socks, vests, pullovers steaming on the floor and the fireguard. He had married Lesley for her small inheritance. He neglected to consum-mate the union. He spent her money on hard liquor, his vicious Jack Russell terrier, field sports, maintenance of an Austin A35 and what turned out to be an insalubrious crumbling cottage with an earth closet near Lampeter. It was not a question of his being indifferent to sex. By his first marriage (to a woman whom he drove mad and had had sectioned) he was father to a son and a daughter whose lubricious escapades delighted him. He was a devoted reader of the *News of the World*, which he called

'Crime and Cunt on Sunday': he would bring this newspaper, far more sordid then than in later years, into services he was conducting as a locum and read it during the boring bits. On one occasion he left a service to buy a copy from a nearby newsagent. Except by Lesley, he was addressed as *Padre*.

This was a boon to me, for I was spared the formal *Missis Gamboge, Squadron Leader Mauve* which was my generation's duty. *Mister* with no surname suffixed was uncouth, just not done, hideously non-U (that frivolously snobbish burden that the wretched Nancy Mitford constructed for the fearful middle class). *Captain* or *Colonel* with no surname was just about acceptable if spoken by an officer of superior rank in a strop. The sheer irregularity of the declensions was trying. There were more exceptions to the rules than there were adherents. Of course had I had the nerve . . . but I didn't, didn't dare call Major Worrin *Tigger* as my parents did, didn't even dare refer to him as Tigger or to his Studebaker-driving wife as Peggy, didn't dare address my parents as anything other than Mummy and Daddy: Mummy was still Mummy when I was middle-aged and she was struggling to utter her last dry rasping imprecations with her memory so shot I could have called her anything but didn't.

Too timid, too, to echo the nicknames that were as much a part of their private patois as the doting *Bobie* they called each other. As well as *Alan Arse Smell, Smoothie Derek* and *the Pigbins* there were *Laundry Maidment, The Flemish Mare, Bloodyman Brayshaw, Young Lochinvar, Prig Prior, Eggy Baba, Dafydd ap, The Drug Peddler, Little* N and *Little N, King Duddo, Malcolm Sargent, Offupthathill, Popeye, The Commie, Keep Death Off The Road, Chrissypegs, Fave o'clork, Byron*.

Television afforded endless opportunities: Ronnie Barker was *Len Gill* because of a supposed resemblance to an army land agent of that name; Brian Jones became *Mrs Wormold*, a character in the sitcom *Hugh and I* played by Patricia Hayes, who did indeed share his maxillary armature; football was *The Ladzz*; a moustached, Ulster-accented weather-forecaster *Thonduray*

Wuthuh. It was embarrassment as much as timidity that dissuaded me from adopting these sobriquets: they belonged to their world of two, a world in which I was an intruder.

The titled allowed me the electric thrill of speaking a Christian name (albeit prefixed) whilst face to face with a grown-up. But there weren't enough of them, and their grand houses. Only *Sir Westrow* Hulse, Bt. and *Sir Reginald* Kennedy-Cox.

Hulse was of the seventh generation of his family to reside at Breamore House (Elizabethan, big, mechanical) in the Avon valley ten miles south of Salisbury. He was much married, warm, genial, generous. His land agent, Dennis Stanford, gave me what he assured me was a valuable pre-revolutionary American postal stamp. It turned out to be worthless. Innocently, I assumed this to be a mistake on Stanford's part.

Kennedy-Cox was a self-important dilettante and stage-door johnnie. He described himself as a playwright. George Devine, on the money, described him as 'weird' and 'a rich old queer'. Nonetheless Devine accepted his financial support when setting up the English Stage Company. Kennedy-Cox had been knighted for having established, with Harold Davidson (the future vicar of Stiffkey and circus performer who died without honours), the Docklands Settlement – one of several early c20 public school 'missions' to the East End, which gave men of his class an opportunity to mix with rough boy boxers who didn't wipe their arse for lack of Izal and Bronco: I was not to his taste. He lived in the Close at Arundells (Georgian, dull) and died there in 1967. Eighteen years later the house was bought by a still weirder rich old queer, Sir Edward Heath. The characterisation of this Herculean grudge-bearer as *ill*-mannered is imprecise. He was rather, gauche, quite *without* manners, as though ignorant of their very existence. A visitor, waiting to see Heath and abandoned by the major-domo who had admitted him, went in search of a toilet. The one he found was 'like an abattoir'. Its walls and floor were streaked with rivers of blood, not yet dry.

EELS

In early spring I'd sit at dusk on a willow stump where the rivers join. The floated meadows between them taper to form what my father and no one else called Pritchett's Point, an ever-mutating collision of mud, ducks' nests, branches, several gauges and colours of polythene, whole swollen drowned calf, reeds, sacking, broken chair legs, fleece, treadless tyres, soggy rope, catkins, brightly bobbing plastic, grass cuttings, bones, would-be trees. This inventory should make meliorists of us all: when Constable painted here, at the very spot where I sat, the dark green waters of the Avon and the Nadder were thick with pulp and rags from paper mills and with human faeces. That's what the past smelled of.

My purpose in sitting here was to witness serpentine armies of silvery eels slither across the twilit meadows.

Unlike those south of Salisbury at Britford and further downstream near the octagonal and quasi-carceral Matrimony Farm, most of Harnham's floated meadows were by now in desuetude. Their carriers, spillways and tail drains were blocked with silt. They had been maintained and their waterflow had been controlled by the drowners who operated rudimentary hatches. When I was very young I had a very old neighbour, a veteran of both the First World War and the Boer War. He lived opposite The Rose and Crown, next to Sid the Butcher's shop and rejoiced in the name of Mr Thick. He spoke in the broadest Wiltshire accent, never wore a collar, collected tobacco in his dense moustache. He was among the last of the drowners. He had succumbed to the trade disease of arthritis which had withered his arms and contorted his bullish body. He spent much of the day leaning against his garden gate, gripping the wicket with twisted fingers, waiting for an audience. He captivated me with stories of his watery omnipotence: I believed that he was some kind of weather. He created floods. He delighted me with the information that in foreign parts – that is, a few valleys away – meadows were known as meads and drowners as meadmen. He said serpentine armies of silvery eels slithered across the meadows in twilight.

Sitting on a stump shivering as day after day gloamed into night after night it became apparent that he had once seen something exceptional which, in time, he persuaded himself was commonplace. Or, more likely, he had so wholly succumbed to eel lore that he believed he had witnessed these amphibian migrations which were (and remain) unvalidated. I wanted to believe him. I was fascinated by aquatic peculiarities – the Severn bore and the Garonne mascaret, leaping salmon, Tarn Beck's trout traps, Seathwaite Tarn's sinister blackness, the sluggish hell of Denver Sluice, pikes' omnivorous viciousness. I had come face to jaw with a pike at just this confluence. It had immediately disappeared into waterweed, more scared of me than I was of it. Nonetheless I got out of the water smartish, I knew what these prognathous beasts were capable of. A couple of years previously whilst eviscerating one, my father had found a baby coot in its stomach. The abundant tall stories about pike had a basis in actuality. This particular one about eels didn't. When my parents moved 400 yards from 55 Harnham Road to 4 Watersmeet Road Mr Thick was long dead. I was now fifteen. Yet I still felt inchoately ashamed that my younger self had been taken in, irritated that Mr Thick, whom I regarded as a friend, should have misled me. Had he?[8]

My father was contemptuous of folkwisdom, the bluff of those too idle to observe nature. The notion that a swan could break

8 In 'Night-Time in Mid-Fall' Thomas Hardy was sceptical: 'The streams are muddy and swollen; eels migrate/ to a new abode;/ Even cross, 'tis said, the turnpike road;/ (Men's feet have felt their crawl, home-coming late): The westward fronts of towers are saturate,/ Church-timbers crack, and witches ride abroad.'

a man's arm was nothing more than evidence of indolent credulousness. Eels taking to land were figments of stale imagination. His interest in eels was, of course, as quarry, as a challenge. Living beside a river meant that he could fish every day. It also allowed him a place to set an eel trap, to fish by proxy.

There was, in the 1960s, no diminution in eel stocks or, indeed in the stocks of any of the species which inhabited the rivers of the Avon and Stour basins. Nonetheless licences to trap eels were seldom granted. So he didn't bother to apply for one. Scratch a fisherman and you'll find a poacher. The trap that he built comprised three small bicycle wheels that he welded to an axle about 1.5 metres long. Fine chicken wire was wrapped around them to form a cylinder. At one end of this cylinder was an ever-narrowing funnel which a hungry eel could just squeeze through. At the other end was a removable shelf which would be baited with bones, carcasses, entrails, anything. Once through the funnel the eels could not escape out due to the sharpness of the wire around the aperture: this might be called the pike's teeth principle.

In late March, early April I had to haul this home-made eel trap from the river at the bottom of the garden. I slid into the cold, cold water and clumsily looped two ropes, of which my father held the ends, beneath the cage. Shivering, I got back on to the bank and took one of the ropes. Heave! We hauled the trap on to the lawn. The glistening snakes squirmed in their wire prison. I ran to the house tripping over the towels I had wrapped around me.

My father grilled them on an improvised barbecue. My mother poached them in a court-bouillon which I have never been able to replicate. It is true: there *is* always something you forget to ask. I'd meant to get the recipe from her. Too late now, too late.

EGG BEATEN IN MILK

'The Persian Gulf is the asshole of the world and Basra is eighty miles up it.' That was Harry Hopkins, F. D. Roosevelt's adviser on diplomacy.

Major J. W. Meades of Paiforce (Persia and Iraq Force) commanded No. 3 Petrol Depot outside Basra. Shortly before he was demobbed in February 1946 he had his cook make up a variety of spice mixes. Each mix was then packed into a dozen or so cans the size of a domestic bully beef can. The cans, about eighty altogether, were rendered airtight with solder and numbered. He had also had engineers at this vast depot in southern Iraq weld a hefty iron boat which he used when shooting wild duck on Hammar Lake. The cans of spice, the boat and its unreliable Evinrude outboard motor were brought back to England on an oil tanker captained by Alex Henney, a distant cousin whom I never met. I imagined him to be dashing and moustachioed. He was not to be confused with another distant cousin Alec Rich, an important electrical goods retailer in Coventry whom I also never met. He, surely, was bald with grocer's stripes.

The outboard, whose use was anyway proscribed by the Dean & Chapter, self-appointed ruler of Salisbury's rivers, lay for years in the flaking stalls of Pritchett's old brick abattoir along with worn harnesses, splintered spokes, holed churns, torn sacks, worn shackles, wonky hives. A different section of the small building housed Pritchett's spruce apiarist kit: a sort of frogman's suit, smokers like oil cans, nets, massive gauntlets. This is where the boat was kept until my parents moved in 1962 to the new house beside the river 200 yards downstream of it: the one move they made in their entire marriage. The boat long outlived its matt silver outboard. It lasted till the mid-Seventies when the rusting hull could no longer support the thick layers of British racing green paint.

The spices had given out a few years earlier: there had been no diminution of their potency nor of my father's enthusiasm for a twice weekly 'curry'. That is the word he used. The dish it described had nothing in common with English curry, an aberration of the post-war years confected, apparently, by boiling raw curry powder in condensed milk, pouring this sauce on to leftover meat or fowl which was then reheated. Accompanied by bananas, dried fruits, chutney, coconut. I suffered this at the table of friends' parents: I never commented on the 'sham' but would, in a conspiracy of smugness, laughingly grass them up to my parents who had taught me that this was the applicable word.

His curry was different, too, from the aggressively chilli'd assaults of Indian restaurants, so rare in smalltown England till the mid-Sixties that my father would travel to London specifically to punish his jejunum. On one of the occasions that I accompanied him we discovered that the restaurant we sought had moved from a row of single-storey shops erected on a bomb site at the southern end of Tottenham Court Road to Mitcham. No alternative was admissible. We set off by underground, overground and foot to that distant southern suburb where, miraculously, the customerless restaurant, beside the remnants of a village green, was still open for lunch. My father spoke his still serviceable Urdu to the uncomprehending Bengali staff who, far from being flattered, were bewildered, even offended. We were served a lunch of stinging stew the colour of Cardinal Red tile polish.

His taste for such buccal infernos was at odds with the curry he cooked himself. This was subtle, delicate, fairly dry, and often incorporating rice in the manner of a pulao or pilau or pilaf – the countless names signify that the method is common to countless kitchens. Yet the flavours of his dishes were, it seemed, *sui generis*, anything but common. After the soldered tins had yielded their last he would buy spices wherever he could find them, and later I'd buy them for him in Euston. But even with an arsenal of the full Rajah range he could not recreate the evanescent fragrance of Iraq '46. In 1987, six years after my father died and three years after I had seen him on Lewes railway station, I ate at an Afghan restaurant in a Putney backstreet. The flavours astonished me. They were familiar. They were those of my childhood. They took me back as surely as particular registers of chalky royal blue and metallic carmine, the scent of maltings, Pears's rendition of 'The Foggy Foggy Dew'. Decades dissolved. The Paiforce cook who had prepared the spice mixes must have been Afghan. Had my father not known?

His own curries became increasingly coarse, ever closer to those of the Taj Mahals, Shah Jahans, Agra Palaces and New Bangalores which proliferated in the later Sixties. Nonetheless, he persisted in inflicting them on anyone who happened to be around. Perhaps his palate had become blunted, perhaps he deluded himself. He was touchy about anything he had made himself and enjoyed the rigorously uncritical support of my mother and my dutiful silence. So the curries had to be consumed.

So did the wines.

He had long harboured the desire to make wine, and even whilst the new house was being built he constructed a crude press, skimmed a couple of instructional books and planted vines. The grape was a species of Seyval hybrid, chosen because it was one of the rare red varieties that were adjudged to flourish in the English climate. It flourished all too well. The crop was stubbornly abundant in even the most miserable summers. The vines were resistant to downpours, frost, hail, everything. The wine they yielded was notably nasty: an odour of slum drains presaged a mouthful of soiled tissues in a thin acidic suspension. It was of course no more undrinkable than many of the cheap wines commercially available in the 1960s, wines he would not have dreamed of buying, which he mocked as having been 'brewed from banana skins in the cellars of Ipswich', an epithet which may have been his but was equally likely filched from Cyril Ray or Pamela Vandyke Price. New parenthood blunts discrimination: the child is the world's first-ever child and a marvel. Such blind joy dissipates with nappies, howling, sleeplessness. And so it did with Chateau Riverain, eventually. He ceased to delude himself of its qualities. But he continued to tend the vines, watching the fruits ripen, picking them. He took pleasure in the process of production and continued to vinify the loutish grapes, to another end. With his friend Joe Gubbins, a GP and a JP, he built a rudimentary still which transformed the wine into a crude, dizzyingly strong spirit, a cudgelling anaesthetic fit for the most exigent derelict and doubtless liable to maim. This moonshining malarkey went on for several years until Joe's possibly unconnected death.

Without, of course, having looked into it, they were, so far as they knew, within the law provided that they did not sell the stuff. Still, they were cautious about whom they gave unwelcome presents to. The next-door neighbour but one, John Silver, a meek, nervy, middle-ranking Porton scientist, was perhaps more cautious than most. He was seen surreptitiously tipping a glass that had been forced on him into a flowerbed. His meekness may have derived from his ancient mother's habit of calling

John's younger brother 'my lovely son' whilst John was merely 'my son'.

My father was more cavalier in his earlier illegal pursuits. When I was small he continued his prewar practice of carrying a Lee-Enfield .22 in the car. He'd shoot anything loitering in roadside fields.[9] Outside the New Forest there were few deer in those days. Hares were sometimes abundant near the ruins of Vanity and at Soming, though they were seldom to be seen near roads. Partridges and wood pigeons were more common than pheasants, which were not yet intensively reared. Up on the desolate downs where the shadows of clouds threatened the very existence of day there were rabbits keen for the pot. He would rarely get out of the car. He would take the rifle from the back seat, load a single bullet and fire. The crack of the gun was thrilling. There was no drama in death, death lacked death throes, the quarry flopped over with anticlimactic finality. I did fear that he'd kill Sugary Bun, but the first Posty got there before him.

Myxomatosis and the police put an end to the rifle in the car. The rozzers – an inspector and a silently invasive rookie – made an annual visit to ask him to renounce his gun licence. He would offer them a drink. They understood (comedy moment, man to man) that Sir wasn't the type to be holding up sub-post offices! No! But what if it was to fall into the wrong hands, what then, Sir, eh? He was smilingly unpersuaded, the conversation moved on. He jocularly bid them farewell: 'Look forward to seeing you next year.' Once they had gone – one at a time through that narrow front door and between the trunks supporting the porch – he would castigate their attempted infringement of his liberty, deride their ignorance of sport, fulminate against whatever pompous half-wit or cocky smart-alec happened to be Home Secretary. His irritation was exacerbated by his embarrassment at having being reproved, no matter how mildly, whilst I was in

9 He had a soft spot for a thatcher nicknamed Killer who would turn up with a bleeding sack and a wink: 'I just happened to run over a stag. Fancy a haunch?'

the house, very likely listening at the door. He considered it a sabotage of his paternal mystique – not that he'd have put it thus. He had an instinctive resistance to being told what to do and an empirical distaste for authority. He was hypersensitive to rank, to social class, to the gradations of hierarchy. He wished to believe in the status quo, in the literality of aristocracy – government by the best.

So the inescapable fact that the pursuit of power and the exercise of authority were undertaken by anyone but the best – by fanatics, blackguards, fraudsters, preachers, cranks, liars, bullies, clowns, believers, know-alls, know-nothings, seditious lawyers in loincloths, any lawyer – seemed to him a perpetual betrayal and everlasting truth. Before his posting to the command of No. 155 Petrol Depot near Kirkuk he had spent the year 1942 at Meerut in what was then United Provinces (now Uttar Pradesh). He had arrived in time to witness the outbreak of unrest that followed Gandhi's and Congress's demand for independence and the aggravation of sectarian, religious and racial fissures which Jinnah, Gandhi, Bose and the Princes – ideologically disparate, united in self-interest – enthusiastically exploited rather than bridged. The British suppression of civil disobedience and riots was selective along religious lines. Hindus were targeted. The Muslim minority was spared, its loyalty was bought so that it might provide necessary, willing, non-mutinous cannon fodder.

He was thirty-three, old to be learning about politicians' duplicity and the gulf between their interests and those of the masses. But he did learn. He would subsequently rail against Mountbatten for his inability to foresee the predictable conse-quences of clumsily hurried partition. He equally resented Mountbatten's most vigorous and astute critic, the by now dotard Churchill. He was convinced that Churchill's government had, early in 1945, maliciously betrayed him. It forbade a handful of Paiforce officers – him among them – to accept the Order of the Patriotic War, First Class, in recognition of their having supplied the Red Army with petrol and aviation fuel through the Persian

Corridor. He was chuffed by the honour, miffed not to receive it. What he most rued was the loss of its attendant perks. These included free travel for life for him and his family throughout the USSR and its satellites, a pension in roubles, a vodka allowance.

That Churchill might have been otherwise occupied and not personally involved in this vindictive decision he dismissed as ridiculous. He voted Labour. The new government would surely be more sympathetic. He wrote to Manny Shinwell, one of Attlee's several Secretaries of State for War, a Red Clydesider, faded now to pink maybe but still a fellow traveller, a friend of the USSR, our ally. No reply. He wrote to John Morrison, since 1942 Tory MP for Salisbury. Many months later the future First Baron Margadale's letter arrived. He had looked into it with all the resources available to him but there was, regrettably, nothing that he could do. The decision was irreversible.

It was all too clear that Morrison had succumbed, he had adopted the evasive habits of the political class of which he was now a member.

Which was a disappointment, for was not Morrison sound? After all, he was a keen sportsman, he wore a bristling moustache, he had held the rank of major in the Royal Wiltshire Yeomanry, the regiment into which my father had been commissioned. This presumption of fellowship on my father's part was a sentimental delusion. The accidental parities of wartime had swiftly evaporated.

Morrison went back to being a multimillionaire landowner.

And my father went back to being a sales rep in a rented house.

Its floors were uneven, its heating was inadequate, its hot water limited. His wife was suffering breast abscesses, his newborn baby's nappies froze on the washing line, his company car wouldn't respond to the starting handle in the coldest winter of the century. His job depended on that car. Had it been discovered that, in contravention of Crawford's stipulation, he did not have a *proper* garage, with doors and a lock, but just a sort of lean-to shelter which incorporated next-door's garden gate, he was blithely certain that Douglas, whom he improbably addressed thus (Brigadier Sir Douglas Crawford – another good chap, another brother officer), would have been indulgent towards him and countermanded the transport pool's pen-pushing tyrants.

This rockily founded optimism might be considered an expression of vanity, a symptom of unworldly innocence, an ill-judged or non-judged estimate of other men's beneficence – despite everything he had seen and lived through he believed in the essential decency of mankind. He believed that the man within the MP Morrison or the MD Crawford might overcome the position the man held. For, having no ambition to hold an office (or lacking the wherewithal to achieve it), he could not grasp the congruence of man and office. He failed to see that the uniform or the title *is* the man, but only so long as the man retains the office, *the role*. He styled himself Major till he died, thirty-five years of increasing embarrassment for his son, to whom it was nothing more than an honorific, a faded laurel. It wasn't as though it would have been less embarrassing had he been of higher rank – he was a brevet Lieutenant Colonel immediately before demobilisation but could not style himself thus.

It's improbable that anyone would actually have noticed had he promoted himself: 1945–*c*. 1960 was the Golden Age of the Bogus Major. Even after that a military rank enjoyed a prestige in Civvy Street that did not entirely diminish till the 1980s, when the generation that had fought in the war was no longer dominant. Captains (army), majors, wingcos, commanders, colonels, captains (navy), brigs, gens . . . they littered the post-war stage, hanging on, proudly, to the titular tokens of their service and, desperately, to a time when their achievement had matched their self-estimate, when status was unambiguous shoulder display. These once conscripted men defined themselves by the rank they had attained rather than by their post-war positions. They peppered their life with martial mores, RAF slang, jacktarishness.

Short-fused Squadron Leader Don Fairs married the widow of a lost member of his flight called Mitchell, took over his paint and grout shop, propped up bars, wore a handlebar moustache and addressed his daughter as *Sprogs*. Lieutenant Guy Jessop RN tackled his daily stride down Castle Road and Castle Street to the auctioneers Woolley and Wallis as though it were a route march. He said a wardroom grace before meals, he enlivened parties with his melodramatic Death of Nelson wearing a tricorn fashioned from newspaper: his affable fellow rugby player and daredevil tobogganist Tim Trethewey took the role of Hardy. Had Guy Jessop[10] been a lieutenant in the army he would not have been allowed that courtesy title: insufficiently senior. Jack Powell had been a captain since the age of nineteen in 1918; to his chagrin he spent *the second show desk-polishing*. My father's lexicon included, conventionally enough, *prang, homework, popsy, officer's groundsheet, gopwo, browned off*. His curries, any curries, were links to a provisional, concentrated, heightened life – to a nabob's array of batmen and to hunting boar the size of donkeys certainly, but more to a time when he was part of a venture of the greatest moment, responsible for the lives of a fractiously cosmopolitan body of men, responsible too for the capability of distant armies.

His habitual breakfast was that which he had drunk outside his bungalow in the pipelined desert: raw egg whisked with milk. Armed Russian convoys, having driven for 1,500 miles from the Volga and the Don to the Tigris, would rest at No. 3 Petrol Depot before returning north in their now filled tankers. The commander of one convoy, offered this breakfast, tasted it and called a subordinate who fetched several bottles of vodka from a tanker lorry's cabin. He had assumed that he was being offered

---

10 In the early hours of the morning at a party of my parents, Guy and Tim, high-spirited adolescents in their thirties, blew a hunting horn through the letter box of a famously officious neighbour, the 'ranker' Captain James, who had complained of noise as early as 9.30. When he crossed the road in his dressing gown to remonstrate he was confronted by his commanding officer who told him not to be so petty.

egg and milk to prepare his stomach for a protracted drinking session and if that preparation began at 06.30 – well, what do you expect from these crazy English? In common with most Englishmen of his generation, my father had never consumed this spirit (which was not generally available in the UK till the 1960s). That was his first and last experience of it, so he claimed.

Whether his antipathy to vodka was due to a morning's mutual misunderstanding that resulted in a day's brain-clubbing over-indulgence or of the spirit's lack of flavour is moot. He would still wonder, thirty years later, whether it was an antipathy he would have overcome had his free passage through the USSR been lubricated by free vodka. He thought he probably would have. Towards the end of his life he would pour a shot of brandy into his breakfast and greet me with an approximate rendition of what he reckoned was a Soviet toast, *boootmoo*.

The Russia I had been denied was a red, cyclopean locomotive as high as a house. Steam boluses gusted from it. I would look out on snowbound wooden cabins and people like wizened Sioux who caught salmon with their hands, shared wigwams with reindeers, rode dog-sledges, wore lacrosse rackets on their feet, drank fermented mare's milk. These happy zoophiles were the personae of children's encyclopaedias and of the midget autodidact's ethnographic and mammarial primer, the *National Geographic*. The red locomotive lived in a gaudy colour photograph in a book of railway exotica. On the opposite page was a monochrome drawing of the Maharajah of Gwalior's jewelled model train which chugged around a banqueting table loaded with decanters, sweetmeats, cigars. It was surely the most exciting thing in all India, in my India. I could not understand why my father had not been to visit it: Gwalior is only 200 miles from Jaipur, where he was briefly posted. Nor could I understand why the Russia that he regretted not seeing was so different from mine. And whyever did he long to go somewhere so horrible? What fascinated him about the USSR was what terrified me so much that I hid beneath the bedclothes – losing myself, getting disoriented in a dark maze, longing for uterine solace.

How were Cold Warriors – nuclear-armed berserkers fashioned from jagged ice – to be distinguished from the guinea pigs of the Common Cold Research at Harvard Hospital who walked the downs and took flight if approached by a civvy? I pictured the Red Menace – a cannibalistic giant whose face was impasted with human gristle and blood; bullnecked mass murderers weighed down by medals; bullnecked sportswomen weighed down by medals; cloud seeding; barbed wire; secret policemen; evil scientists; poor Laika who died in space; the secret and fearsome city of Magnitogorsk where heroic robots made of lifesize Meccano strengthened themselves for galactic travel and men and machines were one; informers; torturers; factories as big as cities; insanitary collective farms; starvation; deportations. 'You're going to Siberia!' was a playground taunt of the Fifties. I confused salt mines with the Big Rock Candy Mountain.

My father's curiosity about the Great Tyranny was stirred by its willingness to acknowledge Paiforce's work when the British government would not and by his comradely appreciation of the Russian soldiers he had met and had learnt to beware of after that first encounter. He had no illusions about the USSR. He wanted to visit it in spite of the *Daily Telegraph* and the *Daily Express*, the papers he read and believed, so far as he believed anything in what was not yet called the media. He regarded the *News Chronicle* as untrustworthy, possibly pinko. Wangle's postal subscription to the fellow-travelling *Manchester Guardian* was derided.

Presumably I was nannyless and a babysitter couldn't be found. Thus I was taken to Uncle Cecil and Auntie Rae's, who had bought a telly early in 1953 so that it might warm up for the Coronation in June. We watched Eric Maschwitz's paranoid spy serial *Little Red Monkey*, whose incidental music by Jack Jordan, all shrill whistles and swirling organ, was as nightmarish as the next year's hit by The Stargazers, 'Close The Door They're

Coming In The Window'. My parents had their own television by the time Rudolf Cartier's production of *1984* was transmitted just before Christmas 1954. This was adjudged preferable to the novel, for though it might have been as stodgy and didactic you were spared having to actually read Orwell's drab schoolmasterly prose. Ambler, Canning, Fleming and, especially, Household were much more the ticket: plots, action, adventure and no preaching, no spelling it out.

We didn't need to have it spelled out. We lived, after all, in Salisbury, the Cold War was being waged all around us. Apart from god the Cold War was Salisbury's defining industry and its true faith.

The red beacon on top of the cathedral spire was a warning to the countless military aircraft that passed overhead day upon day, night after night. Much was hush-hush. So hush-hush that it camouflaged itself with gaudy signs, barred entrances, sentry posts, skeins of barbed wire, concrete roads with a ginger pebble aggregate peculiar to forces' property, lawned redoubts, Donald McGill windsocks, red flags flying to warn of deafening gunnery practice on the ranges, tank crossings, the War Office's timorously utilitarian buildings.

The secret world is vainglorious, it cannot resist announcing its presence, proclaiming its force. The power of the bases was all the greater for being vague, unexplained, unchallengeable. These sites fomented rumours, which were only exceptionally confirmed: Geoffrey Bacon's death from bubonic plague at Porton was such an exception. The Ordnance Survey, based 20 miles away at Southampton, suppressed cartographic probity in defence of the realm. Its numerous omissions were immediately obvious to anyone familiar with the ground. But they were guaranteed to fool the enemy.

This was the front line:

Garrisons at Larkhill (Royal Artillery, the thunder of whose guns was audible ten miles south), Bulford, Durrington, Tidworth, Ludgershall, Fugglestone (HQ Southern Command), Middle

Wallop (Army Air Corps). There were still temporary structures in the grounds of Longford Castle where Field Marshal Montgomery had his HQ through part of World War II.

RN Armaments Depot at Dean Hill (100,000 sq ft of vaulted bunkers excavated in a chalk hillside in 1940–41; munitions for storage were transferred at East Dean station to 4 miles of 2 ft 6 in gauge railway).

RAF Munitions Depots at Fovant, Baverstock and Chilmark (a narrower-gauge railway, 2 ft, connected to a standard-gauge spur at Chicksgrove on the Salisbury–Tisbury line).

The former USAF hospital at Odstock where I had my tonsils removed.

RAF bases at Old Sarum, Upavon, Netheravon, Boscombe Down (Aeroplane and Armament Experimental Establishment. The test pilot father of a schoolfriend took a group of us there to look over a V-bomber. I have no idea whether it was a Valiant, a Victor or a Vulcan. It bored me. The baked Alaska we were served in the mess as a further 'treat' disgusted me. I have never subsequently tried it).

Porton Down (Chemical Defence Experimental Establishment): always called Porton.

These places and the people who staffed them were ours. Our side, our protectors, our friends, our familiars.

Should we not, then, know the enemy that they were defending us against? In August 1938 – a month before Chamberlain was duped at Munich, three months before Kristallnacht, nine months before they married – my parents went to get to know the previous enemy. That, anyway, is how, in retrospect, my father explained their holiday in tidy Freiburg, ten miles from the French border on the edge of the Black Forest. Where – of course – there was excellent trout fishing in the jovial, laughing, rollicking streams. Where there were beer steins so comically grotesque you split your sides. Where every gurning jetty-end and gargoyle spoke of good fellowship and thigh-slapping merriment. Where ribald goblins leered from belfries.

Group activities abounded: games, sports, singsongs, outdoor concerts, parades, dances, hikes, skipping, swimming, climbing. People were *keen*. It was heaven on earth for joiners, for the unreflectively team-spirited, for those who yearn to be at school for ever. What a happy hearty florally garlanded family this nation was, this new nation – 1938 was Year Six, and in Year Six it had no colonies, they had been humiliatingly confiscated under the Treaty of Versailles. Yet the Gasthof owner's courteous son was shortly to begin his second year at a school of colonial administration in anticipation of Germany's imperial destiny. Rather than tanks crawling through the town's streets, rather than ubiquitous armed men in uniform, it was the prospect of this youth's future in *Lebensraum* management that persuaded my parents of the nation's expansionist ambitions and of war's inevitability no matter how cravenly the poodles of appeasement might scrape before Apollyon.

In the Fifties, having lived through two world wars, they were resigned to the likelihood that they might witness a third, not live through it, be obliterated in it. They were of a generation for whom war was a hideous yet necessary norm, a thief of lives who came calling every twenty years, always greedier than last time: 'never again' was as great a lie as 'their name liveth for evermore'. Jumbo Evans was at the bottom of the Atlantic. Mowbray Meades and Joe Baird were Flanders mulch. And the lives it didn't steal it blighted with unbearable bitterness: Jerry Savage killed himself more than a decade after he had walked into Belsen. Pudge Paul had been a POW on the Burma Road and could not bear to be touched by another human. His unspoken, unshared anguish was brusquely admitted: 'Pudge had a bit of a thin time of it out east.' Eric had a metal leg. Wag was in a wheelchair. Mrs Lampard and Mrs Mitchell, young widows, each married a service friend of their dead husband. *The next show* might start at any moment. It appeared to have started one clear winter Sunday night as we returned from Evesham. There was a dusting of snow. The cold groaning Morris

Eight chugged up the snaking slope of the Salisbury road out of Amesbury. It reached the chalk escarpment. The familiar scene beyond the brow of the hill was transformed. What should have been dark downland was illumined by floodlights. I heard my mother gasp.

In the middle distance beyond the ruby strand of tail-lights was a silver structure high as a three-storey terrace, a giant space-beast that had strayed from elsewhere, like Stonehenge and Woodhenge. As we approached it, it resolved itself into a slumped aircraft, the largest aircraft I had ever seen. It was out of its element, a fabulous whale from the sky that had demolished a security fence (concrete pillars and slabs, barbed wire) and some sort of watchtower. The fuselage, with its ranks of black windows and portholes, had come to rest, wheelless, in a field. Its blunt snout lay on the now closed road ahead, visible beyond an ad hoc roadblock of vehicles. It was surrounded by lights, generators, fire tankers, lorries, cranes. Dozens of men in white combat gear, hooded, goggled and armed, stood by on aggressive guard. Soldiers? Members of a crack vanguard of extra-special forces? A group of them manned the roadblock. More of them ran urgently among the cars and vans which were backed up in both directions. Several of them noted registration numbers. Men with headsets squawked language into bulky field telephones.

I feared I was witnessing the start of the Soviet invasion.

I hoped I was witnessing the start of the Soviet invasion.

What opportunities there would be for heroism, spying, disguises, codes and hiding in drainage culverts.

They had taken over. Traffic was directed with curt jerks of sub-machine guns. Terrified drivers complied, left in no doubt of what would happen were they to ignore orders. Two soldiers banged on the roof of a gawping dawdler who had slowed to a halt at the point on the road closest to the aircraft. They furiously indicated that he should keep up with the vehicles in front of him and turn off onto the narrow road towards Catsbrain and Durnford. We were told to follow. The hooded men were twitchy. The frightened eyes in a masticating face that peered into the back of the car were hardly those of a man. The finger on the trigger was a boy's. We could see the distant headlights of diverted northbound traffic making its way by a backroad across the downs towards Idmiston. Our line of traffic moved slowly downhill to the narrow road to the Avon valley.

It was America that my father excoriated. Or, rather, the American presumption that American forces could do as they wished wherever they wished. My mother joined in. They always agreed with each other. They had recognised the aircraft as a USAF cargo carrier. (Presumably a Douglas C-124, confidently named the Globemaster.) It had evidently overshot the western runway at Boscombe Down, almost certainly because of chewing gum, trashy music, absurdly cut trousers and tailfins. What right had these troops to police English civilians? What right had they to impose an extemporised martial law? Here was the full hypocrisy of American imperialism. The vilifiers and destroyers of the British Empire now occupied British soil. Behind it all, no doubt, was John Foster Dulles – the possibly psychopathic, certainly god-bothering, certainly globally menacing sometime Hitlerian and hawk *avant la lettre* who was Eisenhower's Secretary of State and the ideological precursor of such swinishly gung-ho liabilities as McGeorge Bundy ('Ridiculous name!'), Robert McNamara, George W. Bush, Dick Cheney, and the lesbians Donna Rumsfeld and Paula Wolfowitz.

My parents' execrations of Dulles were such that their animus might have been personal. It *was* personal. There is little that's more personal than losing your life because of a distant gambler's addiction to goading an ideological opponent to the point where it becomes a belligerent antagonist. Dulles's coinage, *brinkmanship*, glorified the practice of prodding a bear with a stick and presenting it as a legitimate strategy. He was, too, a traitorous ally: his reaction to the Suez adventure was one of opportunistic betrayal, a further chance taken to diminish Britain. So, according to parental orthodoxy, he entered into an improbable coalition with homegrown anti-imperialist pinkos and treasonable clerks who did not understand the Arab menace, who ignored Nasser's hospitality to SS and Gestapo veterans, who, in their excessive empathy, always took the other side, who were unshakable in their liberal conviction that Britain was wicked.

HARRIS

'I've had my insides removed.' Olivia Harris confided this intelligence so often that it was a catchphrase, now penitential, now triumphant. 'All gone,' she trilled.

The void I imagined was unquestionably disturbing. And the current whereabouts of the insides mystified me. What had happened to them? Where were they? I didn't like to ask. Olivia had been 'on the stage'. *Where* was, again, not vouchsafed. Nor was *when*. Presumably she had been a soubrette before the war. Rep? Concert party? Pierrot troupe? Her voice and accent were regulation-issue theatrical of her generation: breathy; coquettish; exaggeratedly enunciated mock-Teutonic consonants; truncated vowels. I see her in an ivory blouse pouring drinks in a room whose long drawn curtains nonetheless admit batons of churning light. In the late 1950s she was still wearing her assisted blonde hair in the peekaboo style worn by Veronica Lake and Lizabeth Scott at least a dozen years previously. Not that I was then familiar with those reputedly sulphurous femmes fatales. They and their provocative moues and unwholesome hairdos were forgotten by everyone save Olivia, who would already have been in her mid-thirties when the style was fashionable. I listened, I eavesdropped, I overheard, I picked up oblique hints that it was unbecoming for a woman in, at least, her exceptionally late forties (jocular) to appropriate the appearance of sultry ingénues from the age of the low-key light.

Kenneth Harris was dapper, moustached, brilliantined, brass-button-blazered. He retained the honorific 'Captain' and had some undefined connection to the motor trade. His cap's peak was bent, *sportily* bent, to form a triangular pediment. This was a sartorial tic popularised by Mike Hawthorn (the son of a garagist), who would be killed the day after my twelfth birthday: it transformed the flat hat from dull duncher into rakish little number. Kenneth, then, also modelled himself on someone twenty years his junior. And he drove a British racing green Triumph TR2, a car supposedly too young for him, a boy's car, a boy racer's: not a *real* sports car. A few years later several of my wealthier contemporaries would receive a TR (or Sprite or MGA) as a passed-your-test parental gift to be pranged at will. In that last era before the accession of youth-cult, which would eventually see adults dress like toddlers and play children's video games, the Harrises' mildly affected denial of their age was considered risible or presumptuous.

But to me they were a glamorous couple.

And I attached myself to glamour's coat tails, the most desperate of hangers-on. Glamour was in short supply in Salisbury. Thus what passed for glamour there might not have seemed so to the worldlings of, say, Bath. I clung to what I could, inflated it. Whatever it was. Anyone, anything, the barrel scrapings. I was too young to leave in search of it even though from an early age I longed to be somewhere else, somewhere other than home, somewhere other than Salisbury. I longed to take the white chalk track with a middle parting which led over the downs to faraway, to promise, to hope. It's a longing that has seldom left me.

Olivia's and Kenneth's childlessness (no doubt attributable to the missing insides) and the practice of the childless of treating children without condescension seemed glamorous. So too did ginny laughter, casual oaths, languidly waved cigarettes, his suede boots (leather soled chukka, *not* rubber-soled desert).

In the spring of 1955 Kenneth Harris alerted my father to the existence of a 1932 Aston Martin Le Mans for sale. The garage turned out to be a repair shop assembled from holed corrugated iron, planks, bits of pitted doors and abundant asbestos. The car, even then a rarity, was in surprisingly decent condition. My father phoned Hank, who had long desired this car above all others. Hank asked him to buy it for him. And best buy it immediately, before the chance passed, even though the price was high: it no doubt included an ample drink for Kenneth.

My mother, ever mistrustful of my paternal aunt and uncles, advised against this course and suggested that my father wait till Hank's cheque had arrived from Burton-on-Trent. He didn't wait. She was proved right. My father never learnt. He was reluctant to acknowledge the baseness of our race, and familial bonds rendered him especially incapable of discerning his siblings' relentless grasping, scrounging meanness and pious miserliness – even though Reginald answered to Wangle without demur. All too characteristically, despite his many entreaties my father was not reimbursed a sum he could ill afford until a couple of years later when Hank sold the car for three times the sum he hadn't paid for it. He had, then, received an interest-free loan. The car – high off the road with detached mudguards and unincorporated headlights – struck me as ugly and dismally old-fashioned. There was no glamour in wood, in leather. They were yesterday's materials.

Glamour was indissociable from the modern. It was a property of sleek, streamlined sports cars which barely expressed their wings – Austin-Healey 100/6, 100/4, 3000; Allard Palm Beach; Bristol 401 to 405; Frazer Nash Mille Miglia and Sebring; AC Ace and Aceca; Jensen 541 and 541R; all Jaguar XKs. It was a property too of Ice-Cream Rigiani's vanilla Studebaker, an elegant, atypically restrained coupé designed by Raymond Loewy's studio during the years when American cars, familiar sights in Salisbury because of American forces' presence, were items of mobile surrealism: googie, baroque, two-tone, zoomorphic. Their appeal was that of the illicit, the forbidden, the occluded: cutaway collars, elephant trunk quiffs, dark nipples in *QT* and *Kamera*, sex, prostheses. These cars were too frightening, too monstrous, too freakish to be glamorous. Their reptilian chrome radiators snarled, their voracious eyes and excrescent fins terrified me.

André and Renée Ragot (née Kermarec) were among my

grandfather's Breton friends. In the summer of 1957 they came to Southampton for my grandmother's funeral and then on to Salisbury where André would fish with my father. Against their advice they took my parents out to dinner at The Red Lion. Served Yorkshire pudding, André prodded it, tasted it warily and pronounced: 'Mon dieu, c'est du plastique!'

In 1931 he had founded a fly-tying business at Loudéac, a small town in the Côtes-d'Armor. A quarter of a century later Mouches Ragot was known to every fisherman in France and had extended into the manufacture of other lures: plugs, spinners, spoons, all of them gaudier (so more appealing to me) than their naturalistic, almost understated British analogues. My first cufflinks, the only cufflinks I owned till my twenties, were a Ragot promotional device: kingfisher-bright flies suspended in Perspex hemispheres. André's Citroën DS, bought in the first year of that car's production, was the apogee of vehicular glamour. There was a bewildering incongruity between the DS – glassy, sculptural, apparently breathing – and the wonky 150-year-old thatched terrace where we lived. It was puzzling that such disparate objects could exist side by side, juxtaposed time travellers. The lustrous machine was from another world, a world which did not yet exist on this side of the Channel. France's present was our distant future.

As if to prove it my father could not work out how to drive it. In normal circumstances such an inability would have been a mild embarrassment, a failure to be laughed off with a self-mockery which invited sympathy. These were abnormal circumstances.

After showing it off to my father on the long straight roads of the western New Forest at Bramshaw Telegraph and Deadman Hill, André had parked the DS beside an unmetalled track on the Somerley estate between Ellingham and Harbridge. Lugging their rods, reels, gaffs, priests, tackle bags, Mepps spoons, plugs, sprats preserved in reeking formalin etc. they walked three quarters of a mile across fields and fences, stiles and leets to the Avon.

André was some two hundred yards downstream, close by a

clump of willows which partially hid him. So my father, casting into the black-green water, did not see him collapse to the ground.

It was not for some minutes after he had suffered a heart attack that my father wondered where he was and, with no sense of urgency, ambled along the bank. He found him on his side, wriggling feebly, contorted, sweating, wheezing, semi-conscious. A few weeks previously my father, using hip-flask brandy as local anaesthetic, had cut a hook out of the palm of a fellow fisherman with his alarmingly sharp penknife. He reacted with kindred improvisation, vigorously massaging André's chest, loosening his clothes then picking him up and carrying him – now in his arms, now in a fireman's lift over his shoulder – across the fields and fences, the stiles and leets, slipping under the weight of the possibly expiring burden, sinking into unseen troughs. This took a parlously long time. For once the return journey was not quicker. When they reached the car André was all but unconscious. My father attempted further cardiopulmonary resuscitation. Panting like a robber he frisked André for the keys to his car. He unlocked it and lifted him on to the back seat. It is now that he discovers that the technological prodigy from the day after tomorrow is not responsive to the driver of the day before yesterday's Morris Minor.

He spent an incalculable time failing even to ignite the engine: incalculable because clock time's primacy is suppressed by the exceptional. He decided that the only course open to him was to abandon the stricken man and run for help. High summer: but the track was still soft from spring's floods. He eventually arrived at the metalled, causeway-like road and elected to head for Ibsley and the main road even though it was further than Harbridge. Before he got there he recognised a Daimler that was coming towards him and waved it down. André Ragot and my father were thus driven to Odstock Hospital by Colonel Esmond Drury, a fishing writer who had devised The General Practitioner, among the better-known post-war English salmon flies. This approximate symmetry would be sentimentally relished by all three men involved as proof of *l'entente cordiale* and the brotherhood of fishermen. André Ragot was detained for a fortnight. He lived for a further twenty years. The day after he was hospitalised my father directed the garagist Jack Miles and one of his mechanics to the DS. Whilst he fetched his and André's gear from the riverbank the two men, briefed by Citroën UK, had no trouble in starting the car. My father sat mutely beside Jack as he fondly acquainted himself with the alien machine on the road back through Fordingbridge and Breamore: chalk downs to the left, forest escarpment to the right, the bypass at Bodenham not yet built.

He had saved a man's life. Yet his mechanical incapacity dogged him. Not because of the possible outcome, not because André might have died, but because of his perceived vanquishment by technology. He felt slighted, humiliated. His shame was the greater because he was technophiliac. He accepted applied-scientific progress as a given. He was besotted with his fixed spool Mitchell 330 Otomatic reel bought at punishing expense from France before it was available in England. This item of piscatorial modernism was manufactured by a precision engineering company on the Swiss border whose products had previously included watch gears, taxi meters and early electric razors. It sits on a shelf in my office, a predatory insect with a crutch. A memento of my father, of course, also an emblem – like the DS, like Roger Excoffon's typefaces – of that long-vanished France which defined itself as the antithesis of its inglorious recent past, the nation of colourful counter-intuitive objects without ancestors, but with transatlantic cousins. The reel, designed in Year Zero of *les Trente Glorieuses*, was to have been named Michel after its manufacturer's dead brother. Commerce overcame sentiment: Mitchell was reckoned to possess greater appeal to the anglophone market. The yé-yé singer Claude Moine agreed. His backing group retained its French name, Les Chaussettes Noires, and disappeared into obscurity whilst he became Eddy Mitchell, the eternally leather-clad veteran teenager.

My father's embarrassment with the DS was resolved in a peculiar way.

The first model to be regularly seen about Salisbury was lemon and black. It belonged to Alan R. Snell and replaced his Sunbeam Talbot. Alan R. was a dapper and courteous chocolatier with a small factory in Crane Street and, puzzlingly, four shops within a few minutes' walk of each other. Mint crisps, ginger crisps, thin dark slabs: these were delicious, the stuff of treats – grudging treats. Their packaging was as elegant as the man, baby-blue stripes on white with entirely lower case, sans serif lettering. My father referred to him as Alan Arse Smell. The root of his animus was a prep school inter-house boxing bout between me and Alan R.'s son Michael – born to the faintly moustached Tilly in Spiro Nursing Home two weeks after me.

I had no appetite for boxing as either participant or audience. I was more or less obliged to know such names as Dai Dower, Floyd Patterson, Ingemar Johansson etc. One night in 1955 at about two o'clock my father forced me out of bed so that I might feign interest in a crackly transatlantic radio commentary on Rocky Marciano's demolition of Don Cockell, mocked in the American press as 'the barrel of lard'. And he bought me cheap boxing gloves, tried to persuade me of the pursuit's nobility, which I couldn't reconcile with its discomforts. He'd kneel on the big Persian carpet which filled the small sitting room. The idea was that I should land blows with the papery gloves which horribly turned my hands into mute clubs. I failed. He parried every half-hearted effort. It irritated him that my heart wasn't in it. He had yet to learn that I was nothing like him, that I shared none of his enthusiasms; or, if he had begun to realise, he was loath to admit it to himself and perhaps entertained ideas of correcting and conditioning me.

He had judged some of the previous bouts in the Nissen hut gym but had stood down when it was my turn. He was furious that Alan R. did not stand down and remained to adjudicate in my bout with Michael. He cast his deciding vote and gave the fight to his son. Alan R. was, with cause, proclaimed not to understand conflict of interest or fair play. Besides, he knew nothing about boxing.

Worse, a couple of years later both Alan R. and the lightly moustached Tilly took up salmon fishing. My father interpreted this as a provocative slight and mocked their brand-new Barbours, virgin rods and shiny waders. They were, thankfully, never as successful as my father. But then they had their own chocolates to preoccupy them whilst my father merely had someone else's biscuits: to own a business was everything in the petty-mercantile, bookless world of Salisbury and it didn't come much more bookless than Alan R.'s and Tilly's twee Thirties house in a road with the even more twee name of Shady Bower, which culminates in the laughable Milford Manor, built circa 1900 for Gerrish of Style and Gerrish, faced in crazy paving, and subsequently the headquarters of Reed and Mallik, manufacturers of REEMA. This form of systems building blighted much of Britain in the late Fifties and Sixties. Alan R. bought a weekly beat at the Royalty Fishery south of Ringwood. With what was deemed beginner's luck he did *kill* some salmon – that verb was de rigueur among game fishermen; it was coarse fishermen who *caught* pike, tench, barbel and so on and meekly returned them to the river in contravention of the logic of want. That Alan R. (whose confections I enjoyed and whose creepily solicitous kindliness I appreciated) owned a DS proved beyond doubt to my father that this car was flawed. It must be the boastful affectation of smoothies, parvenus, chulakas and their multifarious kin – even wronguns and spivs. Unless, of course, it was driven by a Frenchman.

'I've forgotten what I was going to say.'

I haven't forgotten the first time I uttered that commonplace sentence, the first time that I was aware that thought had suffered stillbirth, the first time I was privy to the sharp frustration which succeeds that loss and to the curse of synaptic butterfingers.

The subject, I know, was to have been the Duke of Edinburgh. The place was the back of my father's Morris 8. I could see the flint school, the white stucco'd convent, the gateless piers of the entrance to Riverside Walk, I can see the yet uncrowned Queen's consort in his dashing naval whites. Then the car turned into St Nicholas Road beside the orchard wall spiked with broken bottles. Ahead, on the corner of De Vaux Place, was the ancient house outside which the splendid Lagonda was no longer parked. To the right, the raised spur of grass separating the road from the sunken pavement and above it, the Close wall.

I've had a lifetime to think about what it was that I was going to say to my parents about the Duke of Edinburgh. I have evidently not thought enough. Maybe the proximity of the convent had reminded me of his mysterious mother, the vision-prone, astral-projecting nun Princess Andrew whose delusional states, surely connected to her name, have resurfaced in her eldest grandson.

Every time I forget what I was going to say an image of the Duke pops up, a protean trickster with as many guises (duncher'd sportsman, Claus von Bülow, bearded sailor, twinkly bigot, plain-speaking flirt, charming curmudgeon) as he has titles, but with a single role in my life – to mock my frail concentration and fallible short-term memory. (It's a more enviable role than his daughter's. Picturing the equine Princess Royal is a sure way of inhibiting orgasm and prolonging enjoyment for everyone concerned, so long as one doesn't picture her for too long and so risk flaccidity. Which is not quite the ticket, Anne.)

There was no doubt something premonitory whirring within my brain, for the only time I have ever seen this admirably tact-less man was here, in De Vaux Place, eighteen months after I had forgotten what I was going to say. Scores of New Elizabethans crowded onto the narrow pavement. Terry Lovell, a couple of years my senior, had been put in charge of me. He told me when I should wave my stiff celluloid union flag. I annoyed him by asking how much longer were we going to have to stand here. Where were they? Why were they late? This was no fun at all.

Then, at last – wave! The young Queen and her handsome balding husband rode past us towards the North Gate of the Cathedral Close in the back of a heraldically pennanted

Rolls-Royce with piebald paintwork lustrous as a racehorse's coat. I got a glimpse of the magical couple. We had waited going on an hour for an anticlimactic fragment of a second which, I told my parents when I got home, represented poor value.

They were not as sympathetic as I had hoped. They reminded me that it had been my idea to waste an afternoon demonstrating my fealty with that gimcrack, now splintered flag from the corner shop. They were as indifferent to royalty as they were to republicanism. Old Acton's dictum on power was fed me with my mother's milk or rather, since I was not suckled, with my Virol and cod liver oil and Farley's rusks and NHS orange juice which shared a name with the fruit but tasted of tarnished coins. My parents were equally indifferent to all manifestations of power. They married in church, at St Mary's, South Stoneham in So'ton. They had me baptised at All Saints, East Harnham – I have a silver mug to prove it, and a piece of paper. My mother taught in Church of England schools for forty years. They sent me to the Cathedral School.

Yet they were not communicant. They attended funerals and marriages out of social obligation. Otherwise they only ever set foot in churches for reredos tourism and choral concerts. One of my godfathers was an atheist, the other a sort of pantheist. 'Churchy' was a word of weary contempt. My parents considered the cathedral's hieratic cadre of Christ's bridegrooms to be pompous, snobbish prigs. They developed an animus against the thin-lipped Dean Haworth who sacked Barry Still from the headmastership of the Cathedral School for no reason other than that he had had the temerity to fall in love with and marry the school's matron. Haworth replaced Still with a holy crony, a lay preacher who eventually took orders. The only churchmen my parents counted as friends were a monstrous sot, Padre, and the indomitable cottager, John Ellis.

It was peer pressure (already so-called though not yet vernacular) that had caused me to wave a flag at the Queen. Adherence to insidious flock conformity also persuaded me to demand that I be allowed to attend Sunday School. In this case the flock comprised the Harnham Road children whom I knew through Roger and whom my parents probably reckoned to be guttersnipes, street arabs, urchins and so on. Several of them belonged to the swarthy Dean tribe; there were three related families of that name living within a hundred yards of each other. There were Helen, Pauline and Sylvia; the ginger sisters Cynthia and Brenda; the Goddard twins; Peter who despite being himself a dull and backward slow-learner was known to try to read for his literally illiterate, religiously fixated parents – he would later use fireworks as weapons.

I was confided to Margaret and Ronnie Smith, children of George Smith, the not much more literate carpenter whose duck-billed 4H pencil lived over his ear, whose house and workshop formed an unsightly adjunct to our terrace. Margaret and Ronnie would show me the ropes at Sunday School. We walked a hundred yards up the road and entered the church. This was my first return to where I had been christened. We sat at the back. It was cold. The seat was uncomfortable. For several minutes nothing happened except timid whispering. Then the congregation stood up and sang. The only hymns I knew at the age of seven were 'All Things Bright and Beautiful' and 'Adeste Fideles'. Indeed it had not occurred to me that there were any other hymns. I was confused by this strange new one. By the time I had found the right page in the hymnal it was over. Next there was kneeling combined with muttering in approximate time with the neighbouring mutterer. Because Sunday School began at 2 pm and my parents did not eat Sunday lunch till some time after that hour I was hungry. A woman with glasses read a boring text for several minutes. I began to cry. The congregation turned to gape. One small girl held a finger to her mouth to silence me. Another woman, this one in a sort of smock, came to ask me what the matter was. I persisted in sobbing. I told her that I wanted to go home. This baffled her. Then she sniffed insubordination. She adopted a simpering pitying churchy surely-not smile of affronted annoyance and told me to pull myself together, to behave: did I not realise that I was in God's house? As soon as she had moved away and the subsequent incomprehensible activity had begun I got up and crept as unobtrusively as possible to the solid door, heaved it open. The hinges squeaked, the foot of it scraped shrilly and shiveringly against the stone floor. I left it open and ran down the road past the phone box, past the entrance to Watersmeet House. I heard The Smock call after me. I ignored her. I had emerged a materialist. So ended my last voluntary attendance at a church.

It was, equally, the first time I had walked out of anything, that I had had the nerve to walk out. Or had been so desperate. Thus was a lifelong habit initiated. Cinemas, jobs, sexual relationships, exams, opportunities, marriages, commitments, professional partnerships, schools, theatrical performances (a speciality), parties, expeditions, dinners, homes, prior arrangements – I've walked out of all of them, often.

Twenty minutes after I'd left I ran in through the back gate. My parents had not even started lunch. They weren't surprised to see me, did not castigate me, merely reminded me that they had warned me: Sunday School was liable to be disagreeable. No doubt they were covertly pleased that I made my break for freedom. My father, especially, considered not joining a mark of individualism rather than a possible symptom of sociopathy. He discounted the modern dictum that loners are necessarily 'troubled'. And he was proud that Jim Laing, whom he liked and admired, should routinely refer to me as 'a one-off'. He had referred to me thus since a day at the new Castle Combe circuit where we watched the young hardly known Stirling Moss in a Formula 3 race (he crashed).

What I had done or said to provoke this epithet was soon forgotten. But I was stuck with it, even though it made me feel freakish, apart, self-conscious – not that I could admit to this because it would have been graceless in the face of what was, as I was frequently reminded, intended as high praise. It was, then, a trait to be encouraged. I had to live up to Jim's estimation. And a way to do so was to dissuade me from belonging to a group, any group, whose collective mores might extinguish my peculiarities and mould me in a way that was not to my parents' liking.

I didn't learn of course. In childhood we struggle to both satisfy parents' expectations and to avoid contemporaries' mockery. And vice versa. The gulf is exacerbated when the very subject of parental counsel is to beware contemporaries' conformist influence, any influence, rather than the predictable bad influence (though that too was to be shunned). Even submission to supposedly good influence was liable to mitigate my specialness. Can it have been that frail? I did not go to Sunday School because of a sudden access of piety. I went because I didn't want to be excluded from a particular group. The Wolf Cubs for instance.

Again my parents were unenthusiastic, for another uniform had to be bought: a green pullover with an integral collar, a green peaked cap, a khaki neckerchief, a woggle. Beyond that they were discouraging because the Cubs and Scouts were organisations. Further they were quasi-spiritual organisations that inculcated pernicious guff.

There was too an element of anti-urbanistic bias. The Scouting movement was intended to teach country lore, woodcraft and fieldcraft to town children who would otherwise be deprived of these important disciplines which I, as a country child, should acquire for myself, as Bevis and Stalky and my father had done, untutored and untainted by greeny-up mysticism. I was preposterously encouraged to think of myself as a country child even though I lived in what was plainly a suburb: I might as well have been encouraged to think of myself as a girl.

A stringy, toothy, kink-haired myope instructed us that we should address her as Akela. She wore a faded green warehouse coat cinched with a belt plaited from fraying canvas which repulsed me. We sat in a circle round an invisible camp fire in the Cathedral School's 'gym', the freezing Nissen hut where Alan R. Snell had the previous winter awarded the boxing bout to his son rather than to me and to which collective imagination could not summon warmth. We swore an oath and chanted. Akela was a believer in the Cub code. And in the manner of believers she wore humility as a weapon. Our life would be blighted if we deviated from the code. It would be an affront to her if we deviated.

Bob-a-Job week in the Easter holiday was the supposed highlight of the Cub year. Small boys in uniform pestered their neighbours to pay them to run errands, wash cars, undertake domestic tasks and gardening chores. The money so raised went to the Cub pack. I set off from home knocking on doors. Most houses were unoccupied. Those that were had no jobs to offer, or already had a fellow Cub working keenly. It was late morning before I found an employer.

Peggy Sanger was mother of one of the many Janets I had gone to school with. Her first husband had been shot down. Her second husband was one of his fellow RAF officers. (My mother confusingly referred to her by her first married name, Lampard.)

She suggested I walk to Upper Street, a few minutes away, on the periphery of West Harnham and try Mrs Fairs. Her first husband too had been shot down. Her second husband was one of his fellow RAF officers. I was loath to importune her, for she made little secret of her dislike of me.

The cause was my having precociously corrected her usage a year or so previously when watching an episode of *Range Rider* with Pauline aka Sprogs. Mrs Fairs referred to the outlaws (distinguished no doubt by their giveaway stubble) as 'the naughty men'. I sensed a twee euphemism, an avoidance of the truth that patronised me because it was trying to protect me (and Sprogs who, being used to it, maybe didn't notice). 'They are not the *naughty* men,' I told her, 'they are the *bad* men.' Whenever I had seen her subsequently she had let it be known to whoever was present that I was too clever by half, a cardinal sin in provincial England, in provincial anywhere. Now she took her revenge. She asked me to fetch some potatoes. From Hands, the corner shop half an hour's walk away, past my home. Surely I could go to Queensberry Stores, a mere five minutes distant? No. Her account was with Hands. She would call to let the shop know I was coming. When

I arrived Hands was about to close for lunch. She had ordered such a quantity of potatoes that I could barely lift them. And the sack they were in was covered in fine dust which made me shiver. I said that I'd return when the shop reopened, sloped home and confessed my plight to my parents, who detected a comic aspect which I had failed to discern.

An hour later my father drove me and the potatoes to Upper Street. Mrs Fairs complained that I had taken too long. She observed that getting a lift in a car was cheating. She grudgingly signed my Bob-a-Job card and gave me a shilling. It was evident that the world of work was arduous and cruel. I quietly took off my uniform, went to play Cowboys and Indians with Roger who was not a Cub and forgot about Bob-a-Job week.

Soon we would hand in our job cards together with the money we had earned. I ruefully sacrificed my two shillings pocket money and added it to the one I had earned. Like a proto-Juppé I invented a couple of fictitious jobs and signed my card with indecipherable monograms. Everybody else had earned at least ten shillings. Akela chided me for my performance, inviting the derision of the pack. That was that – so I thought.

The following week's meeting began with Akela's announcement that she had something very grave to report. A member of the pack had broken the Cub's code. This was one of the most serious breaches of trust that she had ever known. She had rumbled me. She told the pack that Jonathan Meades had committed the unforgivable crime of falsifying his Bob-a-Job card. I pleaded that I had done so to my financial disadvantage. The old witch did not offer to repay me the money which I was too ashamed to ask for. I was no longer a Cub and was never to be a Scout. Somewhere no doubt in a file at Baden Powell House are the details of my crime. That was the first of many sackings. Next up: Dunn's Seeds, then Passmore's petrol station on the Southampton Road.

It was not out of charitable compassion that I went to a League of Pity Christmas party in a grand room at Church House (the Salisbury Diocesan offices), so becoming a member of yet another organisation and the bearer of an enamel badge representing a bluebird blue as ceanothus. The League of Pity was the junior branch of the NSPCC. It encouraged children from supposedly privileged homes to practise a dilute version of noblesse oblige, a bourgeois duty of bountiful care for children from poor homes or no homes at all: waifs, strays, mudlarks, coal gatherers, décolleté ragamuffins of the sort that Alice Liddell dressed up as before she became Mrs Reginald Hargreaves, visits to whose grave at Lyndhurst were, I realised, intended as treats.

This time the group was composed of my new friends at the Cathedral School where I had just started. Again, avoidance of ostracism was my motive. The gradations of social class were daunting as ever. The Harnham Road children, my out-of-school friends, wore hand-me-downs, black plimsolls, haircream. They were grazed, runny-nosed, Wiltshire-accented, out at all hours, i.e. past my prescribed bedtime. Were they the very children whom the League of Pity enjoined me to pity? Or were they merely borderline pitiable? And if so was I borderline pitiable too, pitying when I should have been pitied? I might not have a Wiltshire accent and, siblingless, I had no hand-me-downs. But my parents' domestic circumstances were actually more straitened than the Harnham Road average and they were a world away from those of the families of my schoolfriends, owner-occupiers of interbellum houses with that essential of middle-class middle-brow mid-century domestic desirability – a hatch between kitchen and dining room. They had parquet floors where we had stone or splintering boards. Their floors were even. Their houses weren't porous. Their roofs didn't leak, the part of our roof that wasn't thatched was rusted corrugated iron. We had warped wooden sashes on the ground floor and draughty casements upstairs. They had French windows, wrap-round, horizontal-barred Crittall windows, even portholes and often leaded lights. They had post-war gramophones and cookers, smart cars, central heating, front halls, downstairs 'cloak-rooms', eau de nil bathrooms with shaver sockets, breakfast rooms, long gardens, motor mowers, space.

My mother took me to stay at Erpingham Road, Bournemouth, with her strikingly made-up friend Phyllis Treadgold, the irascible Denis Treadgold and their indulged son Gale ('Gala' in my earliest infancy). His enviable electric train set had an entire room devoted to it. In the distance, beyond sandy pinewoods, rolling stock clanking in and out of Branksome station provided a naturalistic soundtrack.

When we returned home I tried to enthuse my father about the impossibly large house's multiple levels, the winding stone steps which led to its exciting underground garage – underground! As usual I was instructed that such houses were recently built so had no character. Further, because Gale's train set was a plastic Triang, it was not the echt thing, not a metal Hornby 00. This was no consolation: I'd have settled for inferior plastic. When eventually I was given a trainset it was a Hornby, bought secondhand from an overheated semi in Hythe on a grey Sunday. The mains transformer was dodgy and many of the rails were bent. Further, by the time I was twelve I didn't want such a toy: when I was twenty-one Wangle gave me that shunting engine.

As an assiduous eavesdropper I surmised that the Treadgolds were materially ambitious, brash, flashy: bookie's checks and tart shoes – whatever these were – Jaguars, the price of everything, the value of nothing. But were not some of the poor Harnham Road families equally brash and flashy? Look at Derek Brooks's swaggering suits, shoes, Windsor knots, cutaway collars, rings, haircuts.

There were too many markers to figure out:

Wealth, accent, house, manners, school, mode of transport, vocabulary, clothes, job, former rank, domestic servants, address, recreations, resident grandparents etc.

So many tiny signals to be painfully learnt.

Why was game fishing superior to coarse fishing, bridge to canasta, rugby to soccer, napkin to serviette, wood to plastic, opera to musicals, pipes to cigarettes?

Why was Jim Laing's Ayrshire accent not remarked upon whilst Hetherington the Dentist's Morningside bray was relentlessly guyed? 'Goodbay. Ay'll see you at fave o'clork next Wensdeh.' His fillings, extractions and anaesthesia were rather less *refained*: indeed he administered the last so approximately that I coma'd on long after one treatment, dreaming that my father was skinning a pike in his surgery.

Why did Mr Kraft, who reminded me of Hitler (tiny moustache, high-pitched voice) and who was rumoured to be of the processed cheese dynasty's Swiss branch, not drive the primped Standard 8 that stood outside his house instead of wheezingly pushing a bicycle weighed down with Skivertex bags full of root veg?

Why did Mr Reid, a man in his fifties who lived with his mother in a prodigious manor house, dress like a tramp yet talk to himself and to walls in a duke's accent?

What class did they belong to? For a child of a taxonomical bent such oddballs were frustrating. How could I know my rung on the ladder of society if I could not determine its entire scale?

In an era when it was de rigueur to do so, I didn't know my place.

(Years later I would have to teach myself *not* to know my place.)

For the moment the macaronic complexity of the social organism I inhabited was an obstacle that impaired my sense of myself. I yearned for omniscience so that I might know myself, I yearned to know every word so that I might express myself. I did not share the common fear of having been adopted, no doubt because of a bereavement of imaginative self-pity and because my preoccupations were approximately demographic rather than psychological.

However, early one evening when I was nine, in the garden of the next-door house which my parents were keeping an eye on whilst it was untenanted and Mrs Edwards was absent, I told them that I realised I was a burden, that my existence was a blight on their life, that I knew I wasn't wanted, that I was willing to be given away. I didn't cry. Was there a stork strong enough to bear me to new parents?

They stood in front of the lugubrious cliff of cotoneaster that separated the two gardens and made light of it, telling me, 'Oh do come on darling!' Telling me not to be so silly, laughing it off. Here was their characteristic burial of emotional swarf, their refusal to consider that I had, for a moment at least, been in earnest. Their presumption that I was exhibiting deflected symptoms of a different malaise, problems at school, say, was groundless. I was not, as my father suggested, 'a bit browned off'. I was, rather, troubled by a guilty suspicion that I had gatecrashed their marriage.

He would use variations of this formula all his life. 'Down in the mouth . . . off colour . . . not rubbing along too well.'

This habit of stoical meiosis was normal in a generation which denied itself deep immersion in feeling, had not learned to wallow in empathy, understood an outpouring to be the discharge of cloacal rather than lachrymal sewage. The lexicon of demonstrative care had yet to be coined; the people's absurd princess had yet to be born; the mistakenly unaborted Blair had yet to perfect the catch of tremulous sincerity in his voice.

Two world wars, economic depressions, genocidal dictators, material privations, the omnipresence of death . . . enduring such stuff is not propitious for the embrace of affective ostentation, for the desire to get in touch with our inner entitlements (in the manner of the unappealing Mrs Blair), for the infantile need to share our pain, for the comfy validation of our self-pity, for the slovenly luxury of annihilating our restraint, for the quashing of our shame.

The generations which suffered, which had fought for their country's existence and its people's life, would have been disinclined to abide by petty laws of governmentally sanctioned niceness and to indulge the suicide-bombing community's human rights. Our *self*-respect diminishes with the ever-growing number of special-pleading causes, minorities and religions we are enjoined to 'respect'. A French diplomat: 'You had a marvellous country till you buggered it up.' The tyranny of minorities has caused the atomisation of England and the consequent destruction of a coherent society.

The damage is repairable – by state terror or mob rule. But since the state's treasonable clerks are the very cause of the embuggerance we can be sure that it will do nothing. And a mob needs a leader to bring its hatred to the boil, foment its venom, drive it on. It needs the Duke of Edinburgh. Much as he might wish it he won't be around.

KALU

'Bleeding in the brain.' My mother was on the phone. It sounded alarming. I overheard her repeat the phrase. Every day one or other of my parents would push through the gap between the hurdles and the cotoneaster hedge to look in on Mrs Perkins, the genial, stately, impressively amnesiac next-door neighbour who had lived at 53 Harnham Road all her long widowhood. She had the elegant bearing of a standard poodle. Her hair was a white cloud, her skin was powdered white in the fashion of her distant youth, her formal suits were pale.

It was my father who found her unconscious on the bathroom floor. Stroke. That was the state that my mother was tersely describing. I imagined that the bathroom floor was sticky crimson from brain blood. Who would clear it up? It wasn't till Squadron Leader and Mrs Johnson moved in to her house that I realised that Mrs Perkins wouldn't be coming back. Was Mrs Perkins still bleeding? Was there still cacophony in her head? Was she dead? I dared not ask: death was taboo. Where were her belong-ings, her furniture, her beeswaxed table whose mildly undulating surface was so satisfying to the touch? Had she gone to heaven? If she had gone to heaven how did my mother visit her? Where did she visit her?

When I was four heaven possessed a refulgent literality. Maxfield Parrish had devised the mise en scène. Much of it was moss-green and mottled, azurine and dappled. It was always the golden hour. Heaven was horizontally lit by the lowest of low-key lights. There were mackerel clouds and outstretched shadows. The unmitigated sublimity was reward for a life well led. It was deserted. Were the dead invisible? Could they see? With her bleeding in the brain would Mrs Perkins be able to see it? Would curtains of blood blind her? Would she be able to smell the heavenly perfume, to taste the manna, milk and honey? Were all faculties restored once heaven was ascended to? Even had I asked these questions no one would have been willing to respond to them. Did no one know the answers? Or would telling me them cause them to forfeit their place in heaven? I was coming to recognise adults' secrets, their unwillingness to share what they knew with a mere child. I was beginning to cotton on to adults' dissemblance of their ignorance, their desperation not to be found out, not to lose face, their barely suppressed petulance when corrected by a dwarf know-all who was insouciant of the offence he gave and of his supposed precocity. My habit of politely pointing out factual inaccuracies hardly amounted to an assault on the amour propre of the middle-aged but it was frequently taken thus. Similarly, my questioning certain usages: I was my father's son. After fishing, in which I had no interest, the minutiae of usage was the subject he most often addressed at meals. My mother, though a schoolmarm to my contemporaries, didn't share his proscriptive bent. She was inured to the syntactical and grammatical accidents that befell the dull and backward, even

enjoyed them. After little more than a year's tenure Squadron Leader and Mrs Johnson were posted to Cyprus, leaving us their cat Blacky. We got new neighbours at 53. Another RAF family. Squadron Leader and Mrs Ritson-Hoyle. Everything was too much for her. She was always at the end of her tether. She was blinding effing (though whispering) proof that there is nothing genteel about a double-barrelled name or the officer class. Her mucous-moustached son was an animal five or so years my senior. My mother gleefully reported this exchange between them. Whining son: 'But I dund it Mum. I dund it.' Mrs Ritson-Hoyle (sotto): 'Not I dund it. I *done* it.' I noticed that my mother no longer visited Mrs Perkins. Nothing was said. There was never a good time to ask about death. The dead, as I would learn that the French have it, *disappear*. They incite forgetfulness. Even though their name liveth for evermore. It is only the name though. If that, if that. Blacky was renamed Kalu (black or blacky in both Urdu and Ceylonese). My father had had a mongrel dog so named in Iraq. This cat was the most delightful creature. I loved him more even than I loved Sugary Bun, my dove-grey dandy of a rabbit who lived in a cage my father had bodged from a tea chest. My mother had feared that Kalu might attack Sugary Bun. In fact the cat ignored the rabbit. He had other plans. He created a sort of ledge or nest in the springy coto-neaster hedge from which he'd pounce, with a languid flop and boxing paws, on his unsuspecting prey beneath. Hardly a day passed without Kalu bringing a dead or maimed bird into the kitchen. They bled through their feathers as Mrs Perkins had through her brain. They shivered in their throes. Kalu stands over them with hunter's pride. In a moment he will resume his position in the hedge. The garden's little flowerbeds became an avian cemetery. My father was persuaded that all phosphates succour plants. Sentimentally impressed by any form of hunting, he buried the sparrows and tits and finches and thrushes just as he buried pike which hunted down the trout that were, rightly, his quarry. Here was nature's merciless cycle. Kalu was taken to

Dalton the vet to be neutered in a canvas grip. Thereafter the sound of a zip sent him scuttling to safety. It was the only thing that alarmed this fearless predator.

Another forces neighbour: a soldier and his wife. Sandy and Jane Robertson were Scottish, newly married. He was newly promoted. They rented No. 57. I pretended to myself that Jane was my big sister. I wanted to pretend to myself that she was my mother but could not countenance such treacherous disloyalty. But there was a sister vacancy: there always would be, I was resigned from very early on to my parents' unwillingness to make me a sister. (I didn't want to be supplied with a brother.) Jane was young with an excitingly carefree habit of skipping along the pavement whilst I clutched her hand, running to keep up as I knew I must. She took me on shopping expeditions to Sid the Butcher, Hands's corner shop and over the bridges to Mr Batten's where prewar jars of boiled sweets were opaque with prewar dust and the ham was good. It felt important undertaking chores for her, holding a box of clothes pegs whilst she struggled with swollen sheets and dancing shirts, putting tins of cling peaches and fruit salad in the store cupboard, carrying plates from the draining board to the dining room where everything was just so and a dresser displayed wedding presents: lustreware pots, toby jugs, a cow creamer, a docile lion with Edinburgh's coat of arms on its back. Sandy was a handsome Scot, palest ginger, whence, I assumed, came his name – I didn't mention it so no one corrected me. His accent, like Jane's, bore the faintest trace of what I did not yet know as Morningside. He was a young major, a black-sweater'd 'tankie' (a rare breed in Salisbury) seconded to Southern Command at Fugglestone, an unwanted sedentary posting, desk-polishing. He compensated for it at lunchtimes by taking his big black labrador Postman for gusty walks on the downs towards Snake Hill and the descent to the Avon valley. The rest of the day the dog lay with uncharacteristic tranquillity at his master's feet. So many army officers took their dog to work that the Nissen huts at this camp must have been like a kennels. Sandy and my father would rough shoot at weekends on the Gradidge family's farms at Wellow and Whiteparish. Pheasant, partridge, wood pigeon, the odd hare and rabbits, still plentiful in those last years before myxomatosis was introduced to southern England. Postman bounded willingly across fields and through streams. He fetched as a retriever should. My father's admiration for this threateningly boisterous dog increased by the week. He was further trained to flush out birds. And, what is more, he displayed a terrier-like aptitude for seeking out warrens. There was no end to his abilities. My father resolved to get a gun dog of his own, not least because the Robertsons and Postman would soon be on the move again. He pored over advertisements in *The Field* and *Shooting Times*. He wrote letters to breeders. It was decided, by my mother, that if he must have a gun dog then a cocker spaniel would be more domestically manageable than a lolloping enthusiastic energetic uncontainable labrador like Postman. Too enthusiastic. Too energetic. Too uncontainable. And too playful. My mother was in the kitchen chopping or podding. Through the high horizontal slit of the window she noticed that Postman was once again in the garden which the remains of a wicket fence hardly separated from the Robertsons'. She wondered where he'd found the rag doll he was playing with, vigorously, and got back to peeling or seeding. Clock time gets a kicking at this point. The gulf between seeing and understanding is the foundation of the double-take. She understood in a microsecond that lasted a minute what the rag doll was. She ran outside. It was too late. Postman, in terrier mode, had forced open Sugary Bun's makeshift cage. According to my mother he had merely been playful. Too playful. Sugary Bun suffered shaken bunny syndrome. The savage dog had broken the rabbit's neck for fun. He had meant no harm. My mother's attempts at mollification didn't stop me howling. My father buried the rabbit. I hugged Kalu who was imperiously indifferent. Jane hugged me and wiped my tears. She scolded Postman whilst maintaining that he had simply been too exuberant. She said Postman was sorry. I didn't believe her. Postman wagged his tail: that was a fine way to say sorry. He showed no sign of remorse. Sandy clutched my shoulder man to man. Postman wagged his tail. It didn't matter that he meant no harm. He had done harm. He had killed my second-favourite pet, formerly my very favourite pet. I reconsidered: Sugary Bun's loss made him my very favourite once again, for a while. A week or so after Sugary Bun's murder I was being helpful. This, I believed, was one of my strengths. Ingratiation through action. Jane was drying plates and cutlery. I was helpfully carrying them to the dining-room table where, in a moment, she would sort them and put them in the dresser drawers beneath the trophies of her proud marriage. How did it happen? How did it slip through my fingers? Among their wedding presents was an eighteenth-century cruet. (Cruet was a word banned by my parents on grounds of tweeness. But Jane and Sandy had no such inhibitions.) The receptacles were poison-blue glass. They fitted into frilly, squat-legged silver stands, circular for pepper and salt, crib-shaped for mustard. It was the mustard receptacle that I dropped on the kitchen's stone floor. Dropped? Or let drop? The latter was Jane's verdict. She looked at me in fury. I learnt that extreme ire is expressed in a near-whisper. The damage was not just to a mustard pot which was now a former mustard pot – shards and splinters and nuggety lumps. The damage was to her and Sandy and their sacred bond. Tears and anger. I was shooed out of the house.

The presumption that I had taken revenge for Sugary Bun was not discounted by my parents. But they seemed unconcerned. It was just one of those things. They negligently failed to dissemble their indifference from Jane and Sandy. Such a fuss over a piece of glass! My father got browned off with Sandy's pompous Edinbourgeois righteousness and with Jane's fractious self-pity. He had immediately offered to replace the vessel only to be told it was irreplaceable. There was something approaching a row, thick with cruet. I didn't witness it, I didn't hear it through the chalky cob walls. But I realised nonetheless that my parents had defended my maladroitness and – should it have been the case – my motive. In the couple of months that remained before they moved to their next posting the Robertsons were nothing less than civil. We exchanged polite greetings. But I was no longer included in Jane's adventurous shopping trips. An important friendship had been damaged.

They left a couple of days after Christmas 1952. I bravely patted Postman. A few weeks later my father announced that he had found a dog and that we would soon be going to collect it. A dog of our own! My excitement was boundless. On a frosty Sunday morning my father and I took the familiar road through Wilton, past the theatrically castellated lodge to Compton Park, the Fovant badges, the Blinking Owl, the turning to Guy's Marsh, the mesmerisingly straight glinting Sherborne Causeway (fifteen miles from Sherborne itself), East Stour then, at last, Henstridge. My father, as often, followed directions written on paper clipped to a board. At the end of a track we arrived at a drab house. The breeder who greeted us was a strapping pyramid of a woman snugly bandaged in multiple layers of cardigan and checked car rugs. She wore fur-lined bootees with a zip up the instep. We drank tea in her overheated malodorous kitchen whilst she complimented my father on his fine choice of dog and slipped his cheque beneath a mantelpiece clock. She and my father walked across a muddy yard constellated with shit coils to a barking growling yapping former farm building. I waited beside the door onto the yard. The smell was repulsive. There was a large woven willow basket filled with gypsy clothes pegs resting in mire. They reappeared with a dog, the dog, our dog, my dog. A cocker spaniel puppy, a blue roan. But he was black and grey. That 'blue' was a matter of constant exasperation. Why was this species so called? No one could explain it to my satisfaction. As usual no one knew, as usual no one would admit his ignorance. My dog sat on the floor in front of me, beneath the glove compartment. He had large mournful eyes. He was a puzzled dog. His removal from the only home he had ever known at the age of four months prompted a morose resignation. He could not have been less like Postman. When we got home he was shown his brand-new basket and his aluminium water bowl. My mother had prepared a welcoming meal of dog biscuits and boiled meat. This was put before him in a second, enamel bowl. Something happened. Gloomy passivity was shed. Suddenly the dog came to life, to greedy gluttonous life. He was happy. My mother wondered whether he had been insufficiently fed at Henstridge. In any case it soon became apparent that his sole interest was food. The dog was so lazy he wouldn't even fetch a stick. His routine was sleep, eat, sleep, eat. He consented to walkies provided that we processed at snail's pace. After six frustrating months of attempting to train this 'natural gun dog' my father reconciled himself to failure. It served him right for, in the hope that he might share the murderous labrador's sporting spirit, he had chosen to name him Postman.

Did he not realise how much that hurt? He became Posty, my mother's responsibility, and Kalu's whipping dog in perpetuity. But Posty was very easily pleased. Provided he was lavishly fed he showed a constant fortitude in the face of feline oppression, a stoic born of torpor.

KNEE LIGAMENTS

Whilst his father would stay there for six years, coming back for infrequent holidays, Roger and his mother Pat returned from Brazil after only a few months. He brought me a marquetry box containing a deck of cards. It shows Copacabana and the Sugar Loaf, places he had not actually seen. They had hardly left São Paulo where he was frightened by black people, brown people, tan people and the language they spoke. I was selfishly relieved that he had been unable to settle there. We picked up where we had left off, with extra gusto. Our cowboy and Indian games

now acquired a violent edge. We would execute lead (and, later, plastic) models by sawing off their heads. This was no doubt the sado-sexual behaviour of future serial killers; happily we had other vocations. I developed a fondness for hiding under Pat's skirt, inspecting her stocking tops. She indulged me like an amiably unruly pet. Her mother Mrs Dear thought this was a hoot.

Mrs Dear inadvertently taught me the word 'bugger'. She cooked lights for Tiggy the cat. Her favourite film was *The Charge of the Light Brigade*, which she had taken Roger and me to see at a friend's who had a telly. She enjoyed talking football with Sid the Butcher from whom she bought those lights. The day before the 1955 Cup Final – Tony Blair's second birthday – she popped across the road to check if she could invite herself to watch it on our recently acquired telly, so much handier than going across town to Ridgeway Road where the friend lived. I had never heard of the Cup Final, would improbably have watched it had she not been so keen. So it was that I saw my first entire football match. Newcastle United, wearing black shorts and black and white striped shirts, were more visible than Manchester City whose baby blue shirts were rendered pale grey by the primitive monochrome reception. I was hooked from the very start: Jackie Milburn – subject of one of The Christian Bomber's lesser, earlier, but most revelatory lies – scored in the first minute. Jimmy Meadows tore his knee ligaments twenty minutes later. He never played again. The terror on his face as he was carried off was pitiful. I feared that he was going to be put down. Mrs Dear was gleeful that Manchester City would have to play the match with ten men. They duly lost. She had had a bet with Sid the Butcher and would pocket £1 on Monday.

Whilst my parents filled in their pools coupons at random Mrs Dear and Sid the Butcher were assiduous scholars of form rather than connoisseurs of chance. Bradford Park Avenue, Port Vale, Crewe Alexandra, Scunthorpe and Lindsey United, Stenhousemuir, Airdrieonians, Albion Rovers – there was nothing they didn't know about Saturday afternoon's litany of paired names which I now began to understand were more than names, they represented sporting endeavour as well as a dream of untold riches (£75,000) and escape.

'I'll be up that 'ill,' said Mrs Bacon when she left on Friday afternoons, 'I can feel it's going to be my week.' There was no one I would have preferred to receive a two-metre-long cheque from a saucy light entertainer at a gaudy London hotel. Mrs Bacon was a cheery optimist. She chose her numbers from combinations of family birthdays. Her ideal was a newly built bungalow, a dream bungalow, up that hill which rose steeply to the south of Harnham.

This was where I'd go on evening walks with my father and Posty. As we approached the bottom of the long flight of worn steps that led up to Bouverie Avenue he'd often warn me about men who interfere with children. The implication was that such men were liable to be the tramps who slept in the abandoned subterranean munitions stores at the end of the nearby sunken lane rather than nice schoolmasters. Those foggy autumn nights were full of fungal spores, rotting vegetation, cabbages and bonfires extinguished by rain.

In Bouverie Avenue (formerly owned by the Earls of Radnor whose family name that is) there were early bungalows in a vaguely colonial style with wide verandahs. Bouverie Avenue South was tonier. Gen and Mrs Gen, the ecclesiastical architect Robert Potter and Dr Bailes Barker lived there. The last's sumptuous 1920s house had a service wing and an arch to a courtyard with a games room above it.

Close by was Harnham Heights, precursor of a 'gated' community, hidden down beech-shaded lanes where the elderly and fastidious French bachelor J.-P. 'Froggy' Hellmann inhabited one of Salisbury's few moderne houses: he might have been the model for Jules Supervielle's Colonel Bigua, a man of two nations but at home in neither.

Harnwood Road was, Mrs Bacon reckoned, the apogee of

smartness and class. Its earliest houses were large prewar pseudo-vernacular works which might have been designed for Wentworth or Virginia Water: double garages, extensive gardens and, importantly, a hatch between kitchen and dining room. The very largest was bought with what my father considered illicit war spoils. Its resented owner had a company that rewound military batteries. He was certainly uncouth (tomato ketchup on everything, guitar, wife with a moustache), but hardly criminal, and it was probably essential work. The majority of the houses were smaller and post-war. Rather, post-November 1954 when building licences were removed. My parents owned a building plot there. But they procrastinated. Their heart wasn't in it – there was no river. Besides money was, as ever, short. My father constructed scale model houses to my mother's awkward Neaum-derived designs in compensation for the lack of the real thing, their very own and golden house. When Roger's father returned from Brazil in 1960 they built a house there. Mrs Bacon was impressed by the forged metal sign announcing its name, Bom Clima (jocularly, Bum Cleaner; joyously, some people called Bottom built a house on an adjoining plot). She cased the houses noting their foibles, yearning to escape her life of Johnson's Hardgloss Glo-Coat, elbow grease, drudgery, Cardinal Red. She tutted and tutted about an art teacher's house called Topsy Turvey whose bedrooms were downstairs, whose living room and kitchen were on the first floor. That wasn't right. But it was! From the living room and adjacent studio you could gaze across the conjoining valleys at the cathedral and Old Sarum. Nor was it right to install, as my parents did, a bidet in a bathroom. This device, which Mrs Bacon pronounced *biddy*, with repulsed distaste, spoke of sexual abominations.

Alas, it never was Mrs Bacon's week. Wealth eluded her. She lived on in Old Street with her daughter Pammy who had a secretarial job at Woodrow's the ironmongers and had once found a live slug in a school salad. Mr Bacon had been an engine driver in a celluloid-peaked cap. His work clothes shone with coal dust. No doubt it permeated his cancerous lungs too.

She was a generous woman who cut brown bread so thinly that its fibres had to be bonded by slabs of butter. This accompanied tea which was hot water and milk. She used such prodigious quantities of polish that a floor's surface was as hazardous as a skid-pan. When I went a-over-t and put my elbow through a door's glass panel she warned me about my recklessness.

My father sang 'Baa Baa Black Sheep': the little boy was surely me and Old Street was the lane he lived down. It was all puddles, cinders, rivulets, gravel. The back gate, squeezed between our coalshed and next-door's, gave onto it. Each of the four semi-detached pebbledash and red-brick houses on the steep bank to the south had its own flight of steps: here lived the Dredge family (a name more common in Wiltshire than elsewhere), the Newells, the red-headed Norrises and some of the Shipsey catering clan. Mr Latham, the Government House gardener, Mrs Latham, who was permanently attached to a decaying wicker basket, and their two daughters Jean and Barbara lived in a small detached house which had once fulfilled some non-domestic military purpose. Smith the Carpenter's children used the western end of Old Street in lieu of a garden. The other end, where Mrs Bacon lived, was round a 90-degree bend. Some of the fifteen or so houses were borderline slums. This was the pye dog's domain (my father's expression; according to *Hobson-Jobson* it signifies pariah). Whenever I cycled past, the hideous shrieking creature hurled itself from a toxic rookery alley to try to bite my ankles. It wriggled at banshee speed. I shielded my eyes from that alley and the other alleys: their cracked flags exuded leucous venom.

I never knew where to look in Old Street. I hated lingering there. It was a place to hurry through. But because my mother refused to let me bring my bike through the house to the front door I was obliged to broach it even though its dimensions increased with my fear, and its properties grew ever more extreme. The Lovely Queenie's rouge glowed like embers, her powder was flour, her seamed-stockinged calves swelled to thigh thickness, her fat feet bid to escape her GI-pleasing shoes, the dead animal

154

hiding her neck paunch came to life as the pye dog. Mr Thick the drowner's moustache was big as a yard brush. Mrs Bevan's gamboge teeth turned marmalade. Mr Bevan's simian paws dangled beside his shins. His Welsh accent got Welsher. The Bevans were figures from a late Victorian bucolic painting by, say, La Thangue. Like Mr Thick, who had fought in the second Boer War, they had been born around 1880: they were trapped in the dress of their youth and were condemned with the face of their generation (it is not just hairdos which are giveaways of age). The prospect of octogenarian hoodies is one I shall thankfully be spared. Peasants always look old – fatigue, bad diet and so on. My father gave them most of the pike he caught: he considered this fish unfit for human consumption.

LAKER

The off-spinner Jim Laker took nine Australian wickets in the first innings of the fourth test at Old Trafford in 1956. He took all ten in the second innings, the last of them that of the wicketkeeper Len Maddocks, on the late afternoon of the fifth day, Tuesday 31 July.

I learnt of this feat from the six o'clock news on the car radio. We had parked beside a precipitous road on the edge of a golden Snowdonia. Beyond a drystone wall, far below ranks of pines climbing to the light, a river flashed and bellowed in the rocky gorge. My father stared longingly at it. This was one of the days when he had made a sacrifice and had forgone fishing so that I might see something of north Wales. He was smoking a pipe. He indulged me by agreeing that Laker's was a jolly good show.[11] His interest in cricket was confined to players' tics, to peripheral incidents. He relished Ian Meckiff's nickname, 'Chucker'. Hubert Doggart swallowed a bee whilst fielding for Sussex against Hampshire at Bournemouth; it did him no harm – he became headmaster of King's School, Bruton. Laker's fellow spinner Tony Lock often took to the field with his cuffs and collar buttoned: he was likened to an inmate of the Old Manor. A third spinner, the South African Hugh Tayfield who had toured England the previous year, caught his attention because of the pedal ritual he performed before bowling: he called him Tapfoot. I knew however that to his fellow players he was Toey; that was the correct nickname, the official nickname. Tapfoot! Colin Cowdrey was mocked for his huge arse; David Sheppard for his churchiness

11 Anil Kumble took all ten second-innings wickets for India against Pakistan at Delhi in 1999. However Laker's record of nineteen wickets in a test still stands.

(he was an evangelical clergyman, eventually Bishop of Liverpool); Dennis Compton for wearing dripping on his head (he famously advertised Brylcreem and took his gleaming paymaster onto the field with him).

Three days previously we had driven from Salisbury. I derived mild excitement from a signwriter's self-advertising premises at Stratton St Margaret. He advertised his considerable craft by impasting his Edwardian house and workshop with samples of countless fonts, colophons, logotypes, clichés. At Shrewsbury there was a great church built of stone stained by lilacs. We had stopped where the road ran beside a canal, the Llangollen or the Shropshire Union. There were silver birches and a black and white lift-bridge, hand-operated; its benign low-gear winding mechanism allowed tender muscles to hang it in the air at forty-five degrees above the water. Such bridges, rare in Britain, are common in the Netherlands: they are the source of Rietveld's angular, coccyx-trashing furniture. Years later I half-heartedly searched for and failed to find this one. I doubt that I shall ever see it again.

We were staying at The Black Boy in Caernarvon. The ill-wrought inn sign showed a toothy blackamoor, Uncle Tom's nephew who had run away to sea.

We were staying at The Black Buoy in Caernarvon. The ill-wrought inn sign's verso showed a black blob supposedly floating on a blue background (the sea) pocked by white curlicues (waves). The inn still has two names: The Black Boy and, for those who don't or won't speak English, Tafarn Y Bachgen Du. The children who lived across the road, with whom I played on the green beside the town walls and the Northgate, had been instructed that English was not a means of increasingly universal communication but the weapon of an occupying power. Hence when I asked them the word for boy they told me it was mochyn, not bachgen. Mochyn means pig. It was not till three years later that this deception was revealed to me during another and better holiday at Lampeter where the delightful Mr Conti made the best ice cream I had yet tasted. Whilst my father fished my mother read green Penguins and encouraged me to read them too. That was the summer I put Enid Blyton behind me. We walked around the castle, preferring the view of it from the west to the martial actuality of ramparts and portcullises. A fellow guest at the hotel, Major Bismuth-Kerr, a hail-fellow-well-met handshaker, frequently joined us, uninvited. He tried to persuade my mother to send me to the school where he taught, St David's, Congresbury near Weston-super-Mare. She declined glacially. But he was not deterred. He later made the same suggestion to my father, insisting that it would make a man of me in a way that the musically inclined Cathedral School never would.

Llanfairpwllgwyngyllgogerychwyrndrobwllllantysiliogogogoch has the longest place name in Europe. I insisted that we take a bus there. The elegant Menai Bridge and the sinister Britannia Bridge, whose tubular structure was supported on neoclassical pylons, were captivating. Not so the bearer of the longest place name, a village which lived off, doubtless still lives off, its very name. I did not of course admit my disappointment. But it was obvious. My mother was not sympathetic. She disdained anything that smacked of folksiness. That included extravagant place names, the Welsh language, gewgaws and bondieuserie, national costume – particularly kilts worn by expats, regional accents, arty-crafty tat. At Bangor we had tea and rock cakes: never was a foodstuff more aptly named. I put a halfpenny on the track of the North Wales coastal line in the hope that the train hauled by a panting locomotive would so squash it that it would pass as a penny. After the train had passed I couldn't find the coin. Most days it drizzled. The hotel was dark and cramped. My tiny room's dormer window was grimy. Breakfasts were enlivened by a family comprising a ruddy, pompous, tattersall-checked fellow; the apple of his eye – a gleaming 'cyclops' Rover 75; his harassed, nervously exhausted wife; their gurgling, spittle-foaming baby girl. The parents repeatedly tried to feed her spoonsful of egg, crying with increasing petulance: 'Eggy Baba! Eggy Baba! Eggy

Baba!' And the baby repeatedly and enthusiastically repelled them so that her highchair was encrusted with yolk, the floor with toast and albumen. For some years after my father would exclaim 'Eggy Baba' when food fell from a fork or drink was spilled at table. This rather foxed guests.

Fishing the afon Gwyrfai and the afon Seiont had been disappointing. No sewin. In six days he had taken three brown trout (which the hotel had overcooked in Duckham's). There might have been intermittent drizzle but there had been no rain for weeks. The water was low, ad hoc stepping stones had appeared across rivers. So at breakfast on Sunday 5 August whilst watching Eggy Baba's spirited resistance my father announced an unexpected treat.

We would go to the summit of Snowdon on the mountain railway. Bright day!

It proved to be more of a treat than I could ever have imagined. My mother, cautious, insisted that we bring waterproofs: the mountains, you know. We men scoffed. The day was fine, warm, cloudless, mistless. The heights above Llanberis Pass were sharp silhouettes. Scree and slate sparkled. Sheep basked among boulders hurled in battle by angry giants (long ago). Moss turned to velvet. There was a traffic jam, mostly black prewar cars, still commonplace in 1956. I sat in the back fearing my father's impatience: he would turn round and I would never reach the summit of the highest mountain in Wales (3,560 feet – I had that figure by heart, nine times taller than Salisbury Cathedral). Atypically, he managed to restrict himself to drumming on the steering wheel. Nor did he complain when after finding a space in the car park we were obliged to join the end of a long queue for train tickets. However, after a few minutes he marched briskly to the front of the queue counting the number of hopefuls ahead of us. He spoke to a peaked cap. 'We're going to walk.' We would come back by train. My mother sighed. We were not dressed for mountain walking. No one on that bleak mountain was dressed for mountain walking. This was due to a combination of national indigence and national fear of pretension. You walked up mountains in whatever you happened to be wearing that day, no matter how unsuitable; high heels, hats, drainpipes, threadbare blazers whose wire crests were frayed and tarnished, swirly skirts, cheap cotton blouses, flannels, Sunday best suits, pedal pushers, biker's stiff tarpaulins, drape jackets, coiled coifs, oiled quiffs, collarless shirts, (relatively) gaudy holiday shirts whose collars stretched over jacket lapels in an access of informality and seaside fun, garments from war and National Service: combat jackets, blanco'd belts, once spooned boots, pullovers with pips, with stripes, with ARP badges, customised berets, perished Sam Brownes, crudely dyed battledress.

Britain was a raggedly martial nation, making do, improvising uncomplaining. The many who had not been able to get on the train trudged up and up without grumbling, for it was a glorious day. The path followed the narrow-gauge railway, crossing and recrossing the track. It was less than a yard wide, satisfactorily miniature, polished. There were points and passing loops, viaducts and halts, water tanks. My father would stride ahead then exhort us to catch up: 'Rally rally rally!' We looked down on still black lakes and hefty white water churning in straits. Pitted cliffs rose to the blueblue sky. Beside the path stood all manner of cairns: slender as a stylite's pillar; coarse rubble piles; pyramidal garden ornaments; demolition sites; diagrammatic anthropoids; squads of antagonistic zoomorphs; vertical drystone walls.

And then there came darkness. A violently roistering gang of clouds, blueblack as bruises and unmistakably trouble-seeking, lurched from beyond the jagged horizon. These bloated impostors of night switched off the light. The first gouts of fat rain fell. Then there were the water cannons. Crackling runes of lightning. Malevolent cymbals. There was no lapse between them. We were in the storm's core. The path was suddenly deserted. Where had all the walkers gone? To shelter evidently. But where on these barren slopes might shelter be sought? We were not going to find out. Within seconds we had been soaked through.

We couldn't have been any wetter. There was nothing to lose. My father was loving it. So on we went at his behest, now striding, trudging, now paddling, now wading. The path became a torrent, visibility was blighted, scree was shifting, stone and water were belligerently allied. The mountain storm's epic grandeur was however mitigated and mocked by low comic pratfalls and undignified stumbles: sound by Wagner, vision by Charlie Drake. I didn't care that I grazed my shins and bruised my hands, it was such fun. Fun of an unprecedented kind.

At the summit where the railway evidently terminates there perched a café, a cafeteria even, a mid-Thirties structure which might have dignified an important provincial bus station.[12] The windows were densely condensed. Refugees from the storm abandoned reticence. They shared tables chatting excitedly to each other, to strangers whose accent was not theirs – Toxteth spoke to Llandudno, Prenton to Fylde, Tarporley to Bacup. We were the only southerners. Tea-crusted sugar cellars were passed about with generous abandon. They drank in the excitement. I fell for a boy of fifteen or sixteen. Instant crush.

His lank dark hair was parted on the left. A bang fell over his right eye. His cheekbones were just so, his eyes dark and lively, his face frail and starved of light. He carried the germ of young death. He smiled at my mother. I have never forgotten him. His hearing aid was sage-green, coiled wire stretched from it to a transmitter in his windcheater which was the same colour. (Maybe time has dyed it.) I longed for a prosthesis: two years later I would be prescribed spectacles, precisely not the prosthesis I sought. I longed for a squawking, screeching ear-snail or metal callipers (leg preferably, but arm would do) or a correctional neckbrace or an ostentatiously built-up shoe just as I longed for the comradely embrace of this teenager whose disability rendered him vulnerable and romantic. He was more clearly outlined than

12 The architect was Clough Williams-Ellis, who when he abandoned his winsome, cute Portmeirion mode was trite in a different way.

his companions, more vital despite his etiolation, *because* of his etiolation. His redmop friend was certainly no catch. The other members of the group were morose, formless, forgettable. They didn't carry a duffel bag. I relished the few minutes I spent in proximity to this boy. My preoccupation was such that I was only faintly aware of my parents' conversation. Did he notice my fixated gaze? It took me some time to realise that the café had got crowded. The passengers of a just-arrived train jostled each other as they sought tables and places in the tea queue. 'Standing room only!' A couple belied that jovial complaint and pulled their chairs to our table. We silently greeted them, nods and reassuring all-in-this-together smiles. The parts of the panes immediately adjacent to the horizontal and vertical metal bars were clear: condensation is centripetal. My view in the other direction had been obstructed by the milling trippers. When I looked for him again my boy had gone. I stood, scanned the café – too late. The newcomers beside us spoke in incomprehensibly accented stage whispers. They wore motorcycle kit. Unpliable heavily oiled jackets, waterproof leggings. She carried her helmet. He wore his, hadn't bothered to take it off. A pair of goggles was pushed up above the peak like a starlet's shades. Surely this couple must be too hot. They were as much in love as I was, as I had just been. Their love, however, was acknowledged, spoken, reciprocated and impervious to the increasingly clammy atmosphere. Wet breath and reeking urn steam were suspended in the air. Their gaze was tender. They held hands, self-consciously, clumsily, fondly. The lights blinked as the storm flung its electric warriors at the walls. She pretended to wince in fear. He rolled his eyes conspiratorially.

A Walian voice distorted to bronchial gruffness by a hitherto unremarked public address system portentously announced the *indefinite* postponement of the next train to Llanberis Pass. The café hushed. The announcement was repeated with added throat clearance. The café was bemused. How long is indefinite? My father immediately and predictably invited us to agree that walking down would be no chore after that ascent. The return is always quicker. I rued being denied the train ride and was not convinced by his observation that the train is available every day whilst an adventure like this is rarely granted us. But we don't come here every day . . . We shook our drenched macs and put them on over our drenched summer clothes, nodded farewell to our amorous neighbours – she moued 'ooh' at our daring, he gave a bashful thumbs-up – then pushed our way, arms up, from the café into the lugubrious monochrome of obstinately unabated storm.

The downward path was no easier than the upward. We slid, slipped, stumbled, paddled through the dusky day that might still be day, that might now be dusk: climate amends time, an arctic hour is not an equatorial hour. How long had we been trudging when, not far below us, a descending train overtook us, silenced by the stinging gusts? What was happening? The storm was by now even more ferocious, was even less fit for rack and pinion kit. And above that, the carriages were unlit.

John Mattinson was thirty-four years old. His wife Mary was ten years his junior. They came from the Leeds suburb of Wortley. They had left the café at the summit about half an hour after we had. They walked only a few yards. He stood on a cairn. He spotted across the Irish Sea a climatic change that we, by then further down the mountain, were innocent of. He said to Mary: 'Just look at that sunshine over there. Trust us to come to the wrong spot.' Those were his last words. Lightning entered through the goggles perched on his helmet. His death and the portage of his body on the unlit train through the worst storm anyone in north Wales could recall were reported on the front page of the *Daily Mirror*, a paper I had never previously seen. My mother was strict, mock-incredulous, far from sympathetic: 'Well if you will stand on a cairn in a thunderstorm . . .'

MAJOR, BOGUS

October 1986. Warrick Knock employs Bright Clive as his gofer and driver, strictly cash. All I previously knew of Bright Clive was that he was 'an old mucker' (his word) of the tearaway Johnny Dudley, one of whose lesser misdemeanours was to have attempted to shoot the ingénue Tessa Wyatt's caged budgerigar: having missed with six shots he jacked it in and the bird lived. Giving a job to Bright Clive is charitable: he is only recently out after six months in Ford Open. His offence was to put forgeries of antique arms through a 'prestigious' London auction house. As Warrick says: 'Could have happened to any of us.' The swords themselves, made and aged by a bladesmith in Fulda, were convincing. Their provenances – Bright Clive's department – were littered with elementary disparities which contributed to his reputation as The Balliol Dunce. (Had someone taken the entrance exam for him? Had his finals papers got mixed up with another undergraduate's?)

Whatever he learnt at Oxford, it wasn't caution. Ignoring his employer's pleas he is bombing down a road between Cheltenham and Cirencester (the Ciren of my infancy). He runs over a pheasant. He brakes so hurriedly that the vehicle skids. He jumps out, runs back to scrape the multicoloured squash of blood, bone, beak, claw and feathers from the road and hurls it in the back.

'Supper, delish!' he booms fruitily and, without pausing for breath, asks me: 'D'you like post-war thrillers? Black and white. Spivs. Private hotels. John Mills, Nigel Patrick, Eric Portman, those chaps . . . Golden age of the bogus major. D'you know,' he's confidential and wistful now, 'I wish I'd been born a generation earlier . . . then *I* could have been a bogus major.'

He cannot disguise his regret at never having had the opportunity to achieve this touchingly rare ambition.

MAJOR BRAITHWAITE

At the age of four, during a picnic at Pritchett's Point, at the confluence of the Avon and the Nadder where, on the south bank, my parents would build their house ten years later, I pushed Richard Braithwaite into the river whence he had to be rescued by my fully clothed father. The Braithwaites – he was still in the army – were living during that particular south Wiltshire posting in a Britford Lane bungalow subsequently rented by Uncle Ken and Auntie Jessica Southwell. To my embarrassment, and his too no doubt, Major Braithwaite, now cast on to Civvy Street, joined the hopelessly unqualified staff of the Cathedral School in my second year there, 1955–6. He was my first French teacher, and quite the worst. So inept indeed that I spoke better French than he did. He was soon found out by the parents. He was replaced by Barry Still, who actually spoke the language. That faint praise is graceless. This was a man whom I admired even though I often feared him. He mocked my confusion of 'frais' with 'fraise' which caused me to translate 'un petit matin frais' as *early morning strawberry* – this ought to have been praised in a school where David Gascoyne had been a pupil.

MAJOR CHRISTIAN

He rode his bicycle home along Harnham Road as though pedalling through invisible lard. To protect him from mud, segments of engrimed translucent nylon were stretched over the back wheel, a device more usually associable with women's, crossbarless bikes: Miss Ellaby, Pammy Bacon and Rene Bowns all had different configurations of this arrangement but so too did Sid the Butcher's forest-green Raleigh. A forlorn flaccid saddlebag, made of cracked naugahyde and canvas that had lost all its dressing, hung like a crone's tit. He wore a service beret, khaki patchily faded to sand. When he removed it the line of its band was incised fuchsia across his forehead. His fangs were sensationally uneven, misshapen, discoloured as though plundered from dentists' waste. His face was several hues of wan, crosshatched with razor cuts and relieved by clusters of grey stubble that he had failed to see and to shave.

Twice a week before lunch Major Christian bellowed: 'Press, press . . . Fling!' We were lined up, on a wide gravel path between swathes of sacred lawn, in four 'sections', Wilkes, Vaux, Holgate, Kingsbury – each named after a dead cleric. The door to the cloisters was to our right. The Chapter House was behind us. Major Christian stood in front of us. The big yew tree was over his shoulder. His repertoire of exercises was invariable. Stretching here, bracing there, running on the spot, bending, star jumping, shadow boxing. There were a hundred and twenty of us so it was only by chance that he'd spot a slacker. But when he did there followed a villainous pantomime entertainment. He would hurl himself towards the miscreant, skidding to a halt among flying gravel. He'd scream till his temple veins looked fit to pop. Then he'd turn away shaking his head incredulously. He was often like this, struggling to fight back rage. Equally, he was often struggling to fight back tears. The two states were virtually indistinguishable. What horrors had he experienced? The Second World War brain-injured two generations of adults who resolved that it was us who should pay for their lost years.

December 1955, the last week of school term: I awoke to the first snow of the winter. Outside my bedroom a fringe of icicles hung from the thatch. The road was a lesson in monochrome. There was untouched snow as white as whipped albumen. There was shiny metallic snow where traffic had compressed it. There was snow turned into tiny glacial boulders. There was a bank of snow in the gutter outside Mr and Mrs Coleman's where one or other of them had swept the pavement. I shivered as I dressed beside the immersion heater. It was deemed too cold to walk the mile to school. My father drove me in his new Morris Minor. The roads were neither salted nor sanded. Cars skidded on the impacted snow, they drifted gently into kerbs. The marginal slope up to Harnham Bridge became hazardous.

In classrooms we huddled round radiators.

In the blindingly white world outside, the 'lake' froze. It was actually an artificially widened stream. It would be crassly filled in the mid-1960s under the regime of the wretched Dean Haworth in order to provide yet more sports pitches. In the Fifties it remained a delightful vestige of picturesque landscaping and, in such weather as this, a de facto ice rink for those who dared. I never did. I didn't want to get cold or burnt: ice could, supposedly, burn. I didn't want to discover if that was true so I watched from the tribune of the grand Venetian-windowed room called Big School. In the foreground epic snowball battles were fought. White boughs were petrified lace against the cruelly blue sky. There was a ruff of crenellated wall in the distance. On ice scored like pork rind, boys were sliding and tumbling gauchely in dark blue macs that billowed and deflated. They wore unsuitable shoes and shorts that afforded little protection. It was all a fleeting dance made of Balla, Breughel and Start-rite – with English pastoral décor. In John

Constable's *Salisbury Cathedral from the Bishop's Ground* (1823) cows are drinking from the lake's western extremity. It was so cold that even the most hardy skaters gave it little more than ten minutes.

The sports pitches were under snow. There was no possibility of playing rugby. We anticipated an afternoon's free time.

Major Christian had other ideas. He announced that we were going to go on a run. Even to a group of eight-year-olds this seemed a surprising decision. But we unquestioningly obeyed his order to get changed. Of course we did. Fear overcame prudence. Cotton shorts, plimsolls, rugby shirts. I added an outsize cricket pullover, a hand-me-down from one of my mother's friends which I was to 'grow into'. And off we went, sheep in the wake of a short-fused goat.

Our destination was the Race Plain, three miles distant. The pavements were treacherous. The streets were deserted. The few cars had chained wheels which turned them into weapons of ancient warfare. One crept along St Nicholas Road making bone-grinding sounds. The meadows' frozen leets were dazzling. As we passed it I looked longingly at my parents' house, snug beneath its crystalline carapace. We ran up the hill past the lane leading to the wartime bunkers where stinking tramps lay in wait for children who dawdled. After Harnwood Road and the swollen Bayko-ish telephone building much of the way was along tracks across bleakest downland, along declivitous troughs whose high white walls were hedges in hiding, whose smothered ruts and ridges were booby traps. The route of the Old Shaftesbury Drove was not invariably obvious. Snow had drifted high along it. We ran as fast as we could to keep warm and to mollify Major Christian. But the weather was against us, the wind bit and whipped, it hurled stinging powder at our little blue legs. And Major Christian was implacable. He screamed exhortations. He drove us on across unseen ditches, buried banks and gleaming dunes which crumbled beneath us so that we fell on blackthorns and flints. We were failing him. He had suffered and so should we. We reached the Race Plain. The racecourse was signalled by its railings and its grandstand, barnacled with lean-tos with lean-tos of their own. There were intimations of dusk. Major Christian set us to exercising. 'Press, press . . . Fling!' Our frozen limbs were reluctant to respond. Our frozen limbs insulted him. He denounced them. Spiteful crows cackled at our discomfiture.

Whilst the red lamp at its summit shone, the rest of the distant spire began to disappear in the valley's crepuscular broth: the dog's a wolf, the wolf's a dog. It occurred to him as an apparent surprise, an afterthought, that he had to get us back to school. We retraced our tracks, approximately, for fresh snow was hurrying to beat us to them, to cover them for ever, to forge a blank labyrinth. This infinite eiderdown would consume us. The hour and the bladderish cloud combined belligerently. We could hardly move. Major Christian screamed. Mike Speak asked if he could share my pullover. It was so large it fitted us both. We turned into a freakshow specimen with two heads, two arms and four legs, we dragged and checked each other, and lurched all the way back. This was exciting. We were putting on a show. And we were snug, warm: at least, warmer.

The troop of frozen boys was widely witnessed. Mrs Dear, Mrs Sadd and her Bedlington, the Blakeleys and the Beatons, Sid the Butcher Who Missed Nothing, the Goddard twins – they all watched us pass by as though, in Mrs Sadd's and her Bedlington's words, 'The little mites were off to the salt mines'. Some parents complained that we had been subjected to a sort of torture. Not mine, who thought it was a hoot. They had heard about the shared pullover even before I was home from school: Mrs Dear had popped across the road from St Leonard's to tell them. They were indignant when Major Christian was dismissed at the end of that term.

He never found another kindred job which allowed him to give rein to his particular gifts. He worked as a jobbing gardener. I'd dutifully greet him but he failed to see me or didn't want to. Too preoccupied or too ashamed. His bicycle was now unbalanced by hoes, rakes, shears, trowels and a webbing kitbag, the tools of his enforced trade, which was a step down from teaching (perhaps not the word), which was itself a step down from soldiering.

Eight years after he was sacked my mother was bemused to receive a phone call from Mrs Christian inviting her to tea. Although they lived somewhere nearby, my parents knew them merely to say hullo to and never had any social contact. They would improbably have known each other's Christian names and, even had they, would certainly not have addressed each other by them. Tea had turned out to be Marmite sandwiches and stilted conversation. Just the two of them. Why my mother had been asked remained a mystery. She described the Christian home in some detail.

I was soon to see it for myself: a week later Mrs Christian issued another invitation. This time I was included. Neither of us wanted to go, but nonetheless on the appointed afternoon we walked along Harnham Road with the tennis courts' mesh and cries high above us up the sheer bank on the left. Past the boastful, florid, tile-hung late Victorian houses with their curling drives, wellingtonias and cedars. Past 'The Crematorium', the flat-roofed pale-brick double-cube Dr Duff had recently built in the grounds of one of them, Harnham Croft, a nursing home whose acrylic rooms I never dreamed I would one day be obliged to visit. We turned up the slope of Folkestone Road whose gravel aggregate showed through the worn metalled surface. More late Victorian and Edwardian houses, most of them semi-detached. No drives or specimen trees here, merely skewed wooden garages, alopeciac hedges failing to mask front windows, doorsteps harlequined in artificial stone, salt-glazed flowerbed edgers moulded to imitate tarred rope.

I looked up at the attic room where Ham's father had unsuccessfully hidden his copious library of *Solo, Health and Efficiency, QT, Spick, Span, Kamera, Avec Plaisir, Ici Paris* etc. At the age of sixteen I was already nostalgic for my childhood self, for the summers when I had been ten and eleven, knowing they wouldn't come my way again: those days of sunbeams, of Swinging Shepherd Blues, The Mudlarks singing 'Lollipop', of two boys poring over monochrome models whose heavy nipples, the most tempting fruit on earth, promised so much more than kisses sweeter than an apple pie.

Major Christian opened the door of his bungalow.

He staged a well-rehearsed festival of dental caries for my mother. Then he addressed me, surprised me:

'Dick Christian!' He stuck out a hand which I somnambulistically shook. It was as though he had never previously encountered me; if it is accepted that a sixteen-year-old adolescent is merely the same human rather than the same self as an eight-year-old boy, then he hadn't. After brief consideration, he pretended to punch my shoulder, clumsily, playfully, man to man, bonding. This was astonishing, but not so astonishing as his attire.

He wore what was clearly his best – a waisted jacket, just discernible as a sometime item of dress uniform which would have had a Sam Browne strapped across it. It had been subjected to a lavish range of alterations, dressmaker's bricolage, in an attempt to render it apt for Civvy Street and operetta. It had also been dyed. The aim, no doubt, had been to turn garrison khaki into mahogany. The result was a garment which might have been rescued from a fire, scorched but intact. Or it might have been bodged from rare camouflage, adaptively coloured for the darkest forests, a map of blacks, browns, swarfs and charcoals that represented the thing's folds when in the dye tub. The nap was greasily iridescent. His merely faded cycling beret was nowhere to be seen.

Their home was a long, narrow, oxblood brick bungalow with a wooden verandah that would have been confidently labelled 'artistic' when it was new, circa 1905. Now it was rotting. It was the last building in the road, a cul-de-sac which culminated in a high hedge with a wood-framed, lintelled aperture in it. Beyond this aperture, which had worried me as a child because it was so obviously missing a door or gate, was the cinder footpath that ran along the bottom of Harnham Hill. I realised that I knew my hosts' garden. I had often peered from the path through the ragged hedge at the chaos of jerry cans, compost piles, lawnmower blades, wire bales, dog rose, water butts, wringers, hairy twine, formerly galvanised bits, charred planks, burlap-lagged pipes, oxidised buckets, damp sacks, collapsed cloches, troughs, sheaves of cracked panes, enamel stained with dried algae, crippled chairs, glass canines grinning from crumbly putty in window frames.

The interior of the bungalow was also brown. It was the work of the same hand in different materials. Browning newspapers, dun cushions, skeins of shiver-making oatmeal wool tight as a spinster's bun, wicker knitting baskets armed with protruding needles, dark wood tables clambering over crazed leather armchairs, corrugated sisal matting, silt-coloured lino, shelves spilling foxed books and spineless books, earthenware porrons and meerschaum pipes, family and regimental photos in varnished frames, ragged Medici Society prints of plough horses, chipped Staffordshire dogs, teetering shoe boxes on a paraffin heater. A greedy monochromatic obsession was being sated at jumble sales, bring-and-buy sales, in junk shops, in Biggins's father's junk hangar. What wasn't already brown was getting brown – the colour of oldness, fatigue, shit and middens, rot, rust and enervation: adults were forever complaining that they were browned off.

But not Major Christian, not today. Nor Mrs Christian. He was gruffly matey. She was cosy and dumpy with a plump fringe to match and a cough-linctus-colour dress. He asked me how my swimming was going. Training was tiresome. I had perpetual, stinging pink eye. I had just suffered a humiliating defeat by a man mountain barely a year my senior. I mutely resented that, at the age of sixteen, I was still defined by what had been my sole prowess long ago, in childhood. I told him it was going well. I had to hang on to something.

As we walked home after an hour and a half of conversational cul-de-sacs, well-meant smiles, forced chuckles and desperate cakes, my mother wondered out loud why these probably harmless oddballs should suddenly have decided that we should be their friends. What were they up to?

She received the answer within a few days. This time in the post rather by telephone. White card, copperplate print. *Major and Mrs Richard Christian request the pleasure . . . the wedding of their daughter Alexandra . . . to . . . April . . . at Salisbury Cathedral.*

Salisbury Cathedral! Salisbury Cathedral. The cynosure of a bride (or groom's) socially ambitious parents. (Socially ambitious in south Wiltshire.) This was a prize craved by many, granted only to a privileged few. Because he had 'taught' so long at the Cathedral School Major Christian could not be denied it. The invitation was for my parents and me. Again my mother wondered why. She discovered the answer when on a blustery Wednesday afternoon she went alone to the service (my father and I having invented pressing appointments which precluded our attendance). The fifteen or so guests on the bride's 'side' (of the nave) were outnumbered by the clergy and vicars choral. With a handful of exceptions they were of the bride's age. Among that handful were some acquaintances of my mother. They too had been courted with cake and sandwiches by the Christians who, having no friends to invite to their girl's great day, had had to muster some. It was apparently a joyful, untroubled occasion which my mother relished for its felicitous oddness. Major Christian was the very picture of paternal pride, beaming madly. I regretted not having been there.

MAJOR FERGUSON AND MAJOR VEALE

Christine, known when she had successors as 'The First German Girl', woke me, helped me to dress quickly, led me down the wide staircase and out of the barrack-like hotel's front door. I was too bleary to ask what was happening. I never asked what was happening. At the age of three and a half I simply accepted. We crossed the dark yard to a cowshed which smelled of milk, hay, dung, paraffin. A group of adults, my parents among them, were half-illumined by naked bulbs and flickering lanterns. My father and Major Ferguson grasped whisky glasses. My mother took me by the hand and squatted beside me. She told me that a calf was on the very point of being born and that Major Ferguson thought I'd like to see it. Major Ferguson ruffled my hair.

Another novelty! How I adored Eggesford.

My friend the cowman had a ruddy grin for me.

The brown and white cow lay on straw in a wooden pen. She was on her side with her head raised helplessly trying to make out from the corner of an alarmed eye what was happening behind her. Her mouth was open, her tongue flapped, her moos were moos of pain. She heaved and quivered and spasmed and twitched as though she were a great beached fish.

From an aperture below her restless tail poked a head smaller than hers, gift-wrapped in a sort of stretchy transparent rubber. Its little face was puppyishly eager for adventure. The aperture's circumference contracted and expanded like bellows. The wet nose ruptured the rubber. The cowman held out his hand which was duly licked by the calf's tongue. He felt around beneath its breast and smiled triumphantly. The cow responded with an attempted whinny. The calf struggled to escape, its mother pushed with waves of force.

I wondered if my mother had done the same. I hugged her in my excitement at this spectacle which blended zoo, magic, surgery and – thinking ahead – the butcher's. With the cowman's gentle manipulation the calf was prised from its squelchy cave. Its first performance was a slapstick turn: the stage drunk whose legs give way. It was delighted with itself, delighted too to be on the lam and in the light, blinking, guzzling new sensations. Now it revelled in being licked by its mother who treated herself to the transparent rubber as a reward for her ordeal, munching and slurping till it had disappeared.

Do I owe my lack of squeamishness to this exposure? Probably not.[13]

Major Ferguson was inescapable at the Fox and Hounds. Here he is, up to his waist in the Taw's waters casting a fly. Here, still in his waders, he's trudging back from his beat through 'red' mud, fishless but cheerful as ever. Now he's at his table in the dining room with his bottle of hock, beaming. When, timidly, I put my head round the door of the fuggy bar his big bottom is seeping over his stool, his tankard lifted like a trophy before him. He's laughing a throaty man-laugh, smoking a cigarette. I was suspicious of majors who didn't smoke a pipe.

Did he live at the Fox and Hounds? People, especially bachelor majors, lived in hotels in those years. Or did he own it? His manner was proprietorial. Every year we went to Eggesford he was there. The elderly genial dome-headed Major Veale was frequently there too. But he lacked Major Ferguson's magical omnipresence. Even when Major Ferguson was not in sight the tractor would be. The cowman (an agricultural labourer, thus nameless) rode it like an adult on a child's bicycle. It was of course a Ferguson, in that marque's invariable pale grey.

---

13 A few years later, cycling along a chalk path between blackthorns at Paul's Dene on the northern edge of Salisbury, I witnessed a calf trying and failing to make its escape from its apparently unconcerned mother's vagina. I wondered momentarily if I should make my debut as a midwife but really didn't want to get blood on my apple-green jeans (orange stitching) so let nature take its course.

Eventually I would have a plastic model of one, unhappily of a larger scale than the Dinky lorry that my mother bought me in the general stores at Chulmleigh – a grinning S-type Bedford, tan and French navy. The latter colour prompts my brain to vault over the accretions of the decades. It is one of several colours of the Fifties that are sure mnemonic triggers. (There was a water butt in Bohemia, North Yorkshire, in 1991.)

The Exeter–Barnstaple railway, today named the Tarka Line after the celebrity otter, follows the route of the Taw, now on this side, now on the west. Beside Eggesford station, a couple of hundred yards from the hotel, was a level crossing whose mechanisms and polished rails flush to the road tarmac were fascinating even though they were not novel to me.

The rail maintenance gangers' handcar (a hydraulic pump trolley) was, however, unlike anything I had ever seen. I had yet to witness silent cinema where these vehicles were a staple. It was an apparatus to marvel at. And it was of course Major Ferguson who pulled rank with the linesmen, cajoling them to show me how to operate it, pushing the handle up and down to propel it, pushing so that on its return it lifted my feet off its dark base fashioned from sleepers. Whilst the gang ate lunch (sandwiches from tiffin boxes) I rode it back and forth on jolting metal wheels along a stretch of line on top of an embankment. This became daily routine. Christine would accompany me from the hotel to the railway line. We passed big-tongued, fly-eyed cows and their calves. The 'red' earth didn't absorb the surface water. Our path was a series of retreats across tufted islets. But where the path passed beneath the embankment there was no avoiding the deep mud. As I played on the track Christine would attempt to sweet-talk the reticent linesman while ostentatiously scraping mud from her legs. They had no time for Germans or flirts.

It was worth the long walk up the dark sunken lane under a cat's cradle of coppiced boughs. We emerged into sun beside the shining ruins of the Earl of Portsmouth's Eggesford House

– multi-chimneyed, multi-crenellated, fractured, haphazard, jagged, melancholy, exhilarating. An intact neo-Tudor mansion would not have been remotely so affecting. The abundant rabbits had crewcut the grass so it was as springy as Dunlopillo. I rolled blissfully on it as I did on Major Veale's velvet lawn when we visited him at Romsey.

What my parents called 'the lawn' at home was a pat of mud with grass seeds forlornly scattered about it. It wasn't a lawn but a grown-up's lie, just like 'red' earth.

MAJOR HOWELLS

Bachelor history *master* – apter than *teacher*, which would be an exaggeration of his pedagogic capacity. Cathedral chorister, baritone. Brown Bedford-cord jacket, regimental tie. Black hair and moustache, pale skin – a combination which I learnt to identify as Welsh. Slight limp due to an injury he had sustained during the war. He had, presumably unintentionally, discharged a revolver into his right foot. He would sit beside the school swimming pool in a pair of blue woollen trunks and invite us to inspect the site of the lost toe. This seemed normal behaviour. So we scrutinised a stub which, because it lacked a nail, appeared blind and aggressive, a Beardsley foetus. Until 1959 he was accepted as the school's de facto deputy head, a position which he had assumed for himself. But late in the summer term of that year Barry Still was, to general surprise, appointed to that previously non-existent post. Why was Major Howells passed over? Had Still's elevation merely been the means devised by the newly arrived and already intriguing Dean Haworth to ensure that Howells would leave? If so, it misfired. Howells did indeed leave, in a bate, to sulk in St David's for evermore. However, a few weeks later Mr Griffiths died and Still, *faute de mieux*, was hurriedly appointed headmaster. It took the meddling shit Haworth two years to find a reason to dismiss *him*.

MAJOR JOHNSTONE AND MAJOR CORLETT

In 1936 Ted and Dorothea (Dot, Dotty) Craven paid £45 for a ruinous bothy at Seathwaite in the high Duddon valley in Furness. Over the next few years they rebuilt it themselves during their long holidays – he was head of classics at Westminster, she taught at a nearby primary school. At the outbreak of war Westminster was evacuated to three sites in and around Bromyard. Ted joined the Royal Navy and became a submariner. Dorothea took up a post in Salisbury at Highbury Avenue School, an industrial-modern building which looked across the Avon valley to Old Sarum and whose neighbour, Nestlé's factory (pron. *Nessels*), was known, to my father at least, as The Mosque due to its minaret-like chimney. Among her fellow teachers were Nancy Short and my mother, with whom she formed a friendship and soon went to lodge. They would cycle to the school along the Town Path, the causeway across the water meadows where the morning mists are white wigwams. In the Easter holidays of 1942 they made the first of half a dozen trips together to Furness, some 300 miles north. Travel by train was restricted, slow, uncomfortable, unreliable. It involved numerous changes and protracted waits. After they arrived at Foxfield station beside Duddon Sands they had to walk ten miles to Seathwaite unless they could hitch a lift – which was unlikely, for the very absence of vehicles was what made the Duddon valley so plentiful and so attractive in those years of stringent rations. The gradients of the roads at either end of the valley were such that lorries could not enter it to collect the abundance produced there. The people of the valley lived off the fat of the land: partridge, pigeon, pheasant, deer, duck, chicken, egg, lamb, beef, pork, milk, butter, buttermilk, cheese, mushrooms, honey, fruit, vegetables, even flowers. There were brown trout and sea trout in the Duddon and in Tarn Beck, where a rudimentary (and illegal) fish trap had been constructed among whitewater rocks. My mother, Dorothea, Mary Sutcliffe (also a lodger) and a mutating band of other young women ate as much as they could. They camped in Dorothea's still primitive bothy and its garden.

The last time my daughters saw their grandmother they presented her with a photograph I had taken of them beside the deep, green, strangely still pool immediately downstream of Birks Bridge. In her terminal dementia the name wouldn't come, her

face contorted in agonised frustration although she could recognise the place. 'Birks Bridge, Grandma.' It was here that she had been photographed bathing with Dorothea and Mary many summers ago: they looked healthy, glowing, athletic, like companionable Land Girls.

Tarn Beck generated the electricity which lit the Newfield Inn: pub, hotel, restaurant, post office, village shop, farm. Jack and Mary Longmire who owned it brewed beer which they flavoured with damsons. My mother called it 'a piece of heaven in a time of hell'. Seathwaite, Birks Bridge, Harter Fell, Birker Fell, Cockley Beck, Troutal, Wallowbarrow, Walna Scar, Under Crag, Long House Gill: when I was tiny she would recite to me the names of these places she loved, places I had been to but had yet to see. When my father returned from Iraq in the spring of 1946 Ted and Dorothea lent my parents the bothy. That was where I was conceived. The 0.2 mm intra-uterine version of me saw nothing, heard nothing, felt nothing. It did not even yet own an amniotic sac. By the time my parents-in-waiting attended the City of Salisbury's Welcome Home to Members of the Forces and the Merchant Navy at the Guildhall on Monday 13 May 1946 it was almost a centimetre long. It shared my mother's soup, roast turkey, stuffing, sausage, baked and boiled potatoes, green peas, Christmas pudding, crème (*sic*), trifle, ices, rolls. Not yet able to hear, it missed The Spotlights, produced and compèred by Dick Clark: 'A Show Built for the Forces by arrangement with the War Office Central Pool of Artists and Major Harwood of Southern Command'.

It was not till 1954 that I saw the place where my pre-life had begun, where the prospective creature of wartime's epistolatory longing called Jonathan had at last been fertilised. We drove through the night following a route that Norman Short, a member, had ordered bespoke from the AA (Automobile Association). The railway viaduct across the Severn at Worcester; Kidderminster, where Peter Collins's father's garage was – the promised visit would never occur; Bridgnorth's sleeping low town and the silhouette of its high town which one day I'd reach by funicular – I still haven't; Tarporley; doucely half-timbered Wigan; Chorley; treeless streets of back-to-backs in Preston's first light; red-brick encrusted with black smuts; millscapes, chimneys stretching to the sky; Garstang; Carnforth, yet to be globally celebrated as the birthplace of Cecil Parkinson; Newby Bridge, the signpost to Grange-over-Sands.

The Morris Eight grumbled up the hills after Broughton, spluttering and wheezing. And, then, there, spread before us was my mother's heaven which was my heaven too. I had never seen a landscape of such grandeur, such drama. There were haphazard boulders in boggy fields, tufts of tussock grass, drystone walls, layered slate walls, dazzlingly green fields, packhorse bridges, spring upon spring, sheep, whitewashed houses, white water leaping down mountainsides, bright lichens, rushing rivers. Matching places to the names I had learnt from my mother was sheerly joyful. She pointed them out with girlish delight, with a relief at finding it all as it had been before the presage of parenthood, still the land of plenty. (Although fifteen years of food rationing had officially ended two weeks previously the actuality in Salisbury, as in most other places, would not change for a couple of years.) At Seathwaite the end of rationing was an irrelevance.

The childless Longmires doted on me. I rode in Jack's tractor's trailer, tried eagerly to help with harvests, gaped in awe at his huge hands which were leather tools. Mary was happy to have me skiv for her in the Newfield Inn's wonderfully scented kitchen. She cured green bacon; in its fat she fried eggs, kidneys, pluck, brown trout till the skin was crisp. She boiled (i.e. simmered) beef, carrots, potatoes, soups. She steamed dumplings and rich steak and kidney puddings. She baked bread, chicken pies and batter puddings (this was proudly Lancastrian Furness). She moulded great forms of tart white Lancashire cheese and rounds of yellow butter. There were crocks of cream for trifles, fools, fruit tarts, treacle tarts. The wood-fuelled Aga she worked at was an immense vessel. She swallowed draughts of strong tea, smoked an occasional Park Drive and tutted over the *News of the World*'s stories of sexual intercourse and molestation. Now and then she hugged me. The best food I'd tasted away from home was served in a charming corrugated-iron dining room, a prefabricated structure presumably intended as a colonial mission hall. As a special treat I was allowed to wait on certain indulgent tables, but not that of Sir Ian ———, a grocer-striped Latin-reading Whitehall mandarin who seldom condescended to speak to fellow guests and was thus known as Silent Knight.

Late one lowering afternoon whilst my father set off to fish, my mother and I went for tea at Dorothea and Ted's bothy (no longer really a bothy but a snug cottage). After cake, Ted clapped his hands and suggested that I be shown the tarn. Tarn was an unfamiliar word, not part of my mother's Duddon litany. Maybe it was an abandoned chapel. Or a charcoal burner's oven. A shepherd's shelter? It was perhaps the proper name of a distinctive rock, something along those lines. It was a fair climb from the former bothy. Pewter skies above white houses. Velvet green turf. Stern grey karst. The higher we walked the darker and more thrilling grew the lumbering clouds. They obstructed the sun's shafts, they became indistinguishable from the peaks ahead. The stony path was rough, bumpy, steep, blistering.

Then at last there was relief from the hard going. The incline decreased. But, in front of me, at eye level, was an immense lake of the utmost blackness, polished as jet. I was shocked, scared. To have walked uphill for a mile and a half, then to come upon an expanse of water that defied gravity . . .

Expanses of water are meant to be in valleys, not high above us in the fells, which were also black but matt, unreflective. This was a site of unmitigated horror. The water might burst through the old dam at any moment. My mother and the Cravens sat down to contemplate it. I turned away, looked back to safety, to distant wooded crags where there were still bolts of sun, of hope. But this terrible place had done its work, it had glued itself to my retina. It was inerasable and would indeed contaminate my dreams for years to come. This was the first occasion when, due to the weight of water above me, I suffered a sensation akin to vertigo. It was only in sunshine and in the care of a level-headed daughter that I dared return to it forty years later.

A further vertiginous alarm would shortly occur. A big day out was in store, a treat, a trip to Eskdale where we would ride on the narrow-gauge railway to Ravenglass. My father drove upstream beside Tarn Beck and the Duddon to Cockley Beck where he took the turning to Hardknott Pass, mighty Hardknott, the steepest road in Britain, he informed us. My mother had mentioned this a few minutes previously. As though in confirmation the Morris Eight shrieked its mechanical distress. As it crept forward it was overtaken by walkers and scraggy ewes. I assumed that in a battle between machine and nature, machine would win. I was mistaken. Alarmingly, the car began to roll backwards down the snaking road, to roll backwards increasingly quickly. The crest that filled the windscreen receded, the brackened fells moved the wrong way, roadside rocks hurtled slowly upwards. Even more alarmingly my father struggled to prevent the free-falling vehicle leaving the metalled surface. Twisting to gape through the tiny back window he succeeded in keeping it on the road, just. But at some cost to his amour propre. His embarrassment seemed, absurdly, to verge on shame. A cheerfully sympathetic family trudging up the slope offered well-meant Lancastrian-accented commiserations. He looked at them as though they had mocked him: he failed to take into account that north of the irony curtain 'hard luck mate' is liable to mean just that. He was silent as we headed back.

Dimp was packaged in a shallow cylindrical tin of the 1930s – eau de nil, vertically emphatic sans serif off-white letters. It took its name from dimethyl phthalate. It repelled head lice, pubic lice, ticks, chiggers and midges. My father daubed his forehead and face with it before he fished at night, every night. The Duddon midges knew their way into the apiarist's jungly net helmet he wore. This device was a construction of non-porous manmade fibres, a head sauna which caused the smeared Dimp to melt and trickle into his eyes which itched then stung then burnt then closed. Abandoning his rod and kit he staggered across hardly familiar fields, tripping and stumbling till he reached the deserted valley road and grasping the wall that ran beside it directed himself to the hotel.

He believed he was going blind.

A Broughton-in-Furness GP resented having been called out, offered little cheer, told him that he had brought it upon himself, suggested he should hold his eyes under water for as long as possible and said it was just a question of wait and see. My father clung to this inappropriate expression and would cite it as symptomatic of medical ignorance and tactlessness. He lay in the darkness of his hotel bedroom with a wet towel over his eyes. Periodically my mother would guide his face into a stoneware basin. Unable to read, he listened to the idiot relation, a wizened valve-radio tuned, mostly, approximately, to the Home Service and, when my mother remembered, to the Light Programme for the delightful Al Read, admired even though he was northern (catchphrase: 'Right Monkey') and Ted Ray's *Ray's A Laugh* (as direly unfunny as the title – he too had a catchphrase: I have forgotten it).

When, after a couple of days there was no improvement, Jack Longmire drove him to the hospital in Ulverston. He returned with his eyes heavily bandaged. It wasn't like blind man's buff: in a book at home was a reproduction of Sargent's great First World War tableau *Gassed*. A single file of soldiers moves its way forward between trenches and the bodies of those even less fortunate than they are. They hold the shoulder of the comrade in front of them to guide them. Many were dressed in the very bandages my father now wore. They would never see again. Would he? I didn't like to ask. The possibility must have occurred to him, for he was unusually silent. This was an injury which, atypically, he didn't laugh off. The prospect loomed of a noble childhood as a human guide dog of exceptional loyalty and selflessness: I would sacrifice my life to lead him wheresoever he wished to wander, to the riverbank, to the pub. But, before such piety could be observed, we had to get him back to Salisbury. He evidently could not drive in such a state. My mother, no matter what state she was in, could hardly drive. She held a licence from before the inauguration of the compulsory driving test in 1935. Had a licence been conditional on passing a test she would not have had one. When I was three, seatbelts did not exist. Had they existed I would not have been propelled into the dashboard by my mother braking hard for no reason, I would not have had the opportunity to discover the balmy solace of cool moss picked from the Forest roadside and applied to a forehead's bulging shiner.

There was no option. Humiliatingly, my father had to obtain permission for her to drive his company car. A telegram was despatched to Chas Perry, the chirpy Southampton supremacist and saloon bar chortler who oversaw Crawford's reps south of the Thames. Like much of that city's populace (Aunt Doll, Uncle Eric, Benny Hill, Ken Russell) he was a creation of Donald McGill. He doubtless replied: 'Permission is granted to the Major's good lady.' I can hear him saying it. He spoke in an all but vanished So'ton accent, a pile-up of Cockney cackle and Hampshire farmyard which declined to elide; successive words seemed not to have been introduced to each other. It was like listening to an amnesiac mimic.

So she drove. I sat beside her, my sight had not yet begun to fail. Mine was a pair of eyes to lend to hers. She fought the car, foresaw death in every charging lorry, swerved lavishly, cursed the rain. There was no question of visiting Peter Collins's father's garage. The journey was gruelling, long, ill-tempered. She indignantly rued the presence of other vehicles on the road, railed at stupid old fools and young louts. She got us there in the end.

John Ogg sorted out my father's eyes. And four years later I got to ride from Eskdale to Ravenglass.

Four years too late. At the age of eleven I considered myself too mature for miniature railways, model villages and so on. I defined myself as something other than a child preoccupied by cut-down-to-size representations for the little ones. I resented the indignity of still having to wear shorts to school. My favourite book was no longer John Maurice's *The Iconium Mystery*. I was through with Enid Blyton. I still read the *Eagle* and *Tiger*, and the monthly 64-page adventures of Buck Jones and Kit Carson. But soon the only comic strips I read were Super Detective Library: Buck Ryan and Roderic Graeme's Blackshirt. Nothing, though, remotely matched Alex Raymond's exquisitely drawn Rip Kirby, whose adventures, transposed to England, often involved stern beauties dressed in what I did not realise was bondage kit. They were as beguiling as the pipe-smoking, houseboat-dwelling crone Mrs Malarkey was frightening. I devoured green Penguins. The writers I read were, supposedly, not children's writers: Edgar Wallace, John Creasey (sometimes 'writing as J. J. Marric'), Margery Allingham, Nicholas Blake (C. Day-Lewis), E. C. Bentley, Josephine Tey, Victor Canning, Mickey Spillane, Ian Fleming, John Dickson Carr, A. E. W. Mason, Seldon Truss, Geoffrey Household (whom I have never lost the habit of rereading).

Nonetheless, on the afternoon of Sunday 3 August 1958, I was, despite myself, excited by the cute railway's reek of oil and anthracite, by sudden bursts of steam, by the crisp unsummery wind, by the scarf of smoke that now and again enveloped us. Besides, our fellow passengers were not all children or the parents of children. They also included snugly wrapped fully mature males, smiling never-met-the-right-girl smiles, validating the line's appeal to adults. Having earlier taken the road to Eskdale through Ulpha and across Birker Fell we returned over Hardknott. This time there was no struggle, so no shame: indeed, my father was hummingly smug. The slopes had been within the Morris Minor Traveller's capability, though perhaps not by so generous a margin as he wished to believe.

We got back to Newfield in the late afternoon. Tony Duckworth, an amiable cricketer five years my senior from Lytham St Anne's, was skimming a newspaper in the lugubrious brown lounge. He nodded a greeting.

I settled down with the engrossing *Mystery Mile*. I had been reading for about five minutes when Tony asked: 'Oh, did you hear?'

'What?'

'On the news just now.'

'No.'

'That racing driver, the one you were talking about . . . oh, what's his name – he was killed this afternoon.'

Something electric raced up my spine.

'Who?' But I didn't need to ask. I knew. I spoke his name with dread. 'Peter Collins – do you mean?'

'That's the chap, in uh . . . the—' replied Tony.

'German Grand Prix.'

My body felt unprecedentedly cold, pierced by iced needles. I was a helpless child. I ran upstairs to my bedroom to hide my tears. Peter Collins was my idol. I guess I had a mildly homoerotic crush on him. Dashing blond hell-raiser; glamorous American wife; yacht in Monte Carlo; he lived fast, died like a fated fighter pilot. The death toll among racing drivers of that era was high: Luigi Musso had died four weeks previously at Reims; Mike Hawthorn would die, dicing with Rob Walker on the A3 at Guildford, five months later. Collins died at the Nurburgring in the Eifel Mountains, at a corner called Pflanzgarten. That was the first German word I ever knew: the garden of plants. There'd be no going to his father's garage at Kidderminster now.

That night I dreamed that Winston Churchill had died. Inconsolable, I woke my parents and sobbed, a child in my mother's arms.

The next week I pondered the loss of someone I knew only from magazines, photographs and newsreels: someone, then, whom I didn't know. I hadn't reacted this way when Grandma died the previous summer: indeed, my indifference had caused me to feel guilty. I walked the fells, scrambled up the courses of rushing gills, negotiated the rubble rocks, climbed Wallowbarrow Crag, crossed and recrossed the Duddon by stepping stones and a bridge suspended by ropes. Flat-hatted Harry Braithwaite, the Longmires' single employee, had heard of my chagrin. He clouted me manfully on the back.

The next time we went to Seathwaite, in 1961, the Edinburgh University veterinary student Richard Waters told me that Harry slept with his flat-hat on: he had once been obliged to share Harry's rudely scented single-storey quarters next to the cowshed. His mother, wife of a Middlesbrough GP, proudly confided to me that the pretty girl whose photograph was sellotaped to the dashboard of Richard's Standard 8 was likely to be 'the next Mrs Waters'. I never found out. My father feigned jocular concern about the effect of repeated exposure to hexachlorophene soap on Richard's chapped hands and forearms.

I was fourteen: my voice had broken through the late summer and autumn of the year before. Mary Longmire had heard a rumour that Tony Duckworth had joined the police; now, that was a good career. It wouldn't be long before I left school: what was I going to do? Anything but join the police. Her cooking seemed even better than before – the bacon, the eggs, the kidneys roasted in their suet, the fat chops. I ate voraciously, I was growing at an alarming rate. My trousers didn't reach my ankles, my cuffs stopped short of my wrists, my windcheater rode around my ribs. My sartorial sensibility was offended. My parents argued that I'd outgrow new clothes so refused to buy any till my current ones no longer fitted: it was they who decided on what fitted. This was to be my penultimate holiday with them. I wanted to be with 'young people', especially girls. But my self-consciousness, caused by my freckles (and, I guess, by my very existence), was exacerbated by embarrassment at the joke clothes I was obliged to wear, as though I was still a child.

Mrs Handley (née Marjorie Fox) had married in the tiny church at Seathwaite in 1937. After the war she and her husband

Alec went to Tristan da Cunha as missionaries. She a teacher, he the island's chaplain. One of his predecessors had been Lewis Carroll's brother. Alec Handley was also an amateur vet and, alarmingly, an amateur dentist. He died in 1948. Four years later Mrs Handley returned to England, to outermost north London. In her charge was a girl called Valerie whose island parents wanted her to receive an English education. I had never previously heard of Tristan da Cunha. Soon it became impossible not to have heard of it, for the minor seismic activity (earth tremors, rock falls) the island had suffered was reported in English newspapers. This summer was the first time that Mrs Handley had brought Valerie to the site of her wedding. Valerie's surname was Glass, one of seven the 300 islanders of Tristan da Cunha bear. Richard Waters enthusiastically explained to me the effects of inbreeding. I covertly scrutinised Valerie for telltale signs but found none; not covertly enough – Mrs Handley was rightly suspicious of me. But my sac of testosterone was directed at Francine, Valerie's bored, tanned, short-fringed scholastic exchange from Moulins whom I set out to impress by speaking French. She scoffed and repeatedly corrected me: I, of course, did not dare criticise her impoverished English. I offered her my hand to help her across the beck that tumbled down the hill from White Pike. She refused it. I told myself that this was due to Mrs Handley being present, *tried* to tell myself – I wasn't even capable of convincing self-delusion. When I led them through the woods to the suspension bridge across the Duddon Francine complained petulantly about the metre-tall anthills beside the path. They seethed with stinging 'red' ants, actually the colour of barley sugar. She accused me of subjecting her to potential danger. It was as though it was my fault that they were there. Could we not have taken a different route? I retrieved some pride from her fulminations being cast in French. It was an acknowledgment of our common language, an admission that she could not have begun to express her chastisements in English. My humiliation was mitigated, a bit, maybe.

Early in the morning the day they were to return south, Francine came and sat, less than a foot from me, on a bench outside Mary Longmire's kitchen.

Had we time for another walk in the woods? I foresaw kisses of the utmost tenderness. I longed for the scramble to undress each other – which I *knew* happened offscreen in *Beat Girl* and Troy Donahue's movies. I would gallantly protect her from acidic ferns and those ants whilst making her feel like she had never felt before.

From her purse she produced a photobooth photograph of a wall-eyed youth with quiffed hair and a negligent attitude to skincare attempting to sneer like Eddy Mitchell, himself a laughably failed Elvis. This was Yves. To whom she was committed. Isn't he handsome? I replied maybe, yes, perhaps, to certain girls, possibly. Francine evidently reckoned me insufficiently appreciative of her smalltown *tombeur*. Did I know how old he is? He is seventeen. Seventeen. Almost a man. Not a fourteen-year-old. He smokes American cigarettes: Kent, Philip Morris. He is in the *lycée technologique*. He dances the Twist. He dances the Madison. He owns a Solex. He drinks beer – *from the bottle*.

I tied a knot in the corner of my brain to remind me not to emulate Yves's properties and never to look like the berk, who was presumably training to be a garage mechanic.

After breakfast I waved them goodbye as they set off for Mrs Handley's house between the exotic poles of Friern Barnet and Cockfosters (which my father pronounced Co'Fosters). Valerie returned my wave. Francine didn't. I wished her ill.

My malevolence was misaimed. My hate-rays must have struck Valerie, for less than two months later, after further intermittent tremors, a volcano erupted on Tristan da Cunha for the first time in three centuries and the entire population was evacuated to a former RAF base at Calshot on Southampton Water where a number died from diseases to which, in Atlantic fastness, they had developed no immunity.

Seathwaite in Dunnerdale (i.e. Duddon dale) is not quite as

wet as Seathwaite in Borrowdale, a dozen miles due north, which was said to suffer the highest annual rainfall of anywhere in England. But that August it poured down. For several days I did little but play canasta with three spinsters, the Misses King (sisters) and their friend Miss Hopper – I feared ending up like them. When Ted and Dorothea called to collect my mother to take her to the bothy for the afternoon I looked out of the lounge window. A forlorn girl was sitting in the back of their car. My mother put her head round the door to ask whether I was coming. I was about to say yes when the spinsters replied decisively for me: I was going nowhere when there was canasta to be played. My mother shrugged at my inability to extricate myself.

That evening she told me that Ted and Dorothea would like to see me: their niece too could do with the company of someone of her own age. She was being harassed by Ted because of her northern accent, the accent he himself had sloughed en route from Yorkshire to Oxford at the age of eighteen. The next morning I crept out of the hotel before the spinsters could find me and stumbled through the fat rain's grapeshot to the bothy. Its white-ness was inviting as I squelched towards it. But, on a day that was all dusk, there were no lights on. It was deserted. I walked round to the back door. It was locked. Cursing and resigned I set off back to the hotel. A drenched dog-walking neighbour told me that I had missed them by five minutes. They had just left to take young Susan back to Ripon. Apparently she was 'homesick'.

I slunk back to the hotel. The spinsters pounced.

My father boomed: 'He's coming to Berthe's.'

He directed me to the car. My mother joined us. She told me that I was not to submit to bullying by the *old trouts*.

Major Johnstone and his German wife Berthe lived in a large austere late Georgian house some miles downstream from Seathwaite. They owned a pack of savage Alsatians. Canasta with lifelong virgins seemed a better option than being subject to their attention. I refused to leave the car till they were locked up. Berthe introduced me to the delusional defence that dog-people invariably make of their quadripedal weapons: 'Prince/Rover/Mervyn wouldn't hurt a fly.'

But he might bite *me*, sever an artery, detach a limb, scar my face.

They inhabited a reeking slum. The stench of dog was pervasive: dog pee, dog hair, dog food. The Johnstones were inured to it or didn't notice it. They were perpetually drunk. Their stretch of river was supposedly more abundant in sea trout and brown trout than the Newfield's where, despite the rain, the water was frustratingly low. I suspect that my father had simply turned up at the house and asked if he could fish it. They had welcomed him as someone whom they could ply, competitively, with gin (him) and port (her) whilst they screamed, shrieked, swore, tried to throw things and passed out in their sullied playpen. And if he would insist on fishing then my mother and I could provide the audience their exhibitionist intimacy demanded. The house was wilfully gloomy. There were curtains so old, so weighted with dust that their rods were partially detached from the walls: drifts of plaster bordered the wainscot. Warped shutters didn't shut. Stapled drapes made do. Blinds were skewed. Screens propped each other up parlously. Light beams invaded through cracks. The Johnstones were too lazy, too chaotic to be vampires: it's a calling that demands application. Their marriage was all inchoate bickering and nagging resentment, not hatred, not loathing, yet. On a dusty console table there were framed photos of a handsome young officer and a pretty blonde woman. They were unrecognisable as the couple who now swayed grievously beside that table. Yet even the oldest photos had been taken only a decade or so previously. There were some that were evidently more recent. He in mufti, she with her features still uncoarsened. Their decline had been precipitous. He was now pallid and prematurely white-haired (a sign of charlatanry, according to Max Beerbohm). She was bloated, going on blonde. Her teeth might have been smeared with bitter aloes, they had not recovered from a neglect which had perhaps begun during the war: in its death throes the Third Reich was short of dentists, which caused its cities to stink of mass halitosis.

He had resigned his commission upon inheriting the house, its farms, its river. She taunted him: beside the grand Pomeranian estate her family had fled when the Soviet army invaded, this Dunnerdale estate was a mere *cottage* with smallholdings.

He gently reminded her, as he must often have done, that they owned this house, that they owned everything they could see from it, the fells, the forests. In contrast, the palace near Neubrandenburg was, so far as they knew, now a military police barracks. That was the difference.

One day, she boasted, she would go back to reclaim what was rightly hers. She improbably lived to see that day.

My mother doubted that the palace existed. Or, that if it did exist, it was somewhere she knew from far off and had no familial connection with. She suspected that Berthe was like 'The German Girls' but had got lucky because of her (now lost) looks. 'The German Girls' – my nannies Christine, Ruth, Lotte – were constantly on the qui vive for a husband who might offer a permanent escape from the DDR. If Berthe's past was an invention it was a convincing one. Her husband appeared to believe it. If she deceived him she also deceived herself. They had met in Hamburg, in the British Zone, where she had suffered the humiliation of sharing a one-room walk-up apartment with her mother and sister. This tale of conventional indigence might have been devised to cover up the lurid truth that she was a hostess, even a *Strassenmädchen*. Major Johnstone may have been complicit, he may have drunk vodka to erase the memory of his wife's horizontal ignominy.

As the day drew on their mutual insults became coarser if less barbed. The blunt instrument replaced the stiletto. Major Johnstone's repertoire included no allusion to his wife having been a prostitute. It surely would have done had she been. As he slurred and slumped towards blackout he sneeringly reminded her that she was German. He mockingly reproached himself for having married a German. He dared not accuse her or her aristocratic family of having held Nazi sympathies, though the allegation was implicit. Marrying her, he had married into disgrace and buried culpability, he had married into a squalid nation, he had married into a fallen race. Domestic sniping was interrupted when either party had to refill a glass. This was discharged with such adroitness that the drunkenness it effected might have been an act put on for anyone entrapped in their hellish theatre: they cannot surely have comforted themselves with this sustained animosity when alone.

It was near dusk when my father turned up. In the state of exhaustion he often suffered after several hours' piscatorial concentration he seemed not to notice that his wife was tipsy nor that his son was blotto. Or if he did notice he didn't mind, for he was carrying three glistening sea trout which he displayed with childish pride. I was embarrassed that he felt obliged to justify himself with this catch to an alcoholic landowner twenty years his junior, who had not fought in the war and who had initially gone to Germany to do his National Service, a form of conscription my father routinely mocked, casting himself as a professional soldier. Callow civvies resented being called up when there was nothing to fight for. They considered it punishment. They were a shirking embuggerance which hampered martial order.

Berthe scowled at the fish. She complained that despite the freshness of the fish she could not prepare *Forelle blau*. The fish turns blue, or blueish, due to the reaction of the mucus on its skin with vinegar, wine vinegar, proper vinegar, vinegar unknown to the English who consider malt spirit to be 'vinegar'. Gastronomic barbarians! A characterisation that my mother would, in any other circumstance, have seconded. So began another skirmish. The war was of course still being fought when we returned later in the week.

By then, however, the appeal of the Johnstones' attritional palaver had been eclipsed. A quieter, tenser incident had occurred, one whose ramifications were unpredictable and intriguing.

Again, here was a demonstration of the opportunities for re-invention afforded by the now distant war's chaotic aftermath. Was anyone who he claimed to be? We all knew that the war had changed global power's bias and Britain's social shape – we could read of such shifts every day. The democratisation of affluence was a commonplace. There was another level of mutation. Personal, buried, secret.

Early one evening on the way back from the liquid coffin of Wastwater my father spotted a roadside pub and suggested we have a drink. There was a small gravelled car park. I followed him down several flights of steps between rockeries and loud flowerbeds. He ducked through the door between bottleglass bow windows. The room was lugubrious. The only light was behind the bar. A biscuit-coloured man stood there. His thin baby hair and bovine face and crumpled clothes were chromatically indistinguishable.

He barely looked up from the newspaper spread on the bar to greet us with a bored: 'Evshning.'

At about this point everything goes slo-mo.

He looked up again and announced: 'The boy'll havsh to shtop outshide.'

His voice, although a farrago of sibilants and whistles, was flat. It was a voice that resented itself and the callous pity it provoked. It was a voice like no other.

My father started. Not, it was immediately apparent, because of the man's casual officiousness. He bristled with the incredulity of recognition – but recognition of what? In a gesture of contained rage that I had never seen before he tightened his lips over his teeth. He was absorbed in memorious dredging. He peered at the landlord then walked to the bar.

'Well, in that case we'll push off . . . We've met before, haven't we? Kufi wuk say at cot daykanahi.[14] Corlett, isn't it?' He was amiably accusatory.

14 'Long time no see'. Phonetically.

The landlord had not troubled to register him till that moment. For a grossly stretched second his face locked in mortal puzzlement, an abattoir animal that cannot believe the indignity of getting a bolt to its head. He twitched as though about to sneeze. A subcutaneous tic danced beneath his left eye. He masticated air. He shook his head.

'What? No no. Namesh Lishter. Bob Lishter. No yer mush be mishtakin me for shomeone elsh.'

'Really?' My father did not hide his disbelief.

'Fraid sho.'

'Then Major Keith Corlett of Paiforce' – this was undisguisedly mocking – 'has a double.'

The landlord opened his palms, shrugged: ''Appensh.' He nodded in agreement with himself.

My father glared at him, turned on his heel, clasped my shoulder. As we left he glanced up at the white-lettered notice above the door according to which the licensee's name was Robert Erskine Lister. He was staring at us, his face frozen in a rictus of fearful antagonism.

'Lishter! Lishter!' My father sat in the car guying the man's speech impediment. He had an acute ear, not that it was required in this case. I enjoyed hearing him mock the unfortunate.

A finned Austin, baby blue and cream, entered the car park. A small boy with iridescent black hair got out of the car followed by his mother, a strikingly elegant Indian or chi-chi woman wearing pedal pushers. She glanced at us and smiled whitely. From the car's boot she lifted several cardboard boxes marked with Smiths Crisps' logo.[15] They obscured her path. She walked blindly down the potentially slapstick steps with assured grace. This must be Mrs Lister. Or Mrs Corlett.

'He knew bloody well that I'd rumbled him. Lishter . . . A shlimey piece of work.'

15 Smiths' hegemony was near its end. Golden Wonder introduced the UK's first flavoured crisps – cheese and onion – the next year, 1962, and by the end of the Sixties had become market leader.

War foments war. The Japanese army in Indochina surrendered on 19 August 1945 to the Viet Minh, which had been armed and funded by the USA. In the new world order there was to be room for only one colonial power. So the USA continued to support Ho Chi Minh after he had declared himself President since it wanted an end to French rule: it did not distinguish between the Vichy appointees who had been ousted and massacred by the Japanese and the Free French. Some Japanese troops joined Ho Chi Minh's guerrillas. Confusion reigned. An awkward alliance of a British Indian division under the clumsy Major-General Douglas Gracey and a French expeditionary force was despatched to wrest control of Saigon. So began the war that would end in the American evacuation twenty-eight years later.

In Iraq a number of officers and men of Paiforce awaiting demobilisation were astonished and infuriated to find themselves seconded to Gracey's division. Major Keith Corlett, a pen-pushing quartermaster stationed in Basra, was not among them.

But twenty-two soldiers whom he had invented were. For two and a half years he had peculated the wages of between thirty and fifty non-existent soldiers. Further, he had received money for payments to similarly non-existent civilian contractors. The plan he had devised for covering up his embezzlement was not nullified by the peremptoriness of the order that these troops should immediately embark for Bombay en route to Saigon. It was merely enacted earlier than anticipated.

Major Keith Corlett disappeared.

His absence was not noticed for some days. Even then it was a week after he was last seen that MPs investigated his bungalow. His clothes, his personal effects, his papers, his identity card and passport were all there. He was a heavy drinker, a member of several card schools, a polyglot whose impediment was said to vanish when he spoke Urdu or Bengali – prewar he had worked in Calcutta. It was initially mooted that a) he had met with an accident when rough shooting, which he typically did alone; b) he had been murdered in the Hanna Sheikh market area where he frequented a brothel; c) he had collapsed with alcohol poisoning; d) he had been killed over a gambling debt. When twenty-two soldiers failed to report to the vessel that was to take them to Gracey's HQ at Bombay it was assumed that they had deserted. Over a month passed before the extravagant truth began to emerge. By then Corlett was far away, and he was Lister, as he had long prepared to be.

My father had known him only casually. He had recognised him by his voice. This fluke encounter had shocked him as much as it had Lister, who must now have been living in fear of exposure. If, that is, he was Corlett and my father had not been mistaken, a possibility which nagged at him. He was worried too about what he ought to do. He was steadfast in his conviction that if Lister were Corlett he should face trial. This was a matter of an officer's duty, a gentleman's duty. He rightly discounted the notion that to inform the authorities of Corlett's whereabouts would make him a grass. But what authorities? Paiforce was long disbanded. In whose jurisdiction should Corlett be tried? Barrow-in-Furness's rozzers would improbably be interested in a martial fraud and, possibly, an identity theft perpetrated fifteen years previously in a distant country that had undergone a revolution and was now hostile to Britain. Did the Judge Advocate's department have the competence and legitimacy to instigate proceedings? And what proof could he offer? What was the process? How was it put into motion? He repeatedly discussed it with my mother, who became exasperated with his near-obsession. She believed he'd be wasting his time. He corresponded with Mike Morton, now a tobacco planter in Southern Rhodesia who had known Corlett as well as anyone had and who in future years would refer to Harold Wilson as 'that damned Communist, he's sold us down the river'. He talked to a couple of local India hands, Stewart Vartan, an actor who lived at Orcheston on Salisbury Plain, and Dan Goodman. They all agreed with my mother though were more polite.

They all agreed too that Jack Watts, who in 1945 had been

as astonished as everyone else at Corlett's activities, was the man. Would have been the man. Old Jack would have known the form. But this former major in Paiforce and the Cheshires, Roman Catholic bachelor, Mancunian textile magnate, nephew, though only fourteen years her junior, of Agatha Christie, clubman (White's, Pratt's, Carlton), Conservative MP for Moss Side (Commons catchphrase: 'monstrous injustice'), proponent of corporal punishment, of slum clearance and of controlled immigration, had died at his house in Chester Street SW1 the previous month. He had suffered a pulmonary embolism after breaking an ankle. Although he had spent ten days in hospital, deep-vein thrombosis had not been detected. Certain of Watts's friends, my father included, believed that *there was more to it than met the eye*. Having made a hardly contentious link between Manchester's housing shortage and Commonwealth immigration he had received a number of threats which he took seriously. It is difficult to see how the circumstances of his death might be construed as foul play but that did not inhibit my father from insisting that the Westminster coroner's verdict of accidental death was flawed, a cover-up.[16]

Given that English law allowed no statute of limitations my father had all the time in the world to decide what to do about Corlett / Lister. In later years he would occasionally refer to it. He had done nothing to resolve the matter when he died in 1981.

16 At the subsequent by-election the Union Movement candidate's agent was the twenty-year-old Christ Church undergraduate Max Mosley.

MAJOR McCOLL

The inhumanity of majors to children took many forms. Major McColl breathed booze. His clothes had been steeped in tobacco tars. He appeared to own one jacket, gooseshit-green and hairy. It presumably concealed a flask. He was a former gunnery instructor at the Royal Artillery School, Larkhill, an ugly neo-Georgian camp between Stonehenge and Woodhenge. Full-grown squaddies and bolshie national servicemen cannot have provided so attractive a target as a ten-year-old boy. It took him about three weeks to identify me as his preferred quarry. He pushed my head into a stationery cupboard and beat me with a stick till my bottom bled. He did this often. A rubber had fallen from my cramped desk during maths. He accused me of having dropped it. I had not. He knew I had not. He accused me of talking when I was conscientiously mute. The pretexts for his punishments were risibly flimsy. A smudged exercise book. Looking out of the window. Copying someone else's homework. My hopeless innumeracy. My bottom was bruised. I inspected it in my mother's three-mirrored dressing table when my parents were out. The flesh was broken, blistered, striped; the weals were cutely ruffed with dead skin frills. By that age I was, of course, self-conscious about my body. So my parents would not see the injuries by chance. And I was too ashamed to show them. Too embarrassed. We had to take our punishment like men, like the men who meted it out. I wanted McColl to die even though I was guiltily worried about what would become of his wreck of a wife and his ghostly nervy daughter who shivered even in summer like a diseased ewe. But he didn't die. So much for the power of prayer. By now though he'll have obliged. Fleshy lips dissolved, wirewool hair powder in a cask, cirrhotic liver scarred and shrunken.

Long-term damage? No. An antipathy to military personnel (which evidently has countless other causes) and to the strenuously characterful bow-ties he more usually wore, can hardly be considered damage. Rather, a valuable lesson. I have enjoyed a lifelong mistrust of bow-ties which I cannot but regard as the badge of the sadistic bastard and the fraud. They will have done better than he, they'll have been in and out of Oxfam, have kept coming round, frayed, gracing the necks of further generations of embittered passed-over majors and their heirs.

MAJOR MEADES

An officer who has achieved field rank, major and above, is entitled to retain it as a mode of address after he is decommissioned. My father eagerly did so. He was indignant about those who styled themselves captain, though turned a blind eye to his friend Captain Jack Powell who had been thus promoted in September 1918 at the age of nineteen. And a deaf ear to Jack's wearisome 'rolled on the thighs of a dusky Cuban maiden doncha know', unerringly uttered with every cigar.

What was a proud token of service in the 1950s and early 60s seemed unconvincingly self-aggrandising thereafter, as though the bearer of the title was living on dusty laurels. It did not embarrass him. It embarrassed me. Nonetheless mockery of his style angered me.

MARDEN, CYRIL

Old Fielden, who had introduced gas light to Salisbury many decades previously, died in 1959. Watersmeet House was split into flats. The long-neglected riverside gardens where he used to sit sucking a pipe on a rocking chair outside a summer house were sold as four building plots. My parents bought the westernmost – half an acre of brambles and woodbine. The Fieldens were Quaker textile magnates, radicals, and, in the way of great Quaker families, philanthropists. Their fiefdom was Todmorden, on the Yorkshire/Lancashire border high on the Pennines. That small town's public buildings, churches, chapels and almshouses were Fielden gifts. Beside Watersmeet House there was a handsome barn, a treasure trove of late Victorian prints, Stevengraphs, oleographs and several hundred monochrome postcards of

Todmorden, the great town hall (by John Gibson, among the finest architects of the classical survival), factories, flights of locks, mills, Bacup, the Bridestones, high chimneys, pennyfarthings, brass bands, the moors, fanciful bridges, Broad Clough, the Fieldens' castellated houses, Hebden Bridge, cobbled streets, spires. I spent weeks poring over these unwanted mementoes of a distant life. I dared not take any. Then one day the barn was demolished to provide a further building plot. Its contents were thrown on to bonfires by Old Fielden's unsentimental son Edward, a jobbing builder. Jobbing builder suggests that he got jobs. His reputation – as low as Griffin-The-Humber-Hawk's – was such that he didn't get jobs. The four houses built in the gardens between 1960 and '62 were his work because he made it a condition of purchase of the land. He was inept, borderline bent, charmingly plausible, full of excuses. Among his employees was a slobbering evangelical who foisted leaflets and sacred spittle on anyone who came near him.

Access to the houses was created by extending and metalling a previously unnamed lane that led past a corrugated-iron village hall to one of Salisbury's few essays in art deco. Art deco was not yet current. My mother's rather scornful epithet was jazz modern. Windows: Crittall or 'Daily Mail'. Roof: green pantiles. It was owned by a septuagenarian hotelier named Cyril Marden, who was, coincidentally, in the process of building, in his garden adjacent to my parents' plot, a block of two maisonettes. He and his unflappable wife Pam would move into the upstairs one, let the other and sell the art deco house. Progress was hesitant. Pyramids of sand sprouted grass. Trenches turned into reservoirs. Brickies came and went. It became apparent that this was due to Cyril's blithe disregard of the payment schedule agreed with the builder (not Edward Fielden; Cyril, being one, could recognise one). His pathological unwillingness to pay bills was frequently compounded by an equal inability to pay them: his parsimony was both habitual and necessary. Had he been of a more genial disposition he might perhaps have been accorded the wearisome status of 'a character'. But genial was not the word for Cyril. A man less suited to what was not yet called the hospitality industry is unimaginable. He was misanthropic, misogynistic, grudge-bearing, treacherous, paranoid, laughably mean, ignorant, jealous, resentful, permanently irate, too stupid to be cunning, rude. His qualities were manifest in his face, a sour scowling knot of knolls and crevices wrapped around a reeking cigar. It was made further alarming by a pair of feminine cat's-eye glasses whose sweeping frame was styled with the baroque bombast of a mid-Fifties Cadillac. He never smiled. I liked him.

The Crown Hotel was easily missed even though there was an entrance in the High Street and another round the corner in Crane Street. It belonged, at best, to the lowest division of the city's hotels, a long way behind Laundry Maidment's Red Lion, The White Hart, managed by Mr Ianetta who, to my father's consternation, changed his name to Ian, the beaming Austrian's Rose and Crown, The King's Arms (lobster thermidor) and The Clovelly, an unlicensed guesthouse near the station. The Crown's only competitor in sheer insalubrity was the misleadingly named Claridge's in Castle Street, but at least that pit had a bar-billiards table. The Crown was sordid. It looked more like a decrepit office building than a hostelry. White paint flaked from its exterior. The windows were matt with epic grime and curtained with filthy nylon net. The consequently lugubrious interior was a maze of sitting rooms and lounges furnished with bursting sofas and greasy armchairs. The carpets suffered mange. There was an ambient reek, a combination of noxious sources: brimming ashtrays and driptrays, the kitchen, electrocuted rats rotting behind wainscots, the seldom maintained lavatories. It was doubtless to The Crown's advantage that the delightful Old George Inn across the street had been demolished by Hammersons, vandal property speculators and comprehensive redevelopers, in order to build a rotten shopping 'precinct', precursor of many an ill mall.

Cyril drove to The Crown every morning in his maroon and cream Vauxhall Velox, subsequently replaced by an automatic, primitively clutchless, green Ford Corsair which I would sometimes chauffeur him in when he had overdone breakfast. He never paid me, never thanked me. I'd have been disappointed had he done so. It would have detracted from his guileless mystique. He passed most of the day sitting on a stool at his hotel's oddly well-frequented bar, drinking old maids' sickly liqueurs (Tia Maria, Kahlua, Advocaat), baiting the startlingly seedy barman who was also a waiter in the dining room. This culinary morgue was proof that the English attitude to food was founded in masochistic stoicism rather than the disease called pleasure. The walls were a riot of insipidity, all smeared beiges and fawns. The swirly carpet contained the well-trodden gristle of immemorial meals. The food included imperfectly defrosted, fishmeal-fed fowl from the cash and carry at West Harnham and bottom-of-the-range tinned veg from the Amesbury NAAFI. It was typical of Cyril that, with no legitimate connection to the services, he should have got his hands on a NAAFI card.

Christmas Day 1964. Lunch at The Crown as Cyril and Pam's guests. Why? Whatever can my parents have been thinking of? My parents were hard up, but this? The hotel was smellier than usual because grossly overheated. Nonetheless I sat beside an ill-fitting window and suffered Boxing Day neuralgia as a result. Cyril remained ignorant of the food's aggressive nastiness. Or knew it too well. He ate nothing. He drank copiously and chain-smoked. His wine-stained tutu-pink party hat rested on his spectacle frames, a bandage on a severe head wound. The fellow guests were Cyril and Pam's harassed son Brian and his fractious, beehived wife Vicky; dundrearied Mr Slegg wore a vermilion ceremonial sash and roared; mute Mrs Slegg in a hat on which she placed her paper hat; a jolie laide apprentice hairdresser and her mother Mrs, a venomous bundle of prejudices and asperity, who was clearly suspicious of my intentions towards the invitingly dirty-looking Miggy. Happily, by the time the Christmas pudding had been set light to, Mrs, as keen an enthusiast as Cyril for sweet liqueurs, was comatose. Miggy and I made our getaway, to a fuggy drawing room that smelled of old people and was crammed with bulbous prewar furniture. I stroked her thigh whilst pretending to be captivated by the gossip from Charles of Mayfair, Jean-Noel of Bond Street and Wanda (provenance undisclosed). These were Salisbury's top salons: a punning name was not yet mandatory. Soon they would be joined by Hans of Bond Street *and* Vienna, noted for his mittel-European courtesy. She aspired to work at Wanda. She wasn't sure I should be doing that because she had an *official* boyfriend Greg. Greg was going to get his own sports car in the spring. I silently wished him ill. I persisted. In time Miggy appeared to forget about Greg. The bloated armchair we were sprawled over wasn't made for *heavy petting*, a disapprobatory Sixties euphemism for mutual masturbation. Half undressed we stumbled in furious haste to a lumpy sofa. Consummation beckoned. To facilitate that end Miggy pushed a greasy bolster to the floor. She screamed. Where the bolster had been there was a seething tide of maggots covering one of the sofa's thick cushions. The sight of teeming white larvae turned out to be potently anaphrodisiac. Miggy hurriedly rolled down her skirt from above her waist. I suffered an alarmingly swift detumescence, which was just as well, for her scream had been heard. I had only just pulled my trousers on when the door opened. Mrs stood there, she too was seething. She observed the maggots with distaste and me with greater distaste. She dragged her daughter from the room, scowling at me with mighty malevolence. Unseen by her mother Miggy shrugged her puff-cheeked regret. They left.

When I returned to the dining room my mother smiled in mock reproach and touched her chin to indicate that I should wipe Miggy's labia-pink lipstick from mine. I picked up a napkin. My father was locked in conversation with Vicky's deep cleavage. Brian was clutching a bottle of Cointreau and blowing smoke rings. Mr Slegg was chortling at some joke – doubtless his own, doubtless at my expense, doubtless smutty – which Cyril apparently failed to understand. Pam, the only sober member of the party, told me, without severity: 'You should take care.' Which presumably meant I should have been to the Durex dispenser in the gents before meeting the maggots.

Cyril depended on Pam whilst treating her with contemptuous indifference. She kept the books and mollified the staff. The hotel was held together by her skilful drudgery and by subventions from Cyril's elder brother and his nephew whose company's name he spoke with a proprietorial boastfulness that was delusional: Wheelock Marden was a potent Hong whose businesses included shipping, containers (then in their infancy) and property. George Marden and his son John were massively successful taipans. George had bailed out his brother year after year. Loan after loan had remained unrepaid. According to Pam, John considered that he and his father were more or less blackmailed by Cyril, who was all too aware that a Marden bankruptcy, even on the other side of the world, would stain the family's reputation in Kowloon and New Territories, and across the South China Sea to the Philippines and Australia. Nor was Cyril too proud to beg with menaces from his own son, nailbiting Brian, a manufacturer of packaging equipment in suburban Bournemouth.

Pam Marden was diagnosed with terminal cancer in the autumn of 1966. A shaken Brian Marden was telling my parents the prognosis when I got back from Wellworthy's piston ring factory where I worked as a chamfer machine operator. The next evening I went to see Pam. Her impending death affected her less than did the fate of the children of Aberfan who had died that morning under a sliding slag heap. 'At least I've had my life.'

Cyril, however, was deeply affected. Pam's cancer was a form of treachery towards him; at the very least it was offensively inconsiderate. He was incapable of looking after himself, too idle to look after her. He continued to spend all day in the bar at The Crown. Pam was confined to her bed. A series of nurses was hired. Some left because they weren't paid, others because of Cyril's malicious rudeness. Eventually Bill and Eleanor Adams, the tenants downstairs, found themselves taking charge of Pam's care. Brian and Vicky came at the weekends. When Vicky was around during the week she'd spend the afternoon in bed with my father rather than tending to her mother-in-law.

Nosing around in Cyril's squalid office at The Crown she found a pile of some two dozen recent envelopes addressed to him, handwritten rather than typed. Not the usual invoices, summons and demands. The letters had been replaced in the envelopes. She read them with incredulity. They were replies to a classified advertisement for a wife placed by a 'recently widowed gentleman, respected hotelier with international business interests and property owner of standing'.

Cyril was unabashed when Vicky confronted him. He told her that he had already interviewed two of the respondents but considered neither of them suitably qualified; that is to say they were not wealthy or not susceptible to being enslaved. The ideal, obviously, was a well-heeled widow who was accustomed to being downtrodden. Pam was taken into Odstock Hospital. The day she died Cyril was lunching with an applicant in The Rose and Crown. Wisely, he didn't risk his own hotel. The jolly Austrian manager got used to Mr Marden's successive lady friends whose eagerness caused them to travel considerable distances to meet him. They came from Kingston-upon-Thames, from Reigate, from Daventry, from Tiverton. One was so wide a special obesity chair had to be found for her. A second, alert to widowers' ways – and by now he really was a widower – shrilly accused him of being a gold-digger. At which point Cyril confirmed the accuracy of that estimate by announcing that he had forgotten his wallet and storming out of the dining room.

When Marjorie read Cyril's ad she was revisiting the country of her birth for the first time in over thirty-five years: she had migrated to Australia from Derby in 1930 after her fiancé broke off their engagement the week they were to be married. Three years later in Adelaide she had met and married a mechanical engineer. Post-war they established a small business to manufacture the knitting machines which he designed and patented. Their only child, a son, was killed when a scrum collapsed in a university rugby game. When her husband died she sold the thriving, much-expanded concern. The cottage industry in a workshop was now an exporter with a purpose-built factory.

Marjorie didn't have the makings of a mug. She had presumably been an astute businesswoman. But loss and loneliness weighed on her, rendered her vulnerable. She blamed herself for her misfortunes. Her reunion with her socially immobile sister's family and proletarian cousins had not been happy. They resented her affluence, her worldly success, her immunity from wartime privations, her accent, her expensively tailored clothes. She told my mother, whom she would perforce befriend, that she had not been looking for a husband. She had been reading the classifieds as an entertainment; she was taken by their boastful desperation. It was the mention in Cyril's ad of 'a property commanding John Constable's world-famous view of Salisbury's historic cathedral' that sparked her curiosity. Although she had never visited the city, framed prints of certain paintings by Constable had, in her exile, represented an ideal of the England she had left behind. There was a sort of piquancy in the contrast with the Adelaide suburb called Salisbury, a roughneck, meat-pie sort of place, a world away from Glenside where she had latterly lived.

Constable painted more than a dozen *world-famous* views of the cathedral. They are his own. His duty was to his inventions rather than to topographical fidelity. Thus Cyril's claim had, for once, been not entirely mendacious, nor had his boast to Marjorie that Wheelock Marden was 'the family firm'. He was, after all, of that family and massively in hock to it. They married three months after meeting. For Cyril it was like hitting the jackpot. For Marjorie it was the beginning of a sentence in hell. Not that she realised it immediately. On the contrary, she was enchanted by the rivers, the meadows between the rivers, the spire beyond the rivers. Whilst she sat contentedly on the balcony or ambled about the cathedral and close clutching a guidebook, Cyril set about devising ways of redistributing her wealth.

Initially he requested 'loans' to help him through problems at the hotel. He claimed that these were caused by governmental mismanagement of sterling. The sums requested soon increased in size. When Marjorie began to demur he resorted to self-pitying tears: he would lose his hotel, they would lose their home. He locked her in the spare room, hardly larger than a cupboard, till she agreed to sign cheques to him. She would sit with my mother and howl. Her face was puffy from tears and blows. Cyril might be old and scrawny but he didn't allow those qualifications to inhibit his taste for domestics with a purpose. In little more than a year Cyril peculated and menacingly obtained over £25,000. This was a sum far in excess of the handouts he received from his brother and nephew. He swindled to satisfy his avarice, his craving for hoarding. The hotel was not refurbished; he did not replace his now rusting slum of a car; he continued to wear the same shiny threadbare suit day in day out. A year after their marriage Cyril was admitted to hospital suffering pleurisy. Marjorie seized her chance and returned to Australia, partially fleeced but entirely relieved. For several years she sent my mother letters. Sometimes they included a photo of a brightly coloured flower. She was happy. Then they stopped.

Cyril had been surprised by her defection. He couldn't believe it. It took him some time to understand what had happened. When his confusion abated he realised that what he had feared at the time of Pam's terminal illness had come to revisit him. He was alone with no one to bully and abuse, no one to skiv for him, no one to pick him up whenever he collapsed, an ampersand of bony malnutrition. Vicky volunteered to spend part of the week with him. Thus she was able to renew her affair with my father. I was by now so seldom in Salisbury that I knew nothing of it. One time I was there she said of Cyril: 'If he ate anything he'd be incontinent. He'd be in nappies. But he only drinks so he just pisses himself.' He was not so drunk that he didn't realise what his daughter-in-law was up to. He grassed her up to Brian who, with his usual force, confronted my unsuspecting mother rather than my father. Could she please please possibly get my father to desist? I arrived late one weekend morning as Brian, clumsy and tearful, and Vicky, a haughtily unrepentant culprit, exited from my parents' front door. Vicky ignored me. Brian smiled desperately, sort of kneeled.

My father and mother watched them go. He was all sheepish bluster. She was furious. No one said anything. He disappeared to tie some fishing flies. She mixed a jug of gimlet. Perplexed but no doubt recognising what was going on, I went down to the river's edge and laughed at the boiling stream. I was not privy to what had passed but it soon became clear that Cyril had been removed so that Vicky would have no cause to trou-serloiter. He went to live with them in the northern sprawl of Bournemouth. They swiftly tired of his presence. So began Cyril's vagabondage. That conurbation's numberless sunset homes were unable to cope with his ever-increasing delinquency. Time and again he was asked to leave. He died in the brown hall of an establishment in Branksome Park whilst he was waiting for Vicky to drive him to the next place, which he would now never terrorise.

MARKET PLACE

What a spectacle! What a din!

Fearful calves penned between wooden hurdles. Sheep spinning this way and that, sensing something was amiss. Insouciant pigs, happy and snuffling. The market superintendent whose face was a synthesis of farm animals – please note the cavernous nostrils and their stalactites of bristle. Hay, straw, shit in several coalescing forms. Gullible kine snorting and mooing and peering winsomely. A sense of the chaos to come when one of the condemned breaks its bounds.

Till the mid-Fifties the centre of the Market Place was devoted on Tuesdays to livestock.

Prewar trucks, slatted-sided lorries, demobbed Jeeps and the oxidised bronze statue of him apart, the scene could not have changed much in the century since Henry Fawcett – political economist, radical reformer, Postmaster General – last saw it before he was blinded by his father whilst shooting partridge on Harnham Hill. There were still horses tethered outside the pubs along Ox Row. There were still smallholders' dog carts parked by the Guildhall.

Along the northern side of the square, beside Blue Boar Row, where Fawcett was born, stood two rows of stalls and vans. Boiled sweets, suspiciously coloured cakes, jams, canned goods from the Commonwealth, dirty veg, fruit, meat, wet fish and fish and chips. The hygienic probity and the quality of the goods were variable. The air was thick with the stench of the subterranean public lavatories, their disinfectant and unidentified frying agents. But here was Johnson's cockle stall. Threepence a plate. A drop of malt vinegar, a shake of white pepper. This was a kind of bliss, amplified by being forbidden. The First German

Girl, Christine, who initially took me there, warned me not to tell my parents. The Second German Girl, Lotte, was too conscientious to succumb to my demands and had no appetite for such things. She left to marry Mark Young, a Communist electrician who renounced the party for a career as an ETU official and eventually became General Secretary of BALPA. Her short-lived replacement Lynn arrived bearing a gift for my father: a moleskin waistcoat made not of that cotton fabric but of the fur of moles trapped by her father, a professional mole catcher on Lambourn gallops. As well as fur the garment was composed of drops of dried blood, bone shards and desiccated ligament. Much of Lynn's day was taken up listening to Frankie Laine's 'Do Not Forsake Me Oh My Darlin'' ('The Ballad of High Noon') whilst putting on make-up to entice squaddies, one of whom soon impregnated her. She blithely revealed to my horrified mother my fondness for cockles and was duly forbidden to take me there. So too was her successor, The Third German Girl, Ruth, who did as she was told. However, because she had not been told not to give a six-year-old boy half a pound of melted butter for breakfast she did so, granting my request without demur, assuming no doubt that this was a commonplace English dish: a not unreasonable assumption given that I used to eat tubes of supposedly fruit-flavoured Punch and Judy toothpaste. Her more usual repertoire included stuffed cabbage braised in stock, silverside with dumplings, potatoes fried with cubes of bacon.

She had an insatiably sweet tooth. She assuaged it with Tyrozets, cough-sweets packaged in translucent marmalade-coloured cylinders, and frequent visits to the half-timbered Cadena Café on Blue Boar Row where the éclairs and doughnuts were cheaper than The Bay Tree's or The House of Steps's. This chain of cafés had artistic pretensions. In certain branches a trio was said to play at teatime. Here there was no music but a mural which acknowledged local sensibilities: the cathedral spire rose behind chalky downs. The style was whimsical, Festival of Britain, akin to Barbara Jones's. The foreground represented agriculture as a far from pastoral, mechanised industry: combine harvesters and tractors driven by dungareed workers, rectilinear cowsheds, Dutch barns. There were glowing sheaths of corn among pylons. This picture of neatness bore no relation to the Market Place's muddy disorder, lowing cacophony and heavily accented bonhomie. It might have been a fellow traveller's happy dream of a collective farm on the road to Amesbury.

The spectacle of the Market Place took many forms. Muir Martin and Higgins: chemists of contrast! Mr Higgins's shop was a relic of long long ago when tiled floors were coloured by the sun's rays refracted through gigantic vials on shelves in the window, when banks of drawers contained the ingredients of remedies that would be mixed and pounded and fired and pressed into pellets by a pharmacist who had trained to do something other than sell nappies and shampoo. Each drawer was marked with gold lettering in a signwriter's hand from the days of gaiety girls and Skindles. And Mr Higgins himself lived in St Marie's Grange, a house at Alderbury considered to be the last word in ugliness. No matter that it was the work of the young Pugin, who had built it for himself on a site which looked upstream to the cathedral and downstream to Longford Castle. No one knew who Pugin was. Half a century after the Queen and Empress had died Victorian architecture's reputation was at its very nadir. To claim an interest in it was regarded as mad or pretentious or both: there were exceptions such as the neo-Romanesque church at Wilton, the classical survival villas of Clifton and Cheltenham, but as for the Gothic! The Dean and Chapter's typically oafish, typically vandalistic removal of George Gilbert Scott's and Francis Skidmore's reredos and rood screen from the cathedral excited hardly a murmur. This prodigy of the metalworker's craft, installed during Scott's restoration, had lasted less than a century. It was bought by Bert Shergold, a blacksmith who presumably used pieces of it in the patio doors, garden gates and distinctive barbecues for which he claimed to be noted. (The Shergolds were one of the tribes of south Wiltshire – others were the Gullivers, the Moodys, the Chalkes, the Dredges.)

Cecil Kent was a pharmacist. Rae Kent was a character. He was shy, she wasn't. She had moved to Salisbury with her south Walian parents and accent when her father had bought Muir Martin. Cecil had been employed as an assistant. He married into the business. When his father-in-law retired he took it over. He in turn employed an assistant who was known as Living Wage. The attraction of the shop to me resided in the large bowls of shampoo sachets manufactured by a company called French: they were like jewels, taut, distended, sexy. The attraction of the Kents themselves was her effusive generosity and his bemused geniality: they gave countless parties where he was a wallflower and she got badered. Life and soul was their Gannex-clad friend Mac, who had never had time to get married because he was so busy building up one of the most important chains of dry cleaners in Hampshire and Dorset. His dog was incontinent. The Kents moved house often, on two occasions to houses I knew through their previous owners. This troubled me.

Cecil owned a succession of oddball cars which I would get to ride in. My only experience of travelling in a rumble seat was in his Triumph Roadster. Years later he had a Facel Vega which he drove with thrilling recklessness. The Kents' three children – older than me by at least a decade – led admirably independent lives. As soon as he had finished an apprenticeship Martin left England to work as a marine engineer in the eastern Mediterranean. Sandra the youngest married a literally lowbrowed marine who died in a road accident. Pat's acceptance by Guildford Art School's photography department, the first in the country, was regarded with awe, reported in the *Salisbury Journal*: tertiary education was not a commonplace. Then, whoops, she eloped with a beard called Jimmy. Fellow students indicated that they had gone to Paris. Poor Cecil, who had never been out of England and spoke no French, obtained a temporary passport so that he might track them down. Improbably, he succeeded. A neighbour belonged to the same regiment as a member of the British military attaché's staff. This fellow had good contacts in the French intelligence agencies. A moonlighting DST[17] officer had no trouble in finding the indigent young lovers and, misunderstanding why they were being sought, treated Jimmy to some good old-fashioned coppering. The marriage didn't last. Their photographic portrait business floundered. As they grew out of being off-the-peg beat-niks[18] they grew out of each other. They divorced. Rae, following an agony aunt's advice, sent Pat on a cruise in search of a new rich husband. She found a suitable man forty years her senior, older than her parents.

The broadest frontage on Blue Boar Row was that of the ill-named Style and Gerrish, a startlingly tatty department store where in his grotto Father Christmas, too pissed to grope, merely burped Empire sherry fumes at Roger and me; where, at the age of three, I panicked and screamed when I found myself separated from my mother in a dark forest of legs on the move (thinner trunks than today's); where I bought a Tootal Silver Blade hori-zontally striped tie (navy, cerise); where a plate-glass window was broken during a fight between a dozen girls from rival schools and two were hospitalised. Leaving the store one day when I was thirteen I saw a youth of nineteen or twenty with the malnourished, high-cheekboned face of Jet Harris. He wore ice-blue jeans and grey winklepickers. Grey! I had never previ-ously seen grey winklepickers. I wanted a pair even though I knew the smartest feet were now in chisel toes, I wanted those jeans, I wanted his tight bumfreezer, I wanted to be him. Or if not him one of the proto-Mods with Roman haircuts and short iridescent bronze macs who loitered in Sutton's record shop with its advanced, perforated-hardboard listening booths. It had moved a hundred yards from straitened premises in a dark courtyard where there still stood the skewed outside staircase of

17 Direction de la Surveillance du Territoire.
18 Like every other small town Salisbury had a number of coffee bars for the sandalled and bearded to waste their days in: The Two Bare Feet (opposite the Art School – I never dared enter), The Man Friday (desert island décor), The Orchid (bullfight posters).

a late mediaeval pub. Now it occupied a tile-hung building's roomy ground floor which granted the bearded owner sufficient space to embarrass his young clientele with fits of finger-clicking, dig-the-sounds hepcattery. The Spanish girls (or town prozzies) pointed and mugged silent laughter at him. Whether or not they were Spanish is moot: all that is sure is that they were barely anglophone. One had a baby. They were both swarthy. They wore dauntingly tight skirts, thick mascara, moustache-size false lashes, scuffed stilettos. Their vigorously sprayed and back-combed beehives were skyscraping mantillas reminiscent of the patissier's craft. They prompted rehearsal of what I did not then know to be a commonplace urban myth, prompted as much by the nominal association as the vertiginous construction itself. Insects or nits or spiders, maybe beetles or bees, were said to have nested in the cavernous inner recesses of their hairdos and were already boring into the skull. One summer the Spanish girls were always around. Then they vanished. Their brains pocked and holed no doubt.

Pinder's was an ironmongers which sold tacks and nails by weight and wrapped them in shiny brown paper cones. Opposite on the north-east corner of the market square stood a hamfisted lump of tudorbethan gigantism which may have fooled someone but didn't fool me: I knew very well that it wasn't of the sixteenth century, and I was a child. It housed the tartan-carpeted Caledonian Club whose walls were antlerscapes, whose members were, according to my father, pompous, self-righteous bores. (One of them, a sometime 'gaiety girl', had the temerity to telephone my mother to tell her to tell me to get my hair cut.) His despisal of kilts was disproportionate to the visual offence they caused him. I didn't realise that his contempt was not so much levelled at the garment as at the bogusness of 'traditional' garb and sectarian affectation.

By mid-Georgian standards the Guildhall is wild. I was beguiled and repulsed by its primitive rustication, which broke through the smooth ashlared stone like petrified suppuration. It recalled the strawberry-mark borne by the Old Mill's owner. Beside it was Whaley's outfitters. School uniforms, Cash's name tapes sewn in the font of your choice, Lee Cooper jeans, eau de nil jeans, check jeans, snake belts (though none of them compared with my Dan Dare belt whose elastic was printed with space ships and ray guns, whose buckle incorporated the pilot's helmeted head – a masterpiece of moulded plastic).

The Saturday market pitch outside Whaley's was occupied by Billy Hector, a Bournemouth knocker. His job was to read death notices, to discover the address of the departed and at a suitable interval after the funeral – as much as two or three days – to knock on the bereaved's door and attempt to buy the departed's unwanted possessions, the ones that are cluttering up everywhere and that, just getting in the way, inconvenient like Missus and watch out for some of them dealers from elsewhere, Southampton, Totton – bad lot. He was a charming, heavy-eyebrowed, gregarious loose-wallah, whose market stall was laden with the junk that he was obliged to take along with the occasional treasures he uncovered. Those went straight to auctions conducted by supposedly respectable houses. The junk comprised hideous gewgaws, book club books, airport novels, dead men's cracked shoes and shiny suits. Greater Bournemouth, with its tens of thousands of slobbering geriatrics and nonagenarian kerb crawlers, was a fecund source of death's gifts. My father witnessed Billy greeting an evidently regular customer, telling her that he had just the salad tongs she had been looking for. The customer beamed as he proudly brandished a pair of delivery forceps. Sold.

The adjacent greasy spoons, caffs and pubs were unappealing. I ate Stoby's chips on a single occasion. Of the city's five fish and chip shops, one for every seven thousand inhabitants, it was the least enticing. My loyalty was divided: Yorkshire Fisheries' chips were the best but Bedwyn Street had an incomparably showy fryer, a smalltown James Dean with a vivacious blond quiff, with a pack of cigarettes folded into his T-shirt's sleeve, with a muscular shovelling action. He was fearless in the face of flying fat. The tiny outfit smelled good and the chips were crisp. Whereas Stoby's were pale and flaccid and the stale smell had powerful outreach.

The smell of Scats was more like it, mysteriously sperm-like, though in infancy that was not revealed to me. The seed of grass smells like the seed of man. This seed merchant was at the western end of the Market Place. There were bulbous sacks stacked high. A staircase corkscrewed to unseen offices above. The light was dim. The air was brown. Every shade of brown was represented in that shop. From baby's first try to spraint – scat does mean shit. (It also means whisky and heroin.) For many years I obstinately confused Scats with Spratt's, manufacturers of birdseed and brownish dog biscuits. Spratt's advertised their products with an ingenious logotype. The seven letters of the name were eased by the designer Maxfield Bush into the profile of a canary or, more commonly, a Scottie dog. This was achieved without the laborious contortions that habitually characterise such devices. Why, I wondered, did Scats not display Spratt's' logo? I didn't lose any sleep over it. I set out to emulate Mr Bush. I learned from John Bennett, editor of the *Salisbury Journal*, that this sort of visual pun was called a calligram. My efforts at devising them were at least better than my shamefully maladroit attempts to build model aircraft or carpenter anything other than a wristwatch stand in the impenetrably accented Mr Usher's woodwork class. My limitations were apparent to me even though I lied to myself as I did to the world. It alarmed me that my brain's response to three-dimensional demands and spatial riddles should be to close down, to take industrial inaction; that was something to keep to myself. Calligraphy and its derivatives appeared to be as rigorously one-dimensional as cartography, thus as exciting, as alluring: here were forms that I might actually master. Such exercises might culminate in something other than frustration at my wretched incapacity.

Chronology was baffling. Salisbury teemed with evident ancientness. Elsewhere there were things that had been made in another time, in the recent past, which confusingly appeared to belong to tomorrow. I didn't know that these were emblems of a puzzle called modernism. The past they came from seemed more modern than the present. It was as though the future had already been and gone, before the war. Everything was happening in the wrong order. Gresley's A4 Pacifics, pastel colours, the flat-roofed houses besides the unmade roads at Sandbanks, green pantiles, blue pantiles, wrap-round windows, the lonely High Post Hotel, Poole Twintone pottery – they were all evidently products of an aberrational parenthesis outside time. By the 1950s however, time was under control, normality had reasserted itself: the new police headquarters on Wilton Road was neo-Georgian and pompous; the first stage of Southampton's reconstruction was neo-Georgian and meek.

In the course of that parenthesis the alphabet's letters had been cleaned, sharpened, pared down, shorn of redundant excrescences. Now, once again, letters' modesty was preserved – as it had been long ago in advertisements for meat extracts and vaudeville – by flourishes, tails, curlicues, tendrils. An austere sans serif font was associable with the austerity of war and rationing. The reaction against it was swift. All of a sudden it was the typographical equivalent of going out in public with no clothes on: not done, worse than not done.

My efforts to create calligrams, my efforts to design display letters were connected to and hampered by my efforts to achieve an individualistic handwriting which was mine alone, which would, when I perfected it, be a facet of my identity. Indeed when I perfected it my identity would be partially revealed to me. My efforts were also informed by my antipathy to a slab serif or egyptian font which, used in its seemingly invariable italic form, had become ubiquitous with astonishing alacrity. Britain suffered a rash of Stymie. It was timidly invasive, apologetically maculating. Even though it was a prewar composition it did not, aptly, find favour in Britain till the middle Fifties. Like much of the design which came to characterise that decade it gave offence for the very reason that it sought not to give offence. It was cowed by such self-abasement that it couldn't even stand up straight, rather it stooped under the weight of its fawning forelock. Italics were doubtless reckoned casual, modest. High modernism had been formal, rhetorical, ostentatious. The first wave of post-war modernism was a dilute, matey, cosy, folksy reaction to what had preceded it. It felt tentatively pre-modern. That chronological conundrum again.

Stymie was the preferred font of welfarist exhortation, yet it was unauthoritative because so implicitly provisional, so liable to collapse. It was the literal expression of the coercive carrot. Come on! This is good for you. Eat your greens. Swim your lengths, that's the way. Please tie your barrel knot. Run on the spot. Tie your granny knot. Press, press, fling – that's a good chap! *Join in!* Youth clubs which no youth wished to frequent, public lavatories, telephone exchanges, post offices, community centres, health centres, swimming baths, council flats, fire stations, dole offices, civic centres. Stymie was the state's means of reassuring us that the state's largesse provided all our needs, for which boastful do-goodery we must be grateful. It was to be avoided. Nonetheless when I drew letters, the strokes of my heavy crayon or pencil never quit the paper without leaving on it the unwelcome promise of a serif to come, the germ of an unwelcome growth. My hand's insubordinate lack of discipline was frustrating.

Till the age of seven handwriting was a matter of isolated letters on, or almost on, exercise books' lines, wobbly pylons and dead trees on a horizon. The margins of those exercise books are decoratively defaced by drawings of Norman helmets which extend over the nose like an exaggerated widow's peak. Joined-up writing was foisted on us by Miss Piercey, a needling spinster whose classroom was off the undercroft where we ate disgusting lunches (fish spirited away in pockets) and Sun-Pat peanut butter at teatime. Learning copperplate was learning by rote. Times tables, county towns, Marlborough's battles, French verbs and vocab, the kings and queens of England, verse by de la Mare,

Lear and Stevenson: learning these through repetitive recitation was a task I undertook with boundless enthusiasm. Housman: 'Let a man acquire knowledge not for this or that external and incidental good which may chance to result from it, but for itself; not because it is useful or ornamental, but because it is knowledge, and therefore good for man to acquire.' Copperplate was not knowledge. It was a set of inflexible rules, a rubric enforced by a disciple of chastity, a property that the Virgin Witch Kitty's example caused me to recognise, if not to articulate to myself, and to mistrust. We wrote with regularly sharpened pencils then progressed to dip pens which were good for us, like prayers or gym. They tore pages, they constellated them with blobs and spots, with drunken diaereses and macrons on the lam, with dolt's Morse. Miss Piercey was swift to slap our wrists. Because I wished her ill I was incapable of appreciating that a grudging submission to her copperplate tyranny might have bent my hand to my will and so allowed me to achieve something other than the inchoate, illegible skein of wisps and curls which passed for my writing after I moved on from Miss Piercey's class and, unchallenged, declared calligraphic independence.

My imaginary friend, my only imaginary friend, Andrew Parker, with whom I would share record-breaking batting partnerships, was a scion of the family that had founded the fountain pen company. I chose him because he was going to be a ready source of desirable, streamlined, hooded nib Parker 51s. I might write illegibly but I wanted to write illegibly in style, with the modern pen par excellence: modern once again meant something created before I was born. I had overlooked the Parker Pen Company's being an American manufacturer. It was a blow to discover that awkward truth: Andrew Parker was, then, an improbable cricketer who breached my rule of an imaginary friend's credibility. Further, in my parallel domestic life, the Parker 51 I yearned for was considered a laughably expensive pen for a child, let alone a child whose lifelong aptitude for losing things had revealed itself early. Instead I was, as usual, fobbed off with a Woolworths imitation. Which became a series of imitations as, in turn, I lost them. The pens – no manufacturer or even country of origin was vouchsafed – had a hooded nib which could be unscrewed, an inconsistent ink flow and a slightly plumper barrel than the Parker: choose from metallic crimson or petroleum blue. They might not have had the status of Conway Stewarts, Osmiroids or even Platignums, but they weren't old hat. Their streamlining allowed them to move across the page with a speed unthinkable in an open-nibbed model. I was very proud of my nameless pens, just as I was of my wallet – *plastic* and British racing green. (I coveted Poth's non-U green plastic clip-on tie with a non-U Windsor knot.) My father owned, though never used, a hopelessly outmoded Parker Duofold of the 1920s, mottled plastic that mimicked marble or blue cheese and with a clip like an oboe's stretched key. He wrote with pencils or Bics which he bought in bulk in St Malo (where there were formica tables, zinc bars, tergal clothes and sans serif letters so pared down that they didn't even extend to the point where a para-sitical serif might append itself: you cannot be too careful). He teased me that were I to be as modern as I wished I too should use a Bic or a Biro. He knew of course that such instruments were strictly forbidden at school on the spurious grounds that they caused children to write with enfeebled hands. Newness was a crime. Rejection of any form of technological advance was Salisbury's norm, derived maybe from the excessive temporal power wielded by the Dean and Chapter: presumably the land on which the Wilton Carpet Factory stood was not subject to that pernicious body's jurisdiction, for in 1957, during the summer of the concert at Wilton House, a weaving 'shed' with a hyperbolic paraboloid roof was erected there to the designs of Robert Townsend. With the exception of that architect's own house in the benighted garrison village of Durrington, it was the only building in south Wiltshire that declined to look backwards.

As my ineptitude as a cricketer became ever more evident Andrew Parker slipped out of my life. I seldom played the game, training more or less daily to improve my swimming, determined to excel at something. It was not as though I particularly enjoyed swimming length after length and being tested by Mr Cooper's omnipresent stopwatch. But swimming fast – freestyle and butterfly – was the only talent I possessed. It defined me as much as my hairdo and my handwriting; the former in a state of flux, the latter yet unresolved. Not playing cricket did not quash my interest in certain aspects of the game. Watching it bored me. Rather, watching players who were better than I was – that is, everyone – bored me. And I was too close to the game to appreciate its lexicon's dash. But scoring was the practice of an engrossing code: I bought books of scorepads and staged games determined by dice in which I amassed centuries or, in modest mood, was dismissed in the high eighties. My appetite for such publications as the *Picture Post Book of the Tests* was undiminished: 'Benaud in the gully takes "the catch of the century" to dismiss Cowdrey for 23'. (Lord's, 1956). I supported no team or country: tribalism wasn't the point. Australia's tour of South Africa in 1957–8 prompted no more or less involvement than Pakistan's of the West Indies the same winter. Lists of cricketers' names – P. B. H. May, P. E. Richardson, E. R. Dexter, and the initialless 'players', the *Untermenschen* from up north, Trueman, Tyson, Wardle, Washbrook – fascinated me. Were Australians such as Norm O'Neill and Graeme Hole, South Africans such as Jackie McGlew and Peter Heine, gentlemen or players? Among the many annuals I bought or browsed was the Playfair. Oh the exoticism of names: there were cricketers called Contractor and Engineer. Must be Parsi my father said – as were such surnames as Barrister, Banker and Cookwala: one of his Paiforce subalterns had been Lieutenant Doctor.

A further attraction was this annual's cover and its title page. The word Playfair was written in a typeface that imitated handwriting. It was compellingly fascinating. This typeface absorbed me. I tried to figure what was so simultaneously strange and familiar about it. I'd repetitively turn back from the Sheffield

Shield match between Queensland and New South Wales to the cover. It suddenly became clear that this was the handwriting that I had been aiming for, this very hand, these very strokes of dashing insouciance. And someone had stolen it from me before I had created it. It wasn't a case, so to speak, of baby-snatching but of foetus-snatching. The unborn letters that *I* would have formed, had I had the chance, the time, inspiration's prod, had been untimely ripped from – from where? I was looking at a usurpation, a plagiarism of my writing, yet a writing which had never existed. It had *almost* existed, I told myself, almost . . .

The artefacts that prompt this spine-bristling, neck-tingling delusion are rare. The sensation is more than a delusion. It calls into question aesthetic independence, individual integrity. It alerts us to reason's limitations. Memory slyly asserts that it is beyond our control. I have been here before. I have seen this bough before. I have felt this murmuring wind before. A few times in our life we are involuntarily enjoined to consider reincarnation as the root of déjà vu. The paranormal bullyingly gatecrashes our conscious. This was the first time in my life – in my current life – that it occurred. At that age I was doubtless susceptible to it, for was I not instructed daily that Jesus was born of a virgin impregnated by god's projectile ejaculation, that he rose from the dead, ascended to heaven, performed miracles and led a life of impeccable paranormality. I gazed and regazed at the seven letters which made up Playfair.

Most probably I had seen this font in France. Had seen it but had not, so to speak, catalogued it. I may have seen it – the verb is approximate – in the way we see the places that become the loci of our dreams. Acquired, so to speak, by the retina but not processed or only partially processed by the brain. This is a possible explanation for dreamscapes being akin to flipped or reversed photographs.

The font, a word I didn't know, was Mistral. The typographer, another word I didn't know, was Roger Excoffon. This was the man who had had the temerity to ape my potential handwriting.

Chapeau! That this quintessentially French font – as emblematic of *les Trente Glorieuses* as cobalt blue, the DS and OAS graffiti – should grace a book on the quintessentially English game of cricket is oddly apt: Excoffon was a dandy with a taste for *le style anglais* – puppytooth suits from Savile Row, Jermyn Street shoes, cravats and so on. What *is* incongruous is that Mistral should have attained such status in France, for Excoffon based it on his own hand, which is wholly atypical of a French hand. It is the very antithesis of the squat cursive web that infant pupils are taught to weave without first having learned to print separate letters. This may be why French writing tends to be ponderous, wrist-achingly laborious. It is certainly homogeneous. And a French person's writing seems seldom to develop with age. Most citizens write as they did when they were ten or twelve years old, as they were told to. Excoffon's exuberantly fluid hand might be English. Most scribes – fonts that imitate handwriting – are based in stylised calligraphy, cursive copperplate or cursive italic. Mistral was as close as a font can be to autobiography. To auto-graph. But whose autobiography? Whose autograph?

As children, once we have heard the name of, say, a dead actor or forgotten scandal – Edmund Kean, Druids Lodge – we hear it over and again, repetitively. We learn to hear it. Once we have gaped at a plane tree's bark long enough for the sight of it to adhere, it recurs. Our eyes are drawn to plane trees that would otherwise have gone unnoticed. On my first visit to St Malo after the revelation on the cover of the *Playfair Annual*, my eyes had been opened. Mistral was unmissably ubiquitous. A Jeep with four GIs drew up beside us. The driver addressed my father. I didn't hear what he said for I was transfixed by the Mistral sign on a café's awning: Le Pharo. The Jeep sped off.

'Bloody cheek!' said my father. 'Chap said [heavy American accent] "Ooh eh la root ah Wren?" Down to the junction and go right. So he turned to his *buddies*, and said: "Hey, the native speaks English."'

There was Mistral on a traiteur's van, a haberdasher's

wrapping paper, a pharmacy's fascia, in letters ten or fifty times the size of Playfair's 20 point.

Flashy, too clever by half, borderline vulgar, lacking discretion, gloriously impure . . . a minimalist's nightmare. And the nightmare's brood is Excoffon's subsequent fonts, Calypso and Choc, a scribe that derives not from mere handwriting but from scrawl, a base element which is transformed by typographic alchemy, it's like making haute couture from denim. As for Calypso – no typeface has ever boasted louder of its maker's virtuosity, so shouted about his uniqueness. These uplifting fonts, literal tonics, are the highwire acts of an artist who has nothing to be modest about, an artist whose appeal transcends the discipline he worked in.

It goes without saying that Mistral became a crib. I copied my ideal self's hand. My writing was touched by the ghost of my father's – upper case only, by Hank's more generally, not, so far as I can discern, by my mother's and by something of Excoffon's, though that something is restricted to the letters A, F, I, L, P, R, Y.

MARTIN, DOCTOR

Ancient Ulsterman a generation older than my parents. In my
mother's eyes kudos attached to him because he was related to
Naomi Jacob, a manly-looking novelist (and sometime vaudevillian) whose work, or fame, she admired. Every autumn Doctor
and Mrs Martin visited Jacob's home in Italy. When at the age
of eleven my sight was adjudged so poor that I'd have to be
prescribed glasses he tried (and failed) to console me by telling
me that although he had grown up only a few miles from them
he had not seen the Mountains of Mourne till his myopia was
corrected. Only then was he able to appreciate their beauty. I
didn't believe a word of it. I was grateful, however, for his gentle
fantasy just as I was for his amusement at my use of the word
duncher (pron. donncha), Ulster patois for flat cap which I had
learnt from the indecipherably accented, endlessly voluble, abundantly moustached, indefatigably jolly, perpetually ravenous
trainee rep called Freddy, a loyal old boy of Portora Royal, who
for several weeks in the autumn of 1956 travelled with my father
learning the ropes and leaving a trail of porkpie crust, cheese
rind, and crisp packets.

NAMES

I made lists.

Why were people called Salmon, Pike, Gudgeon, Whiting, Chubb, Grayling, Roach, Haddock, Spratt, Bass? But not Tench, Minnow, Eel, Lamprey, Perch, Carp, Huss, Plaice.

Why were people called Hogg, Fox, Wolf, Bull, Lion, Lamb, Stoat? But not Horse, Donkey, Cow, Tiger, Weasel, Otter.

Why were people called Salisbury, Winchester, Chichester, Lichfield, Worcester, Lincoln? But not Gloucester, Canterbury, Exeter, Hereford, Peterborough, Ripon.

Why were people called Hill, Vale, Field, Wood, Ford, Rivers (always plural), Bridge, Brook, Park, Street? But not Road, Track, Path, Stream, Ditch, Garden, Copse, Canal.

Why were people called Wiltshire, Hampshire, Dorset, Cornwall, Kent, Essex, Suffolk, Norfolk, Cheshire, Somerset? But not Devonshire, Sussex, Surrey, Warwickshire, Hertfordshire, Berkshire, Rutland, Buckinghamshire, Oxfordshire, Cumberland.

Why were people called Brown, Black, Green, Grey? But not Red, Pink, Yellow, Blue.

Why were people called Jay, Crow, Sparrow, Hawk, Eagle, Finch, Raven, Starling, Robin, Nightingale? But not Buzzard, Chaffinch, Chough, Jackdaw, Magpie, Seagull, Tit, Vulture, Harrier, Kingfisher, Plover.

Why were people called Butcher, Baker, Cook, Smith, Farmer, Fisher, Hunter, Fletcher, Archer, Tranter, Wright, Carter, Scrivener? But not Soldier, Sailor, Notary, Dentist, Driver, Scribe, Alchemist, Ambassador, Minstrel, Furrier, Musician, Navigator.

Why? I asked. The answer was invariable: *That's the way it is. It isn't important.* I was adjudged tiresome or frivolous or time-wasting. Thus adults masked their ignorance and, worse, their incuriosity. My obsessive insistence on the acquisition of what was deemed *useless knowledge* was a goading reproach to them.

NEW CANAL

This central Salisbury street was known simply as the Canal. It was named after a canal which had once flowed here. Flowed may not be the word to apply to what was little more than an open sewer.

Bloom's, at its eastern end, was a drapery and haberdashery store, remarkable for its exceptional dowdiness. The red-brick building was higher than most in Salisbury, a ruddy intruder from the industrial north. Its gauntness was relieved by an attic storey of pedimented windows, a clumsy attempt at the misnamed Queen Anne style. There were entrances in the Canal and in Catherine Street. It retained a system of pneumatic tubes contemporary with the building. The sales staff, also contemporary with the building, put cash and details of purchases in canisters that resembled cartridges. These were placed in an overhead tube which magically transported them to an unseen central accounting department. A further tube propelled change and receipts from that department. Tubes webbed the ceilings, turned corners, crisscrossed staircases. They popped and exhaled and whistled like gusty drafts. It was a rare technological survival, a legacy of the world inhabited by Kipps and Mr Polly, a world of deference, counter-jumpers, shiny brown paper parcels, balls of string slung from the ceiling and folded bolts of taffeta displayed like zoological specimens in curved glass cases.

The nearby branch of Richard Shops with its exciting range of pastel bouclé suits and fur-collared, raglan-sleeved coats was positively *dernier cri* (in comparison).

Whitehead, Vizard, Venn and Lush, solicitors, had premises close by Pothecary's, hairdressers. Both Leo Lush and George Pothecary had sons at the Cathedral School. Their acquaintance would improbably have extended beyond a polite greeting. In the stiff provincial hierarchy a lawyer was many rungs above a barber, even a non-barbering barber-businessman with interests in retail greengrocery (Swanage) and property (everywhere). The lawyer shot game and drove a Rover. George Pothecary drove a Jag 2.4 with spats over the back wheels for added flashiness. Whilst waiting for a haircut in a fluorescent room scented with cologne and lined with shelves of such classy haircreams as Keg 'With Bay Rum' and Tru-Gel you could read John Taylor on clothes in *Reveille* or shock articles in *Tit-Bits*, e.g. 'A Thousand Hell Holes In My Arm' by Chet Baker. You'd be lucky to get that in a solicitor's waiting room. George, his wife (from Braintree – 'there are cornfields for as far as you can see') and son Nigel, my contemporary, moved house every two years. Between houses they would live above the barber shop in a flat which may have had windows.

The Gaumont's façade was lavishly timbered, super-Tudor and, of course, late Victorian. The hall within was lavishly timbered, super-Tudor and, astonishingly, echt Tudor, if heavily restored. A swashbuckling chandelier was suspended from a cat's cradle of beams above a long bare room with randomly disposed stained-glass windows and lustrous floor tiles. Neo-codpiece and halberd tapestries were hung on the walls of the theatre itself. Its unidentifiable omnipresent smell was pleasant. It never occurred to me that this cinema was an incongruous oddity. Salisbury's other two, the Odeon and the Regal, had conventionally off-the-peg moderne façades concealing hangars. They too had their own attractive smells. It is of course possible that some sort of ambient scent was liberally dispensed. Before the advent of indoor bathrooms, launderettes and washing machines humans were frequently malodorous. Crowds reeked. Ubiquitous cigarette smoke had a use, it covered up the stench of multiple secretions. Houses smelled too. Every house had a distinctive smell. Such olfactory signatures were not necessarily unpleasant. Their source or combination of sources was rarely apparent. It was a secret, buried within the building and its occupants, who were so inured to it that they were ignorant of it.

At the *Salisbury Journal*'s offices I passed hours leafing through old editions, now crisp, now turning to dust, sewn into stiff boards. Two incidents at Salisbury railway station so fascinated me that I read their accounts time after time: the 1906 crash in which twenty-eight people lost their lives as a result of a Plymouth–Waterloo train being driven at 70 mph round a curve where 30 mph was the limit; the suicide of the painter Christopher Wood who threw himself in front of the Atlantic Coast Express in the summer of 1930. My access to this archive was sanctioned by John Bennett, the owner and editor, a watercolourist who painted in the idiom of the post-war romantics. His face reminded me of Hals's *Laughing Cavalier*, who wasn't laughing but smirking. Bennett himself however was often laughing. He was genial, gregarious. According to my father he was making up in obstinate good cheer for the barbarities he suffered as an adolescent at Malvern College. Really? It was difficult for a child to believe that the indignities of thirty years ago could still affect behaviour, *adult* behaviour. For adults existed in a world that was not contiguous with that of childhood. My prospective self, the grown-up me, would share my name but little else. Childhood and adolescence would have been long since cauterised, all scars and gaffes sealed in an oubliette, all immaturity excised.

I would no longer frequent Wilton's toyshop whose dapper, suede-shod proprietor was happily named Mr Kidwell. This is where, in the early autumn of 1956 between Suez and Hungary, I bought a tank transporter, a Thornycroft Mighty Antar Tractor (Dinky Supertoys No. 660). Price 17/6. I already owned the Centurion Tank (Dinky Supertoys No. 651) which I would load onto it.

The shop's many rooms also contained: Britain's model cowboys and Indians – the change from lead to plastic circa 1955 was momentous; .00-scale locomotives, trains and track; farms with churns and troughs and trees; Escalado; board games;

Subuteo; Meccano; Minibrix and Bayko building sets; Airfix kits; expensive imported Revell kits, which I coveted. But since I was hardly capable of completing an Airfix Lancaster such sleek modern USAF jets as the Crusader (99 pieces) and the Sabre were denied me. When I was an adult I would no longer be obliged to make my maladroit fingers struggle with centimetre-long tailfins, gun turrets, glue and transfers. Unless, that is, I turned into one of those worrying adults who protract childhood with such hobbies and invite children to share them. I determined to avoid such a fate.

Bobby Stokes's parents were tenants of The Wheatsheaf, next door to Wilton's and across the street from the Gaumont. He wore glasses so I pitied him, but nowhere near as much as I pitied myself four years later when I received my first prescription for severe myopia from an optician who was himself severely myopic, smelly and elaborately sadistic: it goes with the job. My only experience of Saturday morning pictures was in Bobby's company, at the Regal. The entirely forgettable western yarn and detective serial I saw on that sole occasion were not a patch on the delicious lunch that Bobby Stokes's mother cooked in the flat above the pub: grilled lamb kidneys with onions and mash. Nor were they a patch on my then favourite films, *West of Zanzibar* (dhows, piracy, Technicolor) and *Forbidden Cargo* (dunes, smuggling, Tower Bridge). This Saturday entertainment is supposed retrospectively to have been a weekly rite of 1950s childhood. That should be amended to 1950s working-class childhood: hence the lower middle class's fearful eschewal of it. The era's cinema audience was, like football's, predominantly working class. The films they watched were all suppressed emotion and received pronunciation. When at the end of the decade there was an outbreak of Sillitosis and the working class itself became the subject of a grittily sentimental strain of regional cinema the audience changed accordingly.

The gloomy entrance to Clark's shoeshop gave way to a skylit space lined with pale-green boxes. In the middle of it, like an altar, there rose a veneered Pedoscope. This instrument resembled a vertical coffin. The standing customer stood against it placing his shod feet into apertures. An X-ray image of the feet's ever-growing bones and the outline of the possibly, Madam, too constricting shoes was shown on a fluorescent screen on the box's top which my mother and I would take our turn to gape at. The yet unrecognised dangers of radiation were nothing beside the licence to pomposity that the device granted to the sales staff. They considered themselves doctors, scientists or, at least, foot boffins, technicians. They smugged, they chinstroked, assuming that they alone could interpret what the screen showed, they spoke with the portentousness of bad actors in a hospital drama. The assistants in Boots Lending Library, upstairs from the chemists, combined exceptionally low-level literary criticism with an officious attitude towards hygiene. A book being withdrawn would invite captious appraisal of the characters, as though they were 'real'; a book being returned would invite accusatory scrutiny. Had it been sneezed on? Had it been bled on? Had it been . . . Ah, but Boots, Quakers, didn't stock *that* sort of book. Shield-shaped plastic membership tags played some part in each transaction: held by the library till the book was returned?

Robert Stokes's premises were a hundred yards west of Bobby Stokes's home. What tons of fun were to be had from that nominal coincidence! Salisbury's most august grocer emitted a heady odour of roasting coffee beans matched only by that of the shop at the top of Above Bar in Southampton which sold nothing else. Stokes sold everything that was then available. Glacé fruits were strewn like the aftermath of an explosion at Murano. Sacks of dry goods might have been sandbags. It was hushed as a holy place. Hefty rectangles of industrial cheese-style lactic product, cylinders of Gorgonzola, Stilton, Danish Blue. Boxes of stuffing mix, gravy powder, baking powder and custard powder. As a superior grocer it naturally sold wine. 'Roodge which is red. Blank which is white. And rosy which is in between.'

If only it was always so simple. The nomenclature at Castle's

Wine Merchants was more ambitious. Infuriatingly and, no doubt, deliberately confusing. What need was there for such variety? There was nothing complicated about gin which I loathed or whisky and rum which I adored when sugared and watered. But wine! What was the point? It tasted horrible and the vintages were as perplexing as maths. I was enjoined to be proud that my year of birth had been a great year, a puzzling characterisation which didn't accord with my mother's account of its hardships. The names were some sort of litany: hock – a vague term which seemed to denote a multitude of German wines, moselle, piesporter, riesling; Yugoslav riesling; claret; burgundy; tokay; port; valdepeñas; sherry; Empire sherry; chianti in a lampshade bottle; coteaux de mascara; rioja (which I assumed meant red). These were the last years of English bottling, limited travel and qualified ignorance. An ignorance sometimes shared by a pompous caste of double-barrelled, bow-tied connoisseurs, hail-fellow-well-met *merchants* (never mere shopkeepers) and clubman journalists who blithely confused the generic with the specific, kirsch with cherry brandy. They quoted folkloric bores like Mistral, they turned a blind eye to the criminality of the French trade which routinely adulterated its products with *vins médecins* from the Maghreb, they were often both poacher and gamekeeper, twee and hearty. Bonhomie is a tiresome quality even when sincere, especially when sincere.

Miss Pinnegar, a spinster at the piano, gave dancing lessons in The Assembly Rooms. All towns with genteel ambitions built such rooms in the eighteenth century. These, on the first floor above W. H. Smith, had a roof with a cupola and a modillion cornice. Jumping on the sprung floor was fun but didn't accord with Miss Pinnegar's programme of martial daintiness. She thankfully pronounced, unexceptionably, that I was unteachable.

The Bay Tree. Outside, two potted bays and two bay windows. Inside, beyond the shop, was a café, a Saturday treat: vols-au-vent filled with creamy chicken and mushrooms, an éclair to follow. Another treat, this one free: the Southern Electricity Board showroom's window, horizontally concave in order that passers-by might feast their eyes on three-bar electric fires and the vacuum cleaners of tomorrow without their pleasure being hampered by reflections. I was captivated by the smooth geometry. (This 1930s device was also used by Heal's on Tottenham Court Road and Fox on London Wall.)

After I bought the tank transporter I went to The Bay Tree to get bridge rolls for my mother. There was a long queue. I was so thrilled by my new acquisition that I had to have a look at it. I unwrapped it impatiently, carelessly, tearing the Wilton's bag. I took the model out of its yellow box to admire it. Indulgent fellow customers smiled at my childish pride. When I got to the front of the queue I put the tank transporter back in its box and asked the shop assistant to dispose of the torn bag.

W. H. Smith's staff disapproved of my reading comics, news-papers and magazines with no intention of buying them and were quick to shoo me off the premises. They rarely, however, strayed to the back of the shop where I was able to spend as long as I wished browsing the *Wild West Comic Annual*, the *Buffalo Bill Wild West Annual*, the *Eagle Annual*, the *Tiger Annual*, *Charles Buchan's Football Annual*. After an undisturbed quarter of an hour reading I left the shop to get home for lunch.

I was hardly out on the pavement when a hand roughly grabbed my shoulder. I looked up into a woman's lipless face. She dragged me back into the shop where she accused me of having stolen the tank transporter from the toy department. She took it from me. I explained that I had bought it in Wilton's. She hissed her disbelief. Where was the receipt? Where was it . . . I realised that it must have been in the bag which I had torn, the bag I had asked to be thrown away. She said that no one would believe such a story. I was a liar. I was in serious trouble. The shop's manager was called. He was a three-piece rodent. I made his day. He couldn't believe his luck. A child criminal to persecute. What else had I stolen? How often did I steal from his shop? I was evidently a recidivist. He bundled me through a door between bookshelves along an unkempt corridor adorned with lagged pipes to a window-less office the colour of cardboard. I was instructed to write down my name, address and my parents' phone number. The rodent took the piece of paper and told me to wait. On no account was I to leave this room. I stared miserably at towers of trays full of important papers, vital box files, a hefty typewriter as old-fashioned as a sit-up-and-beg bicycle, some unwashed tea cups. After some minutes the lipless woman opened the door. She didn't speak, just stared contemptuously at me. It was indignation as much as fear which overcame me. I told her that she had only to telephone Wilton's to establish the truth. She slammed shut the door. What had happened to my tank transporter? Who was looking after it whilst I was in captivity? Time was surpassed, rendered invalid. How much later was it when the rodent returned to inform me that I had lied about the phone number? It puzzled me that he should reach such a conclusion as a result of there being no reply: perhaps basic intelligence was not among the qualities demanded of a Smith's manager. My father, I told him, was at work and my mother didn't get back from school for lunch till 12.20. He told me again that I was a liar and that for want of a parent present he had called the police. Left alone again I burst into tears. Although the door was unlocked I was so numb that escape seemed impossible. How far would I get? Would I be able to make it through the shop unseen? My sobbing was taken as an admission of guilt by my captors when they came back to let me know that the police were on their way. They gloated that it was little wonder I was feeling so sorry for myself when I was in such trouble. The policeman was dull-eyed and torpidly uninterested. He didn't regard the crime as particularly grave and suggested that if I made a clean breast of it all would be forgotten. But I had committed no crime: I once again went over the events of that miserable morning. This piqued him. If I continued to deny the theft, he threatened me, I would be up before the court, in front of the magistrates and would be taken from my parents and put in a home.

What time was it? I asked. Twenty to one. I implored him to phone my mother.

A quarter of an hour later she arrived, followed within minutes by Mr Kidwell, Wilton's proprietor, in his reassuring mustard doeskin waistcoat. My mother's fury was magnificent. The rodent cowered. The lipless woman's face was white. There was talk of legal action, of wrongful imprisonment, of bullying, of people unfit for their job. Of course all that happened was that she cancelled the newspaper and magazine order and transferred it to Gilbert's. And she persuaded virtually everyone she knew to do the same. I would, for months after, walk into the shop, smile courteously at the lipless woman, daring her to challenge me, knowing she feared me. And I would read comics safe from disturbance.

NO FOOD, FUTURE FOOD

The paper was battledress brown; thick, matt, absorbent, coarse woodpulp. Touching it made me shiver, the way that felt and flour did. My ration book was liberally stamped. The rubber stamp, the jobsworth's tool of choice, was emblematic of those slow post-war years: everything had to be stamped or franked or cancelled. In Mr Batten's shop across Harnham Bridge I would be handed the horrible book so that I, to whom it was issued, might enjoy the important responsibility of passing it personally to the ancient grocer. He stamped with the deliberation of a surgeon or horologist. I enjoyed the ritual as much as I enjoyed my allotted portion of ham, which seemed to me sufficient. I didn't want for ham, didn't knowingly want for anything. Rationing was normal. It did not occur to me that there might once have existed a time without rationing. We were already New Elizabethans by the time rationing was finally repealed in the summer of 1954. Not that it actually came to an end then. Shortages persisted for several years. However, the inadequacies of the English table of the 1950s have been much exaggerated just as its current prowess is much exaggerated.

Nonetheless it is undeniable that privations – six years of war plus a further dozen provoked initially by Stafford Cripps's smug vegetarian asceticism and subsequently by an agriculture founded in economies of scale – were one of the reasons that many English people lost touch with their indigenous cooking. A culture can be carelessly dissipated with extraordinary haste. Memories that witness better times are eliminated. One generation forgets. A second never knows. England's cooking was obliterated by a kind of revolution – vandalistic, governmental, philistine, boorish. It was a victim of the same mentality which sanctioned the destruction of thousands of buildings.

When, after quarter of a century's research, Dorothy Hartley published *Food in England* in 1954, it was already an historical document, something from a distant era, like cars with mudguards. It quite lacked the allure of Elizabeth David's early books which, although their influence is retrospectively overestimated, were a further incitement to the English middle classes to break with their dimly recalled past or pasts (whatever they had been).

Nothing, though, dissolved that link so wholly as the promise of the dawn of the advent of future-food, neo-food, spacecraft-food, *non-food*. A rational, labour-saving regime of pills, gels, capsules, suppositories, injections, drips and powders which would omit gastronomic pleasure. An omission which would hardly be noticed in circumstances where that pleasure was unknown, that is to say much of post-war England. The notion that food might be anything beyond crude fuel was abhorrent to hairshirted creatures such as Cripps and incomprehensible to the downtrodden who were obliged to eat filth in order to live, just about. Food was a resented necessity, a chore to prepare, a chore to consume.

I knew for certain that this ancient form of corporeal succour would soon be replaced by non-food. Plastics were replacing wood; cotton and wool were not needed in the age of terylene, nylon and tergal; open nibs were yesterday's nibs – today's nibs were hooded; transistors would soon vanquish valves.

Chemists' boundless researches into algae's proteins would have boundless ramifications. What had, for half a century, been wishfulness was now, according to excitable magazine articles, making its way from lab to consumer. In the new world just over the horizon there would be no school food, which was an unspoken punishment, a further means devised by adults to torment children. There would be no reeking farms and silos, no animals bred for death, no gristle, no ammoniac fish, no boiled fish, no ointment-pink sausages in Bowyers' window, no gravy like diarrhoea with a skin on it, no windowless long houses for pigs and chickens, no chickens that tasted of cod liver oil, no tapioca, no flour, no fart-flavoured cabbage, no spotted dick or MNT, no marmalade, no foul turnips, no jaundiced fat lagging round bleeding meat, no mincemeat pies, no Christmas pudding, no dining tables.

There were of course countless foods which I'd miss: I had been privy to gastronomic pleasure. But sacrifices had to be made in the name of irresistible modernity.

I would miss my mother's cooking.

It was, when I was little, still based specifically in her mother's cooking, more generally in prewar practice. In pre-Boer War practice: her disintegrating copy of Mrs Beeton's *Household Management* was published in 1888. *Farmhouse Fare – A Cookery Book of Country Dishes* (third impression) was published by The Farmers Weekly in 1936. Her copy, which cost one shilling, is dated 12 July 1939, seven weeks after she married. *Secrets of Some Wiltshire Housewives*, published in 1927, also one shilling, was compiled by the novelist, folklorist and fag-hag Edith Olivier who lived at the Daye (dairy) House in the Earl of Pembroke's park at Wilton. David Herbert described her as 'a fidgety, dynamic rodent with mulberry coloured hair'. The recipe book quite lacks the bitter whimsy of her fiction. It is an earthy reminder that an essentially peasant culture existed in England well into the twentieth century, thrifty, resourceful, unpampered.

My mother was thrifty and energetic. She salted, simmered and pressed beef tongue. She brined beef – brisket or silverside – till it was saltpetre scarlet, simmered it with dumplings and carrots. A weekly ham hock was delivered by Tom Oke, grocer of Milford Street whose business would be taken over by his nephew from far-off Weymouth, ginger Roy Osmond, who turned out not to have inherited the grocery gene. There were demarcation lines, specialisations. Bacon, ham and Bath chaps were grocer's victuals rather than butcher's. Sid the Butcher duly didn't sell them. The hock was boiled and served with buttered greens and mash: its rind was hung out to fatten Kalu's quarry. She made steak and kidney pie and steak and kidney pudding. The pastry and the suet crust were her own, ready-made were not yet available: 'homemade' was a banal statement of fact not a Luddite boast. Tripe and onions simmered in peppery milk was a dish Grandma Hogg often served when we had Saturday lunch in Shakespeare Avenue; my mother's version avoided the creamy excess which Grandma, a devotee of all things lactic, including near-rancid farm butter, strove for. Faggots and brawn came from Pritchett's, they were perhaps beyond Sid the Butcher's capabilities. Brown trout were fried in butter till their skin was crisp yet their white flesh still moist. Herring roes on toast were sprinkled with paprika (apparently its only use). Crab was a treat. Lobster was a treat for the highest of high days; the gratinated combination of Gruyère, cream, mustard and white wine outdid the flesh. We would eat salmon at suppertime for days on end after my father had caught one: grilled with herb butter or hollandaise, in salad, incorporated in a pie with hard-boiled eggs, mashed and fried as 'cakes'. Plaice was fried in butter. Battered fish and chips were deep-fried in beef dripping. So were eggs: in seconds slithery viscosity was magically transformed into a frilly rococo gewgaw. These disappeared from her repertoire after the second incident. She already had form as a chip-pan incendiarist when she put several pounds of dripping on to heat and popped out for a sharpener at The Rose and Crown where she fell in with Sid the Butcher on his lunch break: the house, remember, had a thatched roof.

Due to its expense we seldom had steak. When we did it was served with garlic butter. Chicken was a Sunday rarity. Even then the bird was an old boiler, simmered then finished by roasting. After that it provided first meat for a pilaff then stock and soup, with vermicelli. She made scones, drop scones, cheese scones, macaroni cheese, cauliflower cheese, cheese soufflés. The cheese was mousetrap, maybe Gruyère, there was little choice: forty or fifty English cheeses had disappeared since the beginning of the war. Stilton, Gorgonzola and Danish Blue were available but doubtless deemed inappropriate for cooking. She roasted pork with crackling, beef with Yorkshire pudding, and (very rarely) lamb. Veal was beaten to wafer thinness, egged and breadcrumbed. Lamb's breads were blanched and fried. Lamb's liver, heart and kidneys were staples, pig's kidneys too, and pork chops which had an ear of kidney attached to them. At Christmas there was turkey, tooth-scraping cranberry sauce, chipolatas, bacon rolls, loathsome sprouts, loathsome parsnips – *all the trimmings*, three words that cause the heart to sink. Even though I disliked the flavour of its meat I was disappointed the year that turkey was replaced by a Polish goose from Green's, a butcher with the only art nouveau frontage in Salisbury. The point being that turkey spelled Christmas and goose didn't – I was ignorant of how recent a tradition turkey was and obstinately refused to believe my mother. Christmas pudding repulsed me. Mince pies were sheerly foul.

Pheasants were hung in the kitchen to the point of putrefaction and filled the room with their odour: The First German Girl said that they reminded her of the halitotic stench in Leipzig's air raid shelters, ascribable to the wartime lack of dentists. I learnt to assume that the pheasants tasted delicious. The tongue, like any other sensory organ, is not autonomous, is susceptible to outside influence, to appreciating what it is invited to appreciate.

In the last couple of years of the 1950s her cooking changed. The availability of new produce introduced the notion of fashion, of choice, into the English kitchen for the first time since 1939. Her copy of Elizabeth David's *A Book of Mediterranean Food* was the first reprint of the first Penguin edition, 1956. That author's *French Country Cooking*, a 1959 edition. *Plats du Jour* by Patience Gray (a woman whom Mrs David detested even more than she detested Peter Mayle) and Primrose Boyd is of 1957. The latter looks as though it was rarely used, the same goes for *The Continental Flavour* by Nika Standen Hazelton ('author of *Reminiscence and Ravioli* . . . she loves to travel to different and exotic places').

Paella! Paella of a sort. Smørrebrød! Daube! Pasta! Zabaglione! Avocado vinaigrette! Snails! Artichokes! Breton onions! From the Breton beret with an onion-strewn bike and a smile who pitched up every year having taken the ferry to Southampton. Chicken kiev! A marvel of ingenuity and engineering. Cooked by her for dinner parties in high heels and reeking of Piguet's Bandit or, in times of hardship, Ma Griffe. Chicken à la King! A fricassé of chicken, mushrooms and peppers. I sucked up to Barry Still, my French teacher and headmaster, suggesting that it should be called *au King*. No, he replied, it is an abbreviation of *à la façon de King* – whoever King was, he added, testily. My parents had invited him to dinner with Honor Wigfall, a widow. He seemed to believe he was being paired off.

I would miss my father's cooking. The twice-weekly curries ended when the spices from Iraq were finally exhausted. His taste was for anything that he himself had caught or gathered. Eels from the eel trap, pheasants, hares, salmon, trout – but not pike, never pike. They were, according to the footling English classification, *coarse* fish, in his words 'hot cotton wool full of needles': no doubt it is if clumsily cooked. It was not until I had learnt in my late teens how to make quenelles and beurre blanc that he came to enjoy them. Given his habitually obstinate unwillingness to try foods which he had disliked at first taste this was a minor triumph. He had a particular antipathy to lamb's breads, which I adored. He refused to eat ceps which he reckoned slimy. Field mushrooms were different. At dawn we'd drive over the Ebble, past the Yew Tree and up the long hill to Odstock Woods where we'd park beside a track that led eventually to an isolated (and, most probably, suspicious) house in a bosky clearing. Sometimes the downland fields were so white with mushrooms that they might have been attacked by a hail of golf balls. This was where the sheep who sprang over hurdles in an attempt to lull me to sleep lived. The mushrooms were a prized component of what was not yet called 'Full English' which he'd prepare when we returned to the sound of St Thomas's bells across the misty meadows: pork sausages (not Bowyers), back bacon which he incomprehensibly preferred to streaky and refused to crisp, sauté potatoes, kidneys, fried bread. He enjoyed making dishes from leftovers: bubble and squeak; Sunday night sandwiches of chicken oysters and scraps which were always accompanied by whisky (dilute and sugared for me); shepherd's pie with meat put through a primitive mincer attached to a kitchen shelf, with Guinness, angostura bitters, Worcester sauce, sweated onions *and* raw onions. He furrowed the potato top so that when it came out of the oven it looked like heatwave plough. His omelettes were perfectly yellow: it was a point of honour not to let them brown. His everyday breakfast was egg beaten in milk. At weekends he would add a shot of brandy or rum. The latter came in handy at Christmas. He was wedded to tradition but disliked its flavour. So Christmas pudding would be crumbled and immersed in half a bottle of Lamb's Navy and *not* set light to.

I would miss: Mary Longmire's bacon and eggs, her thick soups and steak and kidney puddings; Beryl Lush's rusks, cooked overnight at the bottom of the Aga beside which Brack lay for warmth; Maureen Slater's confection which I later came to know as pan bagna; Honor Wigfall's jugged hare derived from Big-Boned Brigitte's recipe for lièvre à la royale; The First German Girl's stuffed cabbage; the prix fixe at l'Hôtel du Louvre; the staff's equine lunch at l'Hôtel des Voyageurs; the Marine Café's deep-fried eggs; the Haven Café's crab sandwiches; bismarck herring with cream and apple followed by Fullers cake at the Lyons' Corner House in Coventry Street; gratinated chicken risotto in a tiny Italian restaurant in Carlisle Street off Soho Square; my own TV Toastwich (a toasted bacon and tomato sandwich whose 'recipe' I had found in *TV Times*).

I *would* have missed all of this and more had non-food come to pass. It didn't. It failed because so much of it sought to replicate past food and was found wanting. Energen rolls were airy bread. Coffeemate tried to emulate cream, no one was fooled. This tastes *like* apple, that tastes *like* lamb, here's a potion to *remind* you of tomato. So it went on. It was analogous to Linda McCartney's horrible industrially produced vegetarian products which, many years later, aped horrible industrially produced meat products.

There would be no new foods. There are no new foods. There will be no new foods. There are only rediscovered foods. Save for those from the Midi and the Midi Moins Quart, many of the recipes collected by Mrs David and Jane Grigson throughout France are uncannily akin, in all but name and minor detail, to those in *Farmhouse Fare* and *Secrets of Some Wiltshire Housewives*. Lancashire Hotpot is baeckoff, faggots are gayettes and caillettes, 'A Very Good Supper Dish' – the recipe is from Mrs F. Roberts of Winterslow, a downland village east of Salisbury – is gratin dauphinois. And so on. Recipes that the English forgot or merely abjured in the collective conviction that what came from elsewhere was necessarily superior.

Even if it meant sharing it with the boche, France, a nationalistic nation of 50 million people of whom 55 million were resistants, retained a bloated pride in its kitchen, or kitchens: the cooking of, say, the Artois has little in common with that of the Béarn, nor that of the Dauphiné with Brittany's, the first I became familiar with. Brigitte, the first French person I met, was a gourmande from Vannes. She was indeed, as they used to say, a big-boned girl, employed in an indefinable capacity in exchange for accommodation and English Conversation by Edwina Neck at the shabby genteel house she was renting in the Woodford Valley, i.e. the Avon valley north of Salisbury. Stonehenge was a few miles away. Brigitte compared it unfavourably with Carnac. There's some justice in that comparison. But Brigitte was simply expressing the prejudice of a Breton supremacist. As for English cooking! She sighed, shook her head. And salad cream – it was nothing short of barbaric. She got on with making an educative vinaigrette: 'On fait le mélange . . .' She uttered this mantra so often that my father was thereafter unshakable in his belief that a vinaigrette should be called *un mélange*. She cooked *savoury* pancakes with cheese and scraps of ham and conjured delicious soups from whatever was cheap or scroungeable. There was no money to spare.

Like her friends Mona Godsmark, Dorry Musto, Peta Carmalt and Honor Wigfall, Edwina Neck was a single parent. None of these hardy unpretentious women was particularly concerned to keep up appearances. Rather they wanted to lead a life of the material standard they would have enjoyed had they not been war widows or divorcees or the mother of an illegit (an ugly contemporary usage).

They were powerful characters, middle or upper middle class by birth, intelligent, outspoken, defiantly untwee, mostly deficient in formal education, mostly unqualified for anything other than the housewifery which had lately eluded them. Despite the presence off-stage of well-heeled and often fairly grand relations they were perennially on their uppers. Occasionally there was talk of a man friend but these men friends were invisible men, maybe unpresentable. Peta Carmalt, a radio producer, had more than one man friend and led a fast life – I knew this because she wore plaid trousers and her home was a Maida Vale flat, and flats, especially in Maida Vale (how did I know this?), still retained the dodgy etiquette attached to them sixty or seventy years previously: I had never seen a flat and was uncertain about what such a thing looked like and what the nature of its particular iniquities might be. What was a fatherless son? My appetite for Maida Vale's exoticism would not be sated for many years. More usually Mona, Dorry et al. tended neither to own property nor to have a sufficiently reliable income to rent. They relied on friends, on hard-sought, surprised distant relations. They moved around a lot, taking live-in jobs or ones that at least provided accommodation and maybe an education for the children.

Edwina Neck was employed as matron at a school where boys who could pass neither the eleven plus to a grammar school nor common entrance to a public school were sent by middle-class parents anxious to spare themselves the ignominy of having a son at a secondary modern. Such establishments, founded entirely in fearful snobbery, abounded in the Fifties and Sixties. In Salisbury there were St Probus (uniform: magenta and grey) and, almost adjacent, the confusingly named Modern School (red and green). Nearby were Hurn Court, Embley Park, Stanbridge Earls. Her next job was at a *genuine* public school, albeit one for boys who couldn't get into the public school of their parents' choice. She was jocularly, ungallantly but correctly said to owe this position to having been the headmaster's 'groundsheet' when he was an army officer.

Mona Godsmark was 'companion' to an author. For four Christmases on the trot my parents received an effusively signed copy of Compton Mackenzie's latest. That particular strain of unreadability ceased when she left his employ in Edinburgh to move back south. She then lived with her son in a succession of 'private' hotels.

Now and again one of these women might demonstrate her entrepreneurial ineptitude by helping to set up a language school or taking in PGs (problematic, drunk, broke) or lending a hand at running a restaurant or opening an antiques shop and ending up even more out of pocket than when she had embarked on the misadventure. They sometimes had to do a flit. Gentlefolk? Maybe. But distressed – never! For all their pecuniary worries and their concerns that the covert sources of school fees might dry up they were a spirited bunch who signally disallowed themselves outward signs of despair. Putting a brave face on it was in the grain. The next cloud would be the silvery one. And in the meantime there's always gin-and-It, Seniors, the races.

Among Honor Wigfall's many and dispersed friends was an Admiral Purvis whose house was high above Dartmouth near the Britannia Royal Naval College, a place that I might, it was hinted, one day aspire to. His son, a pupil at Clifton College, had, at the age of sixteen, been diagnosed as diabetic. The school was unwilling to have a diabetic boarder, so the family had temporarily moved to Bristol in order that Andrew could complete the last year and a half of his education as a day boy. The Dartmouth house had been let but the tenants would not move in till late September 1952. Honor, forever on the qui vive for a freebie, persuaded the Admiral to lend it to her for the month of August *so that it would be looked after.*

The party comprised: Honor; Victoria Wigfall (12); Freddy Wigfall (10); Edwina Neck; Jeremy Neck (10); my mother; me (5). There is no game fishing in the Dart estuary. Sea fishing didn't interest my father. So he had declined Honor's invitation.

The house had been let more or less unfurnished. It was Edwardian, tall, uncomfortable. Like all armed forces houses, whether owned or rented, it was neglected, shabby, bereft of domestic imagination's trace. There were two staircases, one for servants, nooks, long built-in cupboards under the eaves, hidden rooms, lofts. It was an ideal playground for children. The other children, however, did not want to play with me. There was after all a five-year age gap between the two boys and me. I was hurt by their shunning me.

'Do you like me?' I asked them and asked so often that they taunted me with those words, 'Do you like me do you like me do you like me . . .' Victoria Wigfall repeatedly sang: 'Peanut sitting on a railroad track. His heart was all a flutter. Along came a train. Choo choo. Peanut butter!' She ridiculed me for not knowing what peanut butter was. When I entered a lavatory whose door Freddy Wigfall had failed to lock he dipped his hand into the bowl he was squatting on and hurled a fat turd at me. It missed, splattered on the already grimed wall. My mother was vaguely aware of my misery though not of the precise humiliations I was subjected to (mostly being shut in cupboards): needless to say I had been forcibly instructed by my tormentors not to 'squit'. It was a relief to walk with her down the steep streets to the quayside where a red-painted World War One mine had been transformed into a collection box in which I put pennies to help dead sailors' families: every time a glass clinked a sailor died at sea. I suffered an increasingly painful earache. One afternoon my mother rowed me – the only time in my life that she rowed me – to a headland where there were caves, inaccessible save by water. I hoped that Freddy and Jeremy did not get to hear of them, fearing they would exploit their potential as a place to strand me. I hoped too that my father would be proud when he learned that I fished from that boat and, subsequently, from a jetty with a nylon line baited with a worm. No takers. My earache was so bad that I cried through the night to the amused irritation of Freddy and Jeremy. Honor caught the rickety garage's door frame on the bumper of her car as she reversed out of it, causing the structure to collapse groaning onto the ground and onto the car's bonnet in a turbid pall of dust and rot. I took solace in the sandy trails through the furze, gorse, heather and pine at Blackpool Sands: this is where the titular character of Masefield's yarn *Jim Davis* encounters night-riders wearing bee-skeps. When I complained to my mother about my earache she ignored me, assuming that I had self-pityingly invented a surrogate for my misery. We visited the lagoon at Slapton. We took the ferry to Kingswear. The children tired of tormenting me. The earache was agonising. When, after we had returned home, my mother deigned to take me to Dr Barker he immediately diagnosed an abscess, hence my lifelong partial deafness. Even though I could understand that my mother had been negligent I was shocked by Dr Barker's accusatory rudeness. I couldn't bear to see her being admonished with boorish pomposity. (Years later he told me that my hay fever was due to my blowing my nose too vigorously. On my sixteenth birthday his Roman Catholic partner with a naval full-set, Jim Drummond, sent my parents a letter advising them to warn me of the dangers of venereal diseases. When my father suffered a strange growth in his throat Barker said there was nothing to worry about although breathing was obviously impaired. Jim Laing took one look at it, put my father in his E-type,[19] drove him to Odstock Hospital, administered an anaesthetic and cut out of his throat an accretion of chalk the size of a golf ball. Such obstructions

19 The car had a Clarence House sticker on its windscreen enabling him to park there whenever he wished. An odd but useful gift from the Queen Mother in gratitude for the splendid face job that Jim had done for her. A few years later he did a second.

were not uncommon in an area where chalk was ubiquitous and water hard.)

Do You Like Me remained Victoria Wigfall's taunt until I was ten, when she relented and gave me a copy of Tab Hunter's *Young Love*. I thanked her by pouring too much water into a glass of lemon barley water so drenching a colander full of salad leaves in the stuff. She married a French hydrologist who worked on a series of politically murky and ecologically questionable agronomic projects in west Africa.

After Sandhurst Freddy Wigfall was commissioned into the 17th/21st Lancers. His first few years as an officer were typical of that era. Drinking, skiing, riding to hounds, riding in point to points, gambling, field sports. Then, in August 1969, British troops were deployed in Northern Ireland.

Jeremy Neck served an apprenticeship on a local newspaper then worked for *Timeform*, *Horse and Hound* and *Sporting Life* before becoming a racing correspondent for a succession of national papers. He marries into his sport: his wife is the daughter of a knighted trainer.

A European couple die in their bed as a consequence of an arson attack on their villa in the Dakar suburb of Mermoz in June 1971. There is no doubt in the mind of the investigating officer that the crime is linked to the husband's occluded Francafrique connections and to government ministers taking backhanders. Indeed there is a sour joke that so many pots de vins *have been offered that a major irrigation project is oenological, that it's turning water into wine.*

Late November 1971. An off-duty army officer in an unmarked car on the way to Stranraer after a weekend's grouse shooting near Moniaive is ambushed. Speculation is that he was stopped by what appeared to be a police vehicle. He is taken from his car and shot twice through the head. The execution bears the Provisionals' hallmark.

A racing journalist writes a sensationalist story in the spring of 1973. It is based on what he has learned from a disaffected stable lad, from an apparently unrelated veterinary source, from a receipt in Portuguese sent him in the post. The story claims that a trainer, whom he does not name, is doping certain of his horses with a performance-enhancing drug synthesised in Brazil for which there is yet no means of detection. A year later he is found dead a couple of hundred yards away from the Lambourn pub where he has had an early evening drink. He has been struck by a vehicle. Not by chance, for it then reversed over him.

The fourth and final part of this entertainment is an account by an evidently damaged, paranoiac, vengeful psychotic of the wrongs done to him as a child on holiday, by three older children, in a house of killing stairs, twenty years previously.

OLD MANOR

Jim Laing – familially and intellectually unrelated to his compatriot namesake Ronnie, aka R. D. – suggested, not entirely frivolously, that there was a national glut of psychiatrists because entry to medical schools was not dependent on manual dexterity. So applicants who had not spent their childhood making models, practising marquetry and macramé, sewing and weaving were admitted even though there was no certainty that they would possess an aptitude for surgery. When they graduated the maladroit had to choose between general practice and psychiatry. Too many chose the latter. The supply of psychiatrists exceeded demand. They were, then, obliged to foment a demand. This meant inventing mental illnesses, novel disorders, detecting previously undiagnosed syndromes in order to create patients.

In the 1970s certain principles of anti-psychiatry were cautiously incorporated into the mainstream of the over-practised discipline. This tentative trickle would, somewhat improbably, be lent momentum by Margaret Thatcher's successive administrations which were ideologically committed to dismantling institutions (professions, including medicine, trade unions etc.) and being seen to cut public spending (hospitals, tertiary education, social housing). Everything should be rendered accountable to the merciless god The Market.

So psychiatric patients became customers of psychiatry. They were released into society, a chimera which didn't require financial maintenance. These *consumers* of Care In The Community whittled their life in squalid B&Bs, spikes, hostels, public libraries, parks, drop-in centres, day centres, shopping malls, churches, McDonald's (which had presciently just arrived in Britain). A few killed. Some screeched and laughed and trembled and fought and geeked and gurned and scratched and neglected to self-medicate in public. The majority, however, exhibited no such bedlamite tics.

Even Stephen Dorrell's wantonly inspired decision that Care In The Community should be renamed Spectrum Of Care could not save it. But for all its flaws its unintended consequences were tonic. It helped quash the stigma that attached to mental illness if only by causing us, the so far unafflicted, to measure ourselves against those sufferers on public display, by persuading us that we all have the potential to go that antic route, by suggesting just how close the drop to the abyss lies. It showed what had, since the institutionalisation of madness, been hidden.

Hitherto those deemed mentally ill existed behind high walls where they might be lobotomised, drugged, straitjacketed, subjected to electroconvulsive therapy. They were neither seen nor heard. And they were seldom heard of. Mental illness was as much a taboo as sex. It was a source of disgrace. It brought shame on families. The lack of sympathy afforded the mentally ill seemed to derive from the comforting assumption that they had brought it on themselves, that they had actually chosen their quasi-criminal sentience and behavioural anomalies. They were bogeys who, in the night, might infect the sane with their bad madness were they not sectioned.

The Old Manor in Wilton Road had previously been known as Fisherton House Lunatic Asylum. According to its historian Gertrude Smith it was a 'private madhouse', the largest such asylum in England. Six hundred patients were detained there, some of them criminally insane. It was *the bin*. The preface *loony* was redundant.

Avert your eyes, madness travels at the speed of light. On both sides of the road there were high, stockbrick walls with drifts of dust describing downward curves against them. No one swept the pavements. No one walked them. It was haunted by spectres of the living. This was a place to hurry past.

The frosty demeanour of a pompous, churchy, tall, short-tempered, dome-headed, breast-pocket-handkerchief-brandishing solicitor carrying a shotgun in a tan canvas and brown leather slip was attributed not to his having a daughter who had been confined to the hospital for more than a decade, but to people knowing about it.

Mr Reid was of my parents' age. He lived with his rich elderly parents in Downton. He 'had been in the Old Manor'. He masticated perpetually, baring perfectly brown teeth. He rode an overladen bicycle dressed in a long dun rubberised mackintosh (slightly perished): were these signs of madness? Was his psoriasis a dermal sign of madness? I feared that my flaking wrists and ankles were the stigmata that presaged a sojourn behind dusty walls.

Lest they land me there I never admitted to suffering hallucinations even though I wanted to understand why, say, trees, huts, vehicles, cows were transformed as I stared at them. They did not become anything other than trees, huts and so on. It was, rather, that they were, suddenly, more themselves, hitting a higher register of existence. Chromatically intense, vital, above all perspectivally anomalous, moving yet not moving – my eyes and brain conspired to reveal objects as they are shown in a dolly-zoom.[20] It astounded and disturbed me, an unasked-for treat that I apparently granted myself yet over which I had no control: oh, to hallucinate at will! I was merely an involuntary illusionist whose rapt audience of one was eager for more. There was an evident kinship with masturbation, another gift from within which was accompanied by the warning to keep it secret because it, too, leads to the bin and to blindness or at least myopia. Sure enough, my hallucinations coincided with a startling deterioration in my sight, which only occurred after I had discovered masturbation.

The Revd Keith Wedgwood, succentor of Salisbury Cathedral,

---

20 I realised the correspondence when I saw the transfixing opening shot of Alain Resnais's *Muriel* (1963), which has a Hans Werner Henze score and locations in the HLMs (social housing projects) of Boulogne-sur-Mer where Franck Ribéry would grow up. The rest of the film is all post-colonial guilt and jump-cuts.

was, after all, right to have counselled against it in the talk about 'things' he gave us the term we left the school (attendance obligatory). He was no doubt charged with this pointless task because he was a scholar of the Christian approach to masturbation, of the theology of onanism rather than its practice. If only I'd heeded him rather than smirk inwardly. But too late, Keith, too late! As if to indicate to us how grown up we were he delivered his grave homilies in the low-ceilinged sitting room of his house beside Choristers' Green and Mr Searle's sentry box. We listened to blatant denials of corporeal inevitability based in Levitical superstition and in the churchy hatred of pleasure. Did this prickly fellow who, 'faith' apart, was not stupid, really believe that we'd observe his ponderous warnings? Quite probably yes. Because we remained straightfaced, undissenting, maybe he was able to delude himself that our genitals would indeed do god's will, that our hands would be stayed by morality's manacles, that fear (of retribution, disease, shame and – top of the pile, always the winner – *uncleanliness*) would trump auto-concupiscence which is actually deflected concupiscence: we do not think of ourself but of the yet unattainable labial lips or buccal lips which will one day replace the ever-strengthening fist – we hope. He enjoined us to not to succumb to the temptations cast by the mysterious practice of something called premarital intercourse, which, unless we were very much mistaken, sounded like shagging and fucking. It was ungodly and against the teachings of the church, it was morally corrupt, corporeally unhealthy, socially irresponsible and not for gentlemen in the making. So, like cigarettes and drink, it was to be urgently pursued.

Wedgwood's relationship to the Cathedral School was close but ill-defined, some pastoral post no doubt. He was sleeker, younger and more urbane than most of the cathedral's clergy. But he had the usual dogmatic piety and the usual preposterous 'faith', i.e. unimaginative irreason, low-grade fantasy, wishful angelism, empiricism's refutation, subscription to unsubstantiatable, half-witted folk myths, the vanquishment of doubt, pitiable certainty. If you are so crass that you believe in god, annuncia-tion, assumption, transubstantiation, in Jesus-the-sometime-mass-caterer rising from the dead and all the rest of the risible, offensive shit, you must find it easy to believe anything, absolutely anything; to believe, for instance, that boys on the point of puberty will observe strictures which their strutting glands are bound to ignore. We were initiates of *Kamera* and *QT*. We envied Gerald Deacon whose father was a newspaper and magazine wholesaler. His warehouse in Brown Street, near the Darby and Joan Club, was a hamper of forbidden fruit. There was nothing we didn't know about retouching. There was nothing we didn't want to know about the retouched. Who were they, these fallen women? (That epithet was still current in 1960.) Where did we find them? Where were they? Were they in St Michael's Home School, a couple of hundred yards from the Old Manor, across the railway lines in Churchfields?

No. The girls there were sad and pallid. They were punished for the mewling consequence of premarital intercourse by being treated as prostitutes and granted 'sanctuary' in an 1860s building girt with fire-escapes. They were fed slops, reminded of their sin, made to march in crocodiles of guilt and submit to religious instruction. Their babies were forcibly taken for adoption. This near-prison, which existed till 1968, had similarities to Magdalene Laundries, those concentration camps with a lilting brogue. The gulf between St Michael's downtrodden inmates and the objects of my sexual curiosity could not have been wider and became a matter of vaguely Gladstonian shame: this was how men (and boys and nuns) could debase girls. Such a realisation would have delighted Keith Wedgwood, for in that moment the desire to be a sexual human was briefly tempered by the incipient Samaritan, the moral rescue dog.

OLD MILL

On Saturday 18 April 1936 about fifty people, among them my
father and Peter Lucas, attended a dance recital given by the art
student Gwyneth Johnstone at the Old Mill Club at West
Harnham. She was accompanied on piano by her mother Norah
Back and watched by her father Augustus John. At 11.20 the
club was raided by several members of Salisbury's zealous police
force. Although there was no hint of impropriety or actual
intoxication Augustus John, Hugh Dixon, Robert Giddings of
The Moat, Britford (subsequent occupants: H. Wilson Sheppard
and Hugh de S. Shortt), Frederick Maitland-Heriot of Timsbury
Manor, Romsey (subsequent proprietor: Oliver Cutts) and Dr
Patrick Wallace of the Machine Gun Concentration Camp at
Warminster appeared before Salisbury Magistrates Court on 26
May. Each was fined £5 for consuming intoxicating drink during
non-permitted hours. The club's proprietor Elspeth Fox-Pitt (née
Phelps) was the daughter-in-law of Augustus Pitt-Rivers, 'a lady
of gentle birth and breeding'. £30 with £60 costs and 'struck off
the register'. (She was a once-celebrated couturier and costume
designer who had been involved in a suit after she was sacked
from her fashion house when it was bought by Paquin in the
1920s.) In her opinion the club ought to have been run by a
fierce sergeant-major, which would have *so* delighted such
habitués as Stephen Tennant, Cecil Beaton, Tom Mitford, Lord
David Cecil and David Herbert. Mrs Fox-Pitt staunchly denied
rumours of 'nudist dancing' and traffic in drugs. The *Salisbury
Journal* was obliged to print an apology stating that even though
they had been present neither Lady Hulse (Westrow's wife) nor

Lady Juliet Duff ('a four mast schooner with mink sails')[21] was a member.

The Old Mill's reputation took years to recover. No one could make a go of it. It changed hands frequently. Even though it had regained a club licence, twenty years after that night it still excited the constabulary's attention. (Architectural-historical aside: John's friend, the stylistically various Oliver Hill had drawn up plans for an extension to this club, The Old Mill, which are shown in Alan Powers's exemplary monograph of that architect. The cause of its not being built is unmentioned; it was almost certainly unknown to Powers, as was the connection which got Hill the commission.)

By the time I had overcome my infantile fear of Dog West Harnham (not least because the dog was no longer in attendance – dead, I hoped) it was owned by a lavishly strawberry-marked man. He was repeatedly denied a full licence, which no doubt accounted for his choleric mien. He wasn't as frightening as the dog had been. Nonetheless he was perpetually and ostentatiously watchful, as though convinced that merely by hanging about near the sluices and weir, gazing at the foaming water, I was determined to inconvenience him. I wasn't. Observing the patterns water makes is like decrypting a log fire. Faces, gargoyles, grotesques are fleetingly created by the flames, the white water and our fancy. That log is a hare in profile. That spume is a lion's head. See the leaping ghosts and dancing primates! I took an innocent delight too in the hydraulic ingenuity of the feeders, carriers, leets and gutters which drew water from the river upstream of the mill and caused it to flow at several levels across the floated meadows. The intricate system had yet to fall into the disrepair it suffered in the Seventies and Eighties (from which it has been rescued). There were still ancient, nearly crippled,

---

21 Duff said that Cecil Beaton was *'like a very successful Parisian madam who had decided to give it all up, move to the English countryside, and take all her bordello belongings with her'*.

forever stooping drowners tending the sluices and hatches: Mr Evans and our neighbour Mr Thick.

My father would row to the Old Mill. Or rather to within sight of it, for in the summer months, the boating months, the river below the mill was wide and shallow. The water had fulfilled its function. It was no longer fuel, no longer worth controlling. It went its own way. So the boat's hull scraped against the gravel bed. I would leap into the water to relieve the load and push it clear. Then we'd float downstream past Alligator Island which wasn't an island but a willowed tongue of land, strictly an artificial isthmus, bordered by the river and a shaded leet wide enough to take the boat if punted with an oar. This was where he was forever Bevis. This was Stalky territory. That anyway is how my father thought of the Old Mill's environs, a world away from a smoky, beery club visited by the police. He had done his utmost to excise the memory of the night of 18 April 1936. When my mother (who was not there, they had yet to meet) once referred to it in front of me he responded with tetchy embarrassment which was surprising given the inoffensiveness of her casual allusion. But I had yet to learn that there is no equivalence between cause and effect, that they can be waywardly disproportionate. I had no conception that recall of a distant incident had the power to wound esteem and, further, the self carefully constructed in the image of the sporting countryman. Besides, I thought a raid on a club sounded rather thrilling. I was easily pleased.

OSMINGTON MILLS

It was a scuddy billowy day when I ate the whale. Not the whole whale – I was only four – but enough whale to get the idea of the whale's quiddity, to get a mnemonic fix, which persists down the years and is ocular and palatal and olfactory and haptic. Grace and Edgar Meluish who cooked the whale in a pie the size of a car tyre were standard-issue bohos of the era. They made bad pottery, sold unprovenanced antiques, ran empty cottage restaurants, welshed on debts, specialised in flitting from one grand ramshackle house to the next dilapidated manor. They rarely paid rent. They often threw parties (bring a bottle!). The whale pie party was on the beach at Osmington Mills close by the chalk-work of George III on horseback which might have been cut by Stubbs. We sat on undulating banks of stones. The cliffs were dirty, pocked candlewick spreads, as though southern England's nature were in mimetic thrall to cheap furnished rooms. Edgar wore earsplitting tweeds and a knotted Windsor. Grace's fubsy arms extended sleevelessly from smocked shoulders to lilac nails. When the two of them lifted the butter muslin from the pie they did so with dance steps, daft pride. The pastry was tan and wan. The English could as surely undercook flour as they could overcook meat.

Edgar had levelled a shelf of stones. The pie, the pale wheel, sat on it in an enamel baking dish that might have been a giant's chamber pot or a vessel for soaking clothes. It was a stench associable with those functions that was released when Edgar made the first incision. A gust struck me, squatting. The smell was that of cat food, of faeces, of bleach. The meat came in grey chunks, mighty dice of eraser rubber. They were set in a dense opaque paste that might have been petroleum jelly. Whale is as gelatinous as pig. It is also faintly granular, another property it shares with pig that has been long cooked. The meat looked smooth and fibreless. The taste was only vaguely marine. It was the oxymoronish combination of the gelatinous and the granular which rendered it so foully emetic. My wedge was about eight inches long and its share of the pie's circumference was perhaps three inches. It was a lot of whale to lose under pebbles. The rest of the party was more candid about its antipathy, although my father, who had eaten hedgehog and badger, tucked in dutifully, and so did Grace and Edgar's teenagers, presumably inured to a diet of exotic species.

Since then I've eaten the tripe of kine and sheep, sea slug (bêche-de-mer), ox brain, lamb brain, pig brain and trotter and ear, duodenum and other intestines, spinal cord, flying fish eggs, beaver, salmon entrails, testicles (*rognons blancs*), locust et cetera. But there is a limit to omnivorous curiosity and carnal abandon. Whale is mine. Not another cubic metre will ever pass my lips.

OWLETT'S END

Please, I'd whine, please don't let's go through Upavon and Pewsey (where the canal is pastoral, unaffecting, harmless).

Let's go through Cholderton and Collingbourne.

This eastern route to Marlborough crossed the Kennet and Avon Canal near Burbage. It was the first canal I'd seen.[22] Duckweed smothered the sluggish water, the decaying water, the foetid water. Duckweed's primacy was threatened by red bloated inner tubes, rusted chunks of metal, armatures of nothing, aquatic scrap. The straightness was unyielding and perverse. It disappeared into a distant tunnel of trees, shrubs. It prompted a thrilling fear that I retain: I longed to see it, I loathed to see it. A few miles away in Savernake Forest, surrounded by cypresses, there stands a creepily lugubrious church redolent of Victorian death.

Every couple of months on a Sunday we visited Evesham, two hours and eighty miles north.

Marlborough and Swindon were fixed points, linked by a Roman road through Ogbourne St Andrew and Ogbourne St George: Og was a satisfying initial syllable. I admired the eye surgeon John Ogg; would be fascinated by the clumsy and delicate pianist John Ogdon; was stirred by the meaningless west country cry of Oggy, Oggy, Oggy. North of Swindon there was again a choice of routes. They diverged in Stratton Saint Margaret at the signwriter's crossroads. Again, the eastern route was more engaging. My father never failed to remind me that the improbably

22 My curiosity about these things which were like rivers but which were not rivers had been aroused by a spoil heap of the uncompleted Southampton–Salisbury Canal, 4 miles SE of the latter at Whaddon. It forms a high bank topped by Scots pines and might be taken for a defensive work.

baroque small town of Highworth enjoyed Betjeman's approval. (It was in this context that I first heard his name.) We crossed the nascent Thames at Lechlade. That town's new public lavatory had been personally inaugurated by the Mayor. The very name of the next village, Filkins, sang of maypoles and ribbons. The name of its squire didn't: this was the despicable Sir Stafford Cripps Bt, sometime ambassador to Moscow, useful idiot, Marxist Quaker and hairshirted fellow traveller who as Attlee's chancellor imposed his highminded asceticism on Britain and who, more than anyone, exemplified the state's usurpation of noblesse oblige.

Burford: a tea shop and wisteria town, all limestone and quaintness, a presage of the Cotswolds to come. *The Countryman* was edited by Cripps's son at premises in Sheep Street. Hank subscribed to this worthy magazine whose covers of rough green paper were as unpleasant to the touch as a ration book. You could feel them doing you good.

All around this fringe of the Cotswolds there was a kind of country which, so far as *The Countryman* was concerned, might as well have not existed. Not the country of oolitic hegemony and picturesquely crumbling walls but of row upon row of Nissen huts in woodland and parkland, besides runways and ranges. Former army and air force quarters, these rudimentary wartime buildings now served as Polish Resettlement Camps, DP camps by another name. Here, Poles who had fled Hitler to join the Allied cause reaped the reward of the freedom they had fought for – ablution blocks with asbestos ceilings. Thus was the promised land. But now that Poland had been ceded to Cripps's chum Stalin they had nowhere else to go other than these forlorn places, reminders of the old country's industrial death plants where many of their kin had perished: so they shouldn't grumble. These temporary dwellings were still there in the 1960s.

Stow on the Wold where the wind blows cold.

And where, according to my father, in 1953 or 54 a prep school vanished overnight.

Many such schools were simply businesses run by bluff

chancers who took advantage of an ample supply of invariably unheated, barely electric'd country houses which their owners could no longer afford to maintain. They took advantage too of an ample supply of otherwise unemployable ex-officers and otherwise unemployable ex-pupils; these sadistic oddballs were transformed into 'masters'. Ignorance was passed down from one generation to the next. Qualified teachers were scarce, graduates almost unknown. The domestic staff were dipso bulldykes. Pastoral care was when Sir invited you to give him a hand job.

The school on the edge of Stow did not own the house it occupied. The rent went unpaid. Local merchants' bills went unpaid. As the debt mounted, the headmaster, on the point of a breakdown, took drastic action. He rented another house, 100 miles south in Somerset, and by cover of night moved the school to it. Pupils, beds, desks, books, goalposts . . . all were packed into a convoy of coaches and pantechnicons. No forwarding address was left. The parents, many of them overseas, were not informed.

Beyond Stow: the open high road north; watercolour clouds; morose sheep; gust-buffeted swifts. This was one of several places which my father would enthusiastically describe as being *on the roof of the world*. Any sensation of transcendence or sublimity was immediately quashed by the low comedy of Snowshill being pronounced Snozzle. Laugh. The Fish Inn's weird pyramidal roof was that of a dovecote or oast. At the bottom of the curling road down Fish Hill lay Broadway, a village of such emetic tweeness that it might be a dream of F. L. Griggs or Norman Jewson – which, of course, it was: a stage set derived from an arts and crafts illustration showing the Village of Yore, the Garth of Days Beyond Memory, a distant paradise of adzes, smocking and deference.

My grandmother's late Victorian terraced house was in Bengeworth – Evesham east of the Avon. It had no bathroom. There was a tin bath in the kitchen, an outside lavatory, two rooms and kitchen downstairs, three rooms upstairs. Her musty, multiply curtained bedroom was at the front. Every surface was covered with fabric. Formless garments on hangers, doilies and samplers, cushions and crochetwork, a complicated abundance of bedclothes, shawls everywhere. The Virgin Witch Kitty's bedroom was in the middle. She had never left home. Uncle Hank's was at the back. He had hardly left home. He returned every weekend of his life from his digs in Burton-on-Trent. He would continue to do so after his mother died in 1962. Only then was the back bedroom converted into a frugal unheated lino'd bathroom smelling of coal-tar soap. My grandmother knitted in winter and gardened in summer in an old person's garden full of old person's herbs and flowers: sunflowers, honeysuckle, hollyhocks, phlox, foxgloves, lovage, thyme, sage. The garden was long and narrow. The rectangular beds were evenly spaced, partially bordered by metal edgers whose lacy patterns were coarsened by decades of paint. Between the beds were the stems of an arterial cinder path that stretched to the garden's end where a high gate in a high hedge opened onto a lane. Here sheds and garages were dwarfed by a green, corrugated-iron, potato warehouse. Its hangar-like scale was boorish, its windowlessness sinister. At that far end of the garden Auntie Kitty grew runner beans and tomatoes. She turned the tomatoes into vinegary chutney and vinegary ketchup. Dozens of seldom sampled jars and bottles were stored in a walk-in cupboard under the stairs. It was my favourite place in this house of tense misery and ancient odours.

Can they have lived, day upon day, in such emotional straits? With such bereavement of pleasure? With such smug incuriosity about the world beyond Port Street?

Possibly that misery only descended on the house with our arrival. Possibly our intrusion into their hermetic world exacerbated the collective despond.

Possibly the awkwardness of their greetings and the familial gaucheness were compounded by my father and, especially, my mother on her infrequent visits. She was not a blood relation so she contended with the insurmountable handicap of not being a Meades, save by marriage. Further, her pursuits were urban and indoors. Worse, she had stolen my father, led him far from bosom and hearth. And he had gone all too willingly, he had chosen her over them.

The place where Uncle Wangle lived might be more distant than Salisbury but this house was still his home and Poor Frail Auntie Ann's too, for she was an orphan and had nowhere else to call home, no one else to call family. Poor Pale Auntie Ann was accepted because she wore no make-up, because she was meek, because she willingly succumbed to the mother-fixated neurosis of Auntie Kitty, Uncle Hank and Uncle Wangle, because she did not question the delusional familial myth that Auntie Kitty had made a 'sacrifice' to stay at home and look after Mum who (my mother suggested) was quite capable of looking after herself. My mother would add that Auntie Kitty was ugly, idle and spiteful, a sponger who had even invented a sickness to avoid any kind of work during the war. She would not say any of this in front of my father, who showed an unreciprocated, groundless loyalty towards these miserable people whose blood he shared and whom he had escaped from.

And he would escape from them again, within minutes.

Those Sundays we would arrive at Northwick Road at about 11.30. The kitchen and dining-room windows would already be opaque with lunch condensation. Uncle Hank would have gone to a pub. We would stand around awkwardly. I would be offered the choice of staying with Auntie Kitty and Grandma or coming to look for Uncle Hank. I opted for the latter. My mother, if present, would come too, in defiance of the code of the Meades. I'm not going to skivvy for that parasite she'd say out of my father's hearing. By 11.45 we were on Uncle Hank's trail. This was far preferable to hanging around Northwick Road. Soon I'd be comforted by those essential staples of period colour, a bottle of fizzy pop and crisps with damp salt in a blue paper twist, sitting in the car outside a pub.

The Crown on the Avon's right bank near the abbey gardens: a hotel of car parks, drainpipes, yards, dustbins and little future.

The Fleece at Bretforton whose landlady Lola was a character, an appellation I assumed to be a synonym for throaty old bag smothered in panto rouge. Had she not drawn chalk circles around the hearth, witches would have come down the chimney. They were evidently easily deterred. Besides, Auntie Kitty wouldn't have fitted into the flue.

The Lizzie at Elmley (never Elmley Castle) where the landlord's nephew Tony, a cruise-liner steward, came to recuperate from a tropical fever and was still there half a century later, his name over the door now.

The Bridge Inn at Offenham. There was no bridge. There was a rope ferry across the river (the ropes were frayed). It had a scrappy 'beer garden' with cold uncomfortable chairs. This was meant to be a treat for me, to sit there with Hank, my father and my complaining mother (if applicable). It wasn't a treat. The car was preferable. The very notion of a 'beer garden' was to be mistrusted. Worcestershire wasn't, still isn't, Bavaria, even if the people are as ugly. 'Worst-looking women in England' was my father's view.

The Fish and Anchor upstream of Offenham. It was peculiarly isolated, the place was desolate, excitingly gaunt. A ford crossed the river above a weir. A lock was hidden behind an islet of willows. The dusty road ran along the riverbank towards a bare hillside. When I was very small I believed that beyond the hill was the end of the world. Later I would learn that beyond the hill was another hill, a higher hill where, two years before I was born, a hedge-layer had been murdered. His throat was slit with his billhook, a cross was carved in his chest, his body was pinned to the ground with a pitchfork. Such signs suggest that he was believed to have been a witch.[23]

One summer Sunday midday Uncle Hank wasn't at a pub. He was, said Auntie Kitty, at Owlett's End.

With *the Hodges*!

Auntie Kitty imparted this intelligence to my father with a heavy emphasis and a . . . what? I noted a change. Knowing smirk. He either didn't notice or chose to ignore it. The name Hodges appeared not to mean anything to him. He was no doubt as accustomed as I was to Kitty's hobgoblin tics. I had never heard of Owlett's End. Owlett's End! The name was entrancing. Like the Owlhoot Trail. It turned out to be less than quarter of a mile away. We could have walked but, as usual, my father strode across the street, got into the car and drove. Over Port Street, past Beach's jam factory in Church Street where all that remained of the church was a porch. Then, after stopping and starting and peering and reversing, we turned past a five-bar gate hanging from a rotting post into a drive. It led beside a portmanteau-ish house of limestone and wings, add-ons and brick, to a yard flanked by former stables, outhouses, sheds, swaying chestnuts in bloom, dapple. We parked behind Uncle Hank's Aston Martin. A burly man who might have been an officer-class chicken farmer – apple-cheeked, tattersall-checked, cavalry-twilled – was showing him a Morgan sports car. His high voice hardly accorded with his man's-man garb. A boy and a girl in their early teens stood beside their father's new acquisition as though it lent them kudos, which it did, to my regret. The man's greeting to my father was distracted, as though he was trying to place him. I feigned an interest in the car even though

---

23 There are echoes of this unsolved case in David Rudkin's *Afore Night Come* (1962).

it looked out of date, almost prewar, stylistically retardataire as though it was contemporary with the Aston Martin: the same detached mudguards and unincorporated headlights, an entire lack of streamlining. But, undeniably, it was not a Morris Traveller. The teenagers ignored me. Their father squeaked about torque, rpm, nought to sixty. Between the yard and the house was a thick, blowsy garden of palpitating shrubs and heavy-breathing boughs. We had been there only a few minutes when a dark blonde, superhealthy, suntanned woman appeared from it with a tray bearing glasses of beer and lemonade. For a long moment, negotiating the uneven path, she failed to notice my father and me. When she did see that her family and Uncle Hank had someone with them she uttered a surprised vowel. She was about to put down the tray on top of a butt when she started and looked again at my father. Her handsome face glissando'd from recognition to astonishment to suppressed fury. This occurred so swiftly that the others, by now gaping at a carburettor or cylinder head, saw nothing of this transformation which was beyond mere mood: she mutated from one person into another. Her husband, immersed in ownership, offhandedly introduced my father, whose name he had forgotten, as Harry's brother and appended me as his nephew. It was not till he spoke his wife's name, Laura, that my father was stirred from his dissembled Morgan envy and realised that they had at least met before. She announced that she would get drinks for us too. She made it sound like a threat. When she returned she remained silent and still, undemonstratively furious. Why? That my father should have possessed the insolence to come to her house? To so dare? If her restrained anger was evident to my father he didn't show it. He did not allow himself to be fazed by such matters.

Had I mentioned it – which, of course, I didn't – he'd have irately brushed it aside. An undertaker of the emotions, he'd have shrugged it off by suggesting that she was a bit down in the mouth. I didn't mention it because I was afraid of his wrath. And because I was puzzled. I didn't understand anything beyond what I had seen and sensed. What did this woman have against him? Whatever could he have done, or not done, to prompt such a dislike? A dislike moreover that she wished not to reveal. It was her secret. It was his secret. Was I really too young at the age of ten to surmise the obvious? To guess, as I did some time later, that they had been lovers, that my father had mistreated her in some way many years ago when she was not yet Hodges, when she still bore her maiden name. Her surprise: why should she have made the connection between this acquaintance of her husband and my father. He, reciprocally, had no idea whom she had married, whose name she had taken (as was de rigueur in those days). He had left Evesham twenty-five years previously and was hardly assiduous about keeping up with old friends, their gossip and news. Again, there was no reason for Uncle Hank to have known about a distant, youthful liaison of his secretive brother.

What were the sentimental and sexual lives of my parents before they met (and, perhaps, after, given their four-year wartime separation)?

A woman who – dark eyes, chaotic hair, negligent dress apart – so resembles my mother that they might have been taken for each other appears with my father in various photos that I found only after both he and my mother were dead.

This, I assume, is Tina, also dead no doubt: there's no one left to ask.

'Daddy was engaged to a girl called Tina . . . She'd have been your mother.'

I knew enough at the age of seven to retort to my mother: 'I wouldn't have existed.'

That worried me. Not my mother's comforting, misguided, silliness but my non-existence.

So I was grateful to Tina for having wearied of fishing trips. Here she is with two plump trout taken at Paxford near Chipping Camden in the summer of 1935. Maybe she wearied of him, or he of her once he had met her better-turned-out ringer. I was grateful for the combination of circumstances that brought my parents together and for having been given the opportunity of life – this egg, this seed – rather than the ignorance of nothingness which a union with Tina would not have inflicted on the uncreature that could not be called me. What luck to have avoided such nullity, such abysmally close nullity. It was fearful contemplation of this nullity's abysmal proximity that made me see early on that religion is merely a desperate form of pattern-making which attempts (and fails) to deny that each individual's very being owes everything to chance, that the lap of the gods is a euphemism for the conjoined groins of human animals.

My father never mentioned Tina. My mother, only that one time. She was hardly more forthcoming about her former boyfriends.

After her death I found some photos of her with a moustached, crinkle-haired fellow (Southsea 1932 etc.). I described him to my aunt, her sister Mary. 'That'll have been Stuart,' she said.

Sometime after, I discovered more photographs of the same man, now wearing academic robes; on the back of several of them he was named as John.

My mother once mentioned (parenthetically, forgetfully) that when she was a probationary teacher at Basingstoke in the early Thirties and he was a policeman, she had known John Arlott 'quite well'. That might have meant anything. It probably meant no more than her having 'gone to a couple of dances' with the young Hugh Casson, whom she had met through his father, University College Southampton's rowing coach.

She didn't row.

She played violin in the college orchestra.

She watched in horror as the front wheel of her friend Gwen Newman's bicycle got caught in a tram track near Bevois Valley on the way to school. The tram, braking hard but unable to stop, bore down on Gwen Newman. She scrambled desperately to get out of its path. Just! Her bicycle was crushed. This incident was often recalled as a cautionary tale, although when I was at my grandparents' house in Southampton I had no bicycle and in Salisbury where I did have a bicycle there were no trams. Its achievement was to intensify my dislike of Bevois Valley where the pavements were piled with dead people's furniture and mangey fur coats, where the collarless totters stank of tobacco and drink, where lorries hurtled and clanked, where the day was dense with gyring smuts and tracks still gleamed in the macadam, lethal souvenirs of the trams they had once guided.

Gwen Newman was my mother's only schoolfriend whose name I knew. And it was heard *exclusively* in this context. Poor Gwen was the near-victim of an accident that was reported in the *Southern Evening Echo*. That was it. That was her one role. What did she do with the rest of her life? Had she excelled at lacrosse? Was she brunette? Did she marry? Was she happy, was she a housewife, did she serve in the war – if so, how? Did she leave Southampton? Did she have a pet as sweet as the fox terrier Rags?

The marriage that my future parents contracted beside the Itchen at St Mary's, South Stoneham on 20 May 1939 was of course a union. It was also a tabula rasa achieved with a Kärcher, a compact to shut out those friends who were his and those who were hers, rather than those who were theirs. This may even have been deliberately plotted, a quid pro quo where the quid and the quo are indistinguishable. It may have been an unspoken treaty. They were strangers to each other's milieu. For different reasons they were not at ease with the other's family.

These are propitious conditions for an enduring marriage so exclusive that its child will inevitably sense that it is an intruder.

The premarital world that was erased that day.

My father went to Prince Henry's Grammar School. He often walked to school across 'Echo Bridge' which carries the railway over the Avon to Evesham station. He roamed on Bredon Hill with Jumbo Evans and Os Edwards: years later he would tell me stories about the imperious Lord Rabbit whose luxury warren was in a quarry there. My mother was insistent that he ought to write them, send them to a publisher.

He and his friend Eric Rae who lived at Rous Lench would, when Rae's parents had gone to bed, push their car from its garage, along a long drive and when out of hearing of the house crank it and glide, high above the hedges, through the silent sleeping Vale to Ab Lench, Atch Lench, Pinvin, Peopleton, Iron Cross, White Ladies Aston. He ate hedgehog baked in clay with gypsy fruit-pickers. He worked for a wool merchant. He got a job with William Crawford and was posted to Bath.

The next-door house in Englishcombe Lane was occupied by James Pullen, an octogenarian widower suffering dementia, his middle-aged daughter Connie, her six-year-old daughter Beryl from her former marriage, and her second, younger, husband Reg Hinks who, according to my father, was 'a classic small-town Lothario, smarmy, bit of a pissartist'.[24] He called himself an electrical engineer rather than an electrical goods salesman – a marginal self-elevation that would improbably be called into question. He had given up work upon marrying. No matter what

24 To that generation *pissartist* signified a braggart rather than a drunk, though the two are undoubtedly congruent.

the weather, he would often push Pullen in a bath chair out into the back garden. The old man would sometimes remain there till after dusk. He screamed and swore and jabbered incontinently. He shivered. His face was knotted in pain. He sat through hailstorms. Anxious neighbours gossiped that it was going to be the death of him. They were repeatedly assured that exposure to climatic vagaries is what he wanted: remember Gramps isn't quite all there in the head, Hinks told them. And besides, he's physically fit – apart from all the falls which caused him multiple contusions. On 1 December 1933 Pullen died. It was apparently a gas oven suicide: something he had repeatedly threatened. Connie was absent when Hinks discovered the body. A postmortem, however, revealed that Pullen had been hit on the back of the head. Reg Hinks was charged with murder, found guilty and sentenced to death. In the condemned cell he received more than 3,000 letters of sympathy, many of them proposals of marriage. Too late. 'The only English murderer I came across – *so far as I know*,' said my father, who had occasionally nodded to him in the street and had observed him in a pub.

By the time Reg Hinks was hanged at Horfield Prison, Bristol, on 4 May 1934, my father had moved to Devizes. He shot at hares on the downs at Bromham with Joe Davies, a policeman whose family owned The Bear Hotel. He fished in the chalk streams to the east and south of Salisbury Plain. This was when he first got to know the city of Salisbury where he would live most of his life.

In the autumn of 1936 he moved to Strathbrook Road, Streatham Common, London SW where he had digs with a family called Ridley. He went to Madame Tussaud's to see the newly installed display of Reg Hinks's effigy together with the actual gas oven from Englishcombe Lane. With his contemporary Norman Ridley he watched the Crystal Palace burn on 30 November. He didn't like London. Maybe he didn't realise that Streatham going on Norbury was not London. He was impressed by how much an acquaintance who worked for the *Daily Mirror* was paid.

Soon after, he was back in Wiltshire, in digs in Salisbury, in Wilton Road. He disgraced himself by eating all the walnuts decorating a cake his landlady had made.

He met the woman who would become my mother.

They spoke of each other as though they had hardly existed before they met, as though they were the ghosts of the beings they would become. They left behind them almost vanished worlds which I learnt of obliquely in repeated anecdotes:

When a Czechoslovakian orchestra visiting University College Southampton played that country's protracted national anthem, the audience, believing the piece to have ended, sat down and applauded only to discover that it was barely halfway through.

In the So'ton suburb of Shirley my mother instructed her class of eight-year-olds to draw a flower seller, which they did. One of them however misunderstood the brief. She drew a cellar full of sacks of flour with rats running over them. This child knew her stuff: she was an over-candid member of the Lowman family which owned bakeries and tea shops.

She taught for a year at Ashurst on the edge of the New Forest. Living with her parents in Portswood she no doubt took the train from St Denys station precipitously perched above muddy hulks in the Itchen. Ashurst was only just developing the arterial roadscape it possesses today. Much of it was still shacks and bothies. In winter a little girl came to school sewn into untreated rabbit furs beneath her clothes. Another was wrapped in newspapers. I used these bucolic quirks in a short story. My mother's only reaction was: 'You left out that business about the couple who claimed the child had caught syphilis from a towel.'

I kicked myself. I had forgotten it.

At weekends in autumn she and her family would gather penny buns (ceps) at Emery Down in the Forest: in the last days of her life, short-term memory shot, she would recall: 'The Forest floor was a carpet of penny buns, a carpet of them.' At weekends in summer they would go to a beach hut at Naish's Farm where Chewton Bunny debouched into the sea. She spent family holidays on the Channel Islands from where they would go on to Brittany. This was unusual for a petit bourgeois family in the 1920s. Pop, my grandfather, her father, worked in the accounts department of the Southern Railway at its pompier High Victorian offices in Canute Road near the docks. The company ran ferries to St Helier and would later run them to St Malo and Le Havre. His family was allocated free passages and cut-rate passages. And because he travelled to these ports on business he had friends in them with whom his family would stay. I, in turn, would benefit from (the now nationalised) Southern Region's largesse towards its employees and often travel on the *Falaise* to and from St Malo.

My grandmother, née Agnes Baird, had numerous relatives around Falkirk and Bridge of Allan: her parents had both grown up nearby in St Ninian's, not yet a suburb of Stirling. My mother spent a miserable school holiday with some uncouth, bullying, perpetually truanting cousins called Taylor near Dunblane. She and her sister had to sleep in button beds – alcoves beside the stove, an arrangement close to that used in Kazakhstan and Turkmenistan where children slept on palettes suspended above stoves. The two sisters walked up to the Wallace Monument of which their great-grandfather had been the first keeper. They hated the food. They refused to go back the next Easter.

That, they hoped, was the last they'd ever see of the Taylors. And it was – for over fifty years, until the late 1970s when an Australian backpacker arrived at my parents' house and announced he was the son of one of those cousins who had emigrated in the 1930s. How, it was wondered, had he got the address? The youth was as callow and boorish as his father had been. After ten days of being waited on he showed no sign of pursuing his grand tour. He was only persuaded to leave when some imminent house guests were invented. My father opened an ancient wound by jocularly holding my mother responsible: the Taylors were, after all, part of 'her' family. She was indignant at this reminder of a buried animus, which would soon be thoroughly exhumed when, within a few months of each other, Uncle Eric and Uncle Hank, who had never met each other, died.

My father predictably spent the day fishing rather than attend Eric's funeral. In revenge, my mother refused to go to Hank's.

QUALIFICATIONS

I was provided with three godparents. Uncle Hank was a DIY pantheist. 'Auntie' Nancy Short was agnostic. 'Uncle' Norman Short was atheist. He was not militant because he had no cause to be. There was nothing to rail against. Religion was not a question in the milieu he frequented. He was originally a Cambridge mathematician, a scholarship boy from working-class Spalding who retained vestiges of a flatlands accent, a collision of East Anglian twang and Dukeries vowels, these veneered with RP. Post-graduation he turned to aeronautical science. He married his childhood sweetheart. He was recruited by the Aeroplane and Armament Experimental Establishment at Martlesham and moved with it to Boscombe Down in the first month of the war. He remained there all his working life save when seconded to USAF testing facilities in California and Colorado. He was the very opposite of my father, who referred to him as 'Little N', obstinately unable to figure how or why their lives should be intertwined. It was through their wives, fellow teachers who had met during the war at Highbury Avenue School. They met as adjuncts of their wives. Thus they endured a thirty-five-year acquaintanceship which pretended to friendship. In my father's eyes Norman was a bloodless, introspective, fastidious, unworldly, antisocial, snivelling hay-fever sufferer. (Norman and Nancy never came to my parents' parties. Either they weren't invited or if they were they declined out of shyness.)

Norman ate the rind of hard cheese, grew vegetables and flew with test pilots, beyond the speed of sound, roller-coasting above the numberless greens and greys, buffs and blues, corkscrewing through the empyrean, *his* empyrean. He was a cold warrior boffin-god with his graphs, charts, diagrams, headphones, allinonecatsuit as shiny as a light entertainer's, a life-support helmet, corrugated pipes, breathing apparatus, valves, wraparound goggles. With feet on land he cut a comical figure. He was, indeed, short, closer to five feet than six, squat, severely myopic, restrained and so calm he might have been under almost permanent sedation. Almost. Major calamities were met with mute stoicism whilst the frailest of causes might prompt a fit of petulance, which may have been a kind of displacement: his first child, a sweet-natured daughter, was severely disabled, whether through a botched delivery or a genetic flaw was unresolved. His son feared the latter and determined not to have children.

Nancy held up her many siblings and, implicitly, herself as paragons of striving and upward mobility. Their father was a cobbler, their mother a cottage hospital cook. They worked hard, passed exams, went to college, achieved, gained *qualifications*. Ruth Misselbrook was a lesbian primary school teacher with an entourage of desiccated elderly queens whom I wouldn't have blown even had I been not as other men (apart, evidently, from the others who are not as other men), Peggy Misselbrook was a lesbian grammar school headmistress, Anthony Misselbrook was a heterosexual senior civil servant in Customs and Excise (one son), Sidney Misselbrook was so senior a heterosexual civil servant in the Inland Revenue that he received a knighthood (one son), Jack Misselbrook was a homosexual civil servant who killed himself by slitting his wrist. There may have been others. They were all good bridge players; Anthony, the best of them, represented Scotland. They were not wholly indifferent to literature, art, music etc. But anything beyond detective fiction, Medici Society prints and saccharine light orchestral music was reckoned to be pretentious and corrosive. Norman and Nancy owned three prints: a horse at plough followed by gulls, downs in the background; a windmill, more downs (chalk is aptly the medium in which to represent them). And one painting, realised with precision: a tile-hung arts and crafts house above a raised pavement. This was said to be a scene in Wheathampstead. On my only visit to that village I failed to locate the site. A further enthusiasm was Compton Acres, a risibly kitsch park at Poole built by a margarine baron and filled with coy 'classical' sculptures. Sir Sidney, a sometime hockey international and minor counties cricketer, was proud that among his fellow commuters from Meopham was the thriller-writing solicitor Michael Gilbert who composed his work on the train. His son, Sidney Tim, a couple of years my senior, once failed to impress me by demonstrating how to leave a tip in a restaurant: the coins were to be pushed by the palm of the hand rather than the fingers under the rim of a plate or saucer. The gesture should be indiscernible.

The Shorts and the Misselbrooks were preoccupied with mores' minutiae, for if they got them right they were entitled, *qualified*, to sit in judgment on those who failed in one regard or another. So any mention of the socially ambitious local horizontal Estelle Tedd would prompt Nancy to hiss: 'Marriage breaker . . . she's got more than a few divorces on her conscience. Or would have if she had a conscience.' As well as the adulterous and the sexually promiscuous, she berated exam failures and idlers and those who had fancy ideas above their station. She assumed that the road accident at High Wycombe in which Ken James's first wife and their unborn child died in 1939 was bound to have been his fault: we all know what sort of chancer – thus driver – he is. (The inquest was shown irrefutable evidence that a spoked wheel's wingnut had suffered metal fatigue.) She denounced Ian Priest as irresponsibly selfish; had he given up playing rugby Kay would not now be a widow with two small sons to bring up on a teacher's salary after he was fatally injured in an inter-services match. The Dowson boy[25] is in trouble again, stealing from his father's firm . . .

My father thought it necessary to instruct me in the difference between a moralist and a moraliser. He said that when he calls someone a loose-wallah or a chelaka or a pansy, he is *describing*

---

25 Subsequently known as 'the parish Nureyev'.

them, not condemning them. He harboured a faint fear that my mother might be infected by Nancy's schoolmarmish fishwifery and that she might take up with Nancy's friends, among them a miserable woman, also a teacher, whom he referred to as 'Keep Death Off The Road', an allusion to the widow in weeds shown in a road safety poster of the Attlee years. He need not have worried. My mother was not much given to judgment. She used the term 'a superior type', but not without irony; she would describe her denser pupils as 'dull and backward', but not without fondness. The Shorts' semi-detached bookless house was excessively overheated. It was furnished with swollen prewar armchairs. The fireplaces were all fudge-coloured tiles. A table by the front door held a telephone and an American plastic address book equipped with an arrow-shaped slide that took one swiftly to whatever letter was required. The house smelled pleasantly enough of Nancy's cooking. That was the best thing about her cooking. It tasted lardy, bland, greasy, underseasoned: the putty colour of a chicken roast at too low a temperature was unappealing. The worst of it was that it was all served with reckless generosity that stretched beyond the table. Norman and Nancy liked to help. I didn't want to be helped with my near-innumeracy so that I might qualify to read physics at Hull like Derek Gibby, son of one of Norman's Boscombe Down carshare group. I didn't want to be taken on holiday to a dismal bungalow in the North Sea resort of Mundesley, a week of killing boredom, chilly beach and gala pie which was spectacularly relieved by a drive to their native Spalding across the fens where black-sailed vessels soared thrillingly on black waterways high above the black earth. The world went widdershins.

RICHMOND, DANIEL & BUNTY

In the early autumn of 1956 my father was offered a promotion by William Crawford and Sons. The job was akin to Chas Perry's in Southampton. My father would oversee the company's reps in the East Midlands and East Anglia. He would be based in Northampton. Early one Sunday we drove to what was to be our new hometown. I was impressed by a taut flag in the brisk breeze in the ironstone village of Rockingham. I was further impressed by being able to buy a half-pint of dilute orange juice in a milkbottle from a milkman on his rounds: this was not, it turns out, peculiar to Northampton but I had not met it before. And though we didn't go there I knew that Fotheringhay was close. The name sent, still sends, a shiver down my spine. I looked forward to moving. Why my father had even bothered to drive to Northampton was puzzling. He must have known that he would never live there. There was no river. The mighty Nene didn't count. It wasn't a chalkstream, there was no game fishing. He wasn't going to sit on a bank with a Thermos waiting for inedible mud-flavoured bottom feeders that would be thrown back. The considerably higher salary, over £2,000 p.a. according to my eavesdropping, was no compensation for the sporting bereavement. He believed himself to be defined by his eternal battle with *Salmo salar*. Not that he could really afford the ever-mounting fees demanded by the fisheries he favoured.

The Breamore estate owns extensive riparian rights on the Avon upstream of Fordingbridge. Down on its luck in the second half of the Fifties, it decided to investigate the idea of exploiting the river as a commercial fishery in the manner of Somerley and Royalty, further south. My father had acquired a minor local reputation as a sort of virtuoso, a consistently successful salmon fisherman on the Avon over the previous decade. He was nevertheless astonished to be contacted out of the blue by Breamore's owner Sir Westrow Hulse, Bt, with whom he had a passing acquaintance. Westrow made him a splendid offer: would he be prepared to fish the river for free for three or four years, in all seasons, to determine whether the proposed scheme was feasible and if so what were the piscatorial characteristics of the water, where are the pools where salmon might lie, what attention should be paid to the management of the sluices, how

it might be organised as beats and so on. Given that salmon fishing is a rich man's sport and that my father was far from rich and forever attempting to sponge a day here or there, this was a gift. And Westrow, whose fortunes were such that he could barely afford to heat his sprawling Elizabethan house, was getting what would now be called expert consultancy for nothing. Deal done.

This would prove to be as much a social as a sporting adventure. Westrow had been apprised of my father's prowess by Daniel Richmond, whom he had originally asked to survey the river. Daniel Richmond was too busy. His name meant nothing to my father. In that case, said Westrow, you must meet him. Thus through my father I came to discover the allure of a singular man with a semi-ziggurat hairdo.

Daniel (never 'Dan') was charming, intemperate, alcoholic, witty, promiscuously bisexual, snobbish, generous, chain-smoking, outrageously rude, usually laughing. For over a decade and a half my father and he would enjoy a friendship marinated in fishing, cars, champagne and black velvet. 'I'm just a gwease munkih,' Daniel would sibilantly murmur, not for a moment expecting anyone to believe him. He was, in fact, a brilliant and inventive engineer. An engineer on the verge of (automotive) fame and considerable fortune. His company Downton Engineering tuned the BMC Mini Coopers which, driven by Timo Mäkinen and Paddy Hopkirk, became the most successful rally cars of the age and won the Monte Carlo three times. They were tested to screeching point on the long straight roads across the Forest: stray ponies tested the brakes. I couldn't, still can't, tell a manifold from a rocker arm. How cars worked bored me. Daniel didn't bore me, nor did his diffident astonishment at his achievement. He was an obsessive tinkerer and maker who succeeded in raising the performance of Alec Issigonis's creation to an unprecedented pitch. Issigonis and Alex Moulton, who designed the folding bicycle and the Mini's suspension, were friends of Daniel's. So too were Jem Marsh who designed and built the Marcos and such once-scandalous figures as his fellow gentleman-engineer Jeremy Fry, Edward Montagu of Beaulieu and the profligate landowner and occasional writer Michael Pitt-Rivers (who despite his marriage to Sonia Brownell was homo rather than bisexual). Daniel's milieu was that of upper bohemian oddballs,[26] black sheep, remittance men, bolters, bankrupts – the sort of people who lived in the villages of Rockbourne and Whitsbury, had indiscreet affairs, gambled recklessly, suffered nembutal and/or seconal addiction and hanged themselves.

Bunty, his terrifying and saturnine wife, was not actually his wife. She had apparently bolted from her husband, a man named Whitaker, after a couple of years' wartime marriage and had not divorced. She was older than Daniel. Together they bought a garage that was little more than a decent-sized shed, a carriage house. It was an extension of Daniel's hobby of

26 Among his close neighbours was the unorthodox entrepreneur Oliver Cutts, sometime owner of the vast late Victorian Rhinefield Lodge, who in reduced circumstances dressed like Max Wall. He once yelled across a river to my father: 'I say John old man – do you know anyone I could pay to see me towards a K?' The fact that he wasn't entitled to did not inhibit him from styling himself 'Sir'.

motor sport – saloon car races, hill climbs (Shelsley Walsh, Snettisham), time trials etc. They hoped to scratch a living repairing and refitting the grand cars of the aristocracy which had been in wraps for the duration. It wasn't the most ambitious of enterprises. They were novices in engineering and business. Bunty's modest private income was hardly a guarantee of security.

Daniel had a gift for friendship, Bunty had a gift for antagonism. He could get away with anything. She couldn't. It can be a fine line; in this instance it wasn't. Her accent was posher than the Queen's. She was bossy, occasionally menacing, impressively touchy and never let anyone forget that she was Somerset Maugham's niece. Which, in fact, she wasn't – her father's sister was married to Maugham's brother. Near-miss. Besides, what kudos did she expect to gain from announcing herself as Maugham's niece in a village such as Downton, a bucolic place whose industries were tanning (Richardson), seeds (the well-named Hickman) and brickfields (the stations and halts of the fantastically slow Salisbury and Dorset Junction Railway were ruddily built of them). Her precise cousinage was improbably challenged, for why should such a connection be fabricated? She was hypersensitively suspicious of the most meagre courtesy shown her. 'Why don't you say what you're fucking thinking?' was her habitual response to any utterance which she reckoned (rightly, wrongly) euphemistic or, signally, which failed to insult her as she believed *she deserved to be insulted*. She abhorred niceness, she despised wanting to be liked: 'Je m'en fous du qu'en dira-t-on.' She gave no other indication of familiarity with idiomatic French. With crashing understatement my mother once remarked: 'Bunty can be really quite difficult.' The rawness, hurtfulness, vindictiveness, palaeolithic crudeness of her demeanour were much more than difficult. This was clinical. Her appearance was a problem. She had clearly once been good-looking – handsome rather than beautiful; but, in the cant of the era, 'she had let herself go'. And how. Her hair was a greasy chaos with a pronounced widow's peak. There was liverish baggage beneath her eyes. She had a puffy indoors complexion, her arms were fubsy with quasi-dropsical flaps that were not yet called buffalo wings. Years later I would see her near-replicated in Ian Nairn. Her frumpy shapeless dresses might have been expressions of self-contempt. Yet she drove a Ferrari (Enzo Ferrari himself owned a Downton-tuned Mini) whilst Daniel drove anything that was around, mostly Minis but also an astonishingly ungainly Morris or maybe Austin Maxi which could accommodate salmon rods. It was lumbering proof that Issigonis had peaked with the Mini. And it presaged the decline of British car manufacture. Since they were unsaleable maybe Daniel had been given his.

His habitats were a) the Works, b) the Bull, c) the House.

The Works was a group of utilitarian, single-storey, light-industrial 1950s buildings to the north of the village. These insipid structures looked as though they had been intended for some purpose other than tuning cars and had been seized upon by Daniel and Bunty as they began to prosper (which he, certainly, had never yearned for let alone expected).

The Bull, still there, was frequented by elderly pub bores: 'Have ye heard mih shtory bowt . . .' The taxidermised pike in a glass box was more entertaining. Under age, I was tolerated because I was Daniel's guest. He was the place's most important, richest client. I'd guess that by the time he sat beside me on a hefty settle and laid the rather delicate hand that wasn't holding a Gauloise on my cock he was a millionaire. I can see my father in his Gannex holding a couple of glasses as though in frozen porterage, a gesture to show that he is en route to another part of the room, a gesture that is blithely unrecognised by the anec-dotard bending his ear at the bar. I can hear myself explaining to Daniel, with a calmness that surprised me, that were I to be taken queer he'd be my first port of call. He agreed that was a good idea. Later that evening as we drove home I recounted this to my father. He merely laughed: 'That's Daniel all over.' His implication (I guess) was that at the age of sixteen I was old enough to look after myself, to make my own choices in such matters.

The House was a narrow, low, perpetually sombre cottage on a steep slope. Its upper storey was level with the road that passed within a few yards. It had been built two hundred years before for foresters, bad-diet folk, hence diminutive. The scale was not appropriate for lurching, fully formed boozers. Other people's homes are as much a mystery as other people's marriages.

Daniel and Bunty's partnership withstood quarter of a century of excess. Excessive lucubration, excessive drinking, excessive infidelity (him), excessive antisocial behaviour (her). What it could not bear was excessive wealth. Their financial fortune changed with alacrity. The cottage industry turned into an industry. The passionate inquiry, inspired improvisation, make-do-and-mend spirit of post-war amateurishness were sacrificed to a professional production line. The years of research had provided them with a golden goose that they dared not destroy even though it was destroying them with boredom and plenty. Daniel did not wish to be an executive. With the swollen tide of royalties that he now received from BMC for the design of components which were incorporated as standard in Mini engines he bought several miles of fishing on the Taw at Chumleigh, a house and a variety of decrepit adjacent properties. He would hole up there for weeks on end. Bunty would join him then return reluctantly to Downton to run the business in which he had lost all interest.

Chumleigh is only a couple of miles downstream from Eggesford. My father was delighted that Daniel now owned water there, further delighted that he should be issued an invitation to stay and to fish whenever he wished: which, of course, this being England, didn't quite mean that. Nonetheless my father gratefully accepted when Daniel suggested specific dates. He drove to Devon for a couple of weekends. The appeal of these exercises in riverbank sodality, initially undertaken with enthusiasm, soon palled. My father found reasons to decline Daniel's subsequent invitations. He observed, not altogether frivolously and with some regret, that the less Daniel was with Bunty the more he seemed to adopt Bunty's characteristics. There is a price to pay for free fishing, this one was too high.

Daniel, the new Bunty, drifted away from the old Bunty. He hardly noticed. He sleepwalked towards oblivion. He became friendly with the elderly Henry Williamson. He took up with a woman who ran a riverside pub. Fishing began to get in the way of drinking. He was a few months short of his fiftieth birthday when he suffered a fatal stroke. Two years later, having meticulously wound up the business, Bunty killed herself with an overdose.

SCUTT, ERIC

'Seventeen times did goalkeeper Eric Scutt stoop to pick the ball out of the back of West Harnham Reserves' net.' My mother asked me what I was laughing at. I read out the exquisite first line of the *Salisbury Journal* match report. (West Harnham Reserves' opponents had been St Osmond's.) 'Eric Scutt. Oh god . . . I used to teach him.' She rolled her eyes.

'Seventeen times did Eric Scutt stoop' became a catchphrase. It signalled preposterous failure.

Other catchphrases:

Not in front of the renchild.

Rally Rally Rally.

Lance says urrgh.

No sooner asked than granted.

Act with all due decorum.

The Ladzz.

Das Ladzz (when Germany was playing).

SEARLE, MR

Mr Searle was the Close Constable. Old, amiably avuncular manner, healthy appetite, consequently bulging dark blue uniform.

Work habitat: a tightfit wooden sentry box beside Choristers' Green: he was usually outside it, presumably because he couldn't squeeze himself inside it. His job was to prevent unseemly behaviour. (How does it go? – '*The buttered buttocks of the bishop's bumboy.*' There wasn't enough of that malarkey.)

He monitored comings and goings and discouraged motorists from using the Close as a short cut – it was the quickest route from the city to Harnham. Harnham Gate (aka De Vaux Gate), St Ann's Gate and the High Street Gate were open till nine or ten o'clock at night. How residents drove in and out after that hour is to this day a mystery. Pedestrian access was through doorways in the gates which may or may not have remained perpetually unlocked. The Bishop's Gate on Exeter Street was always locked and never washed; it gave on to the grounds of the Cathedral School (formerly the Bishop's Palace) rather than on to a public road. It was known to us as Cavy's Gate after Mr Cavanagh. He had been a pupil at the school in the 1880s and had graduated in the 1890s, whereupon he had returned to teach Latin at the school. He lived with his similarly ancient wife in the house that stretched over the gate. Mr Searle's domestic habitat was a house beside Harnham Gate, the only gate that has no quarters above it. Its hefty machicolations are martial – it is a work of fortified exclusion rather than an invitation to observance like the others.

There are three houses conjoined to this gate. Another of them would subsequently be occupied by the lank-haired choral singer Michael Foster who taught me history in my last year at prep school. He had just come down from Cambridge. From the Pye factory, according to my father. In what was presumably a clumsy effort at blokeish ingratiation he called me, to my evident irritation, Gerty. His example was not followed. So he imposed the same crass sobriquet on a slow farmer's boy called Sladen who was less able than I to cope with jocular bullying. His future wife Sarah had been the school's matron; she was the neurotic sister of the cathedral organist, teacher, musicologist and naturist Christopher Dearnley who, when assistant organist to Douglas Guest, had been responsible for bringing both her and Douglas Blythe to Salisbury. The Close was socially and familially tight-knit. The Church of England was not yet a property empire run by alumni of The School of Rachman. The Close was a village with rules. All of the houses were then still owned by the Dean and Chapter. The majority were inhabited by clergy and officers of the cathedral (organists, adult choristers, the Clerk to the Dean and Chapter etc.). Others were let as grace and favour dwellings to observant communicants: Mrs Martin-Jones, a doctor's widow and her two daughters; Mrs Pettiward and her artistic son Daniel, by Salisbury standards something of an exotic; Douglas Pitcairn and his wife Leonora who wrote romantic fiction and books on child care; Margaret Diment, the spinster daughter of a long-dead canon. Others of her ilk lived in the College of Matrons, an almshouse ascribed (not without cause) to Christopher Wren.

Miss Philips (aka Ma Pee) owed her position at the Cathedral School to the fact that she was the headmaster's sister. Given that she didn't share Laurence Griffiths's surname she had presumably once been Mrs Philips. Of Mr Philips we knew nothing. Her morning duties included inspecting boarders' stools before allowing them to flush the lavatory. When she wasn't poking around in foetid puddles of Izal and Bronco she was in charge of the kitchen.

My fellow pupils, the future MP for Salisbury Robert Key and the future progrock guitarist Mike Wedgwood, were sons of, respectively, the suffragan Bishop of Sherborne and the Cathedral's succentor. The latter got a cottage beside Choristers' Green. The suffragan bishop got a finer billet, the Walton Canonry: red brick, early c18, homelier than its stately neighbour Myles Place where Harry and Marjorie Jacobs lived. When Marjorie died, two centuries of occupation by that family ended and the Dean and Chapter sold it.

The heterodoxy of the bishops John Robinson (Woolwich) and, later, David Jenkins (Durham); churches in the round; the New English Bible; vicars with guitars strumming 'Kumbaya'. Due, however, to their coarse mediation and the vague odour of 'controversy' the atypical, as so often, was granted a disproportionate currency. The majority of Anglican clergy, certainly of Salisbury Cathedral's clergy, were not susceptible to dilute modernism. The Close was a bastion of unchallenged dogma, ritual, philistinism, unquestioning belief. The manipulator of millions of minds Joseph Goebbels wrote: 'It is almost immaterial what we believe in so long as we believe in something.' Time and again, those with this promiscuous capacity for credulousness are shown to be those with the equal capacity to promote and sanction atrocities. We repeatedly witness the migration of believers – 'spiritual persons' – from one cult to the next; a religion is merely a heavily armed cult. Believing in something all too evidently means believing in anything. Why should Christians, Jews, Sikhs, Hindus, Muslims – especially Muslims – be treated with anything other than the contemptuous toleration that is visited on flat-earthers and ufologists? Believe in the existence of fairies at the bottom of the garden and you are deemed fit for the bin, for the Old Manor. Believe in parthenogenesis and ascension and you are deemed fit to govern the country, run the BBC, command UK Landforces etc. The notion that these people might be mentally ill is quite overlooked: *quis custodiet* and all that. David Hume was right: 'Examine the religious principles, which have, in fact, prevailed in the world. You will scarcely be persuaded, that they are anything but sick men's dreams: Or perhaps will regard them more as the playsome whimsies of monkeys in human shape.'

The Close's inhabitants – lay and sacred alike – were those monkeys in human shape. They were not blessed with doubt. They were obedient and loyal; both qualities which, like sincerity, are in themselves of no merit. Obedient to who? Loyal to what? It is from the ranks of the obedient and loyal that come our most accomplished state torturers, most deluded freedom fighters, most narcissistic bombers. These were evidently not occupations pursued in the bridge-playing, sensible-shoe-wearing, drop-scone-eating Close. But a chiding sanctimony sprouted like henbane. The clergy were pro-god and anti-life. My parents' lack of observance was noted with priggish severity. And the omission was no doubt exacerbated by my mother's teaching in a C of E school, a C of E school that overflowed from its humble Gothic premises (beside All Saints, East Harnham where I had been baptised) into a wooden makeshift classroom in a field next to the South Canonry, home of the Bishop.

For my parents, baptism and confirmation did not signify an intention that I should become any more of a communicant or joiner than they were. These rituals were merely social. There was no particular hypocrisy attached to this stance. It was the norm, the done thing. I loathed, still loathe, still despise, the liturgical boredom, the sheer balls that was spoken, the crass panto that was enacted, the degrading notion of worship of a hackneyed human construct. Kneeling for no one, blathering in prayer. Self-abasement is the terrible vanity of the unknowing.

I hated the desiccated smell of the cathedral, the ponderous responses, the dirges, the perpetual dusk, the organ, now joyless, now fatuously pompous. Because I had no faith I had no occasion to suffer a crisis of faith. Thus a nugatory adolescent rite was denied me. I vaguely regret that I will never understand the *torment* of losing faith any more than I will ever understand having faith. To do so demands an imaginative leap that I am incapable of. Where does it go when it is lost? Does it infect others? Does faith slip away, does this comfort blanket of the soul self-slough? If you attempt to shed it, does faith threaten that multi-suckered flukes will lay eggs in your soft tissue? If you question it, does faith respond with bolts of molten wrath? My ignorance was a deprivation akin to, say, not having been given a teddy bear when I was little. At the age of fourteen I complained to my mother of the grave psychological damage caused by that ursine absence. In the same spirit of comic exaggeration she bought me one, to teach me how little succour is to be had from such things. Faith, then, is no more than a soft toy, a cuddly companion in make-believe, an imaginary friend that is a false friend. Faith demands a gene, a credulous gene, that was not passed to me. My parents gave me little to rebel against: thus a further adolescent rite was denied me.

The Close continued to be defined by piety, the aggression of unworldliness and the faith of spinsters till the last quarter of the last century when it underwent a demographic shift.

Myles Place was sold to Sir Arthur Bryant, a popular historian and enthusiastic Hitlerite.

Leslie Thomas, a popular novelist and the bloke's bloke, bought the Walton Canonry.

Arundells became the home of and, after his death, an insipid shrine to the former cottager Sir Edward Heath who, taking advantage of a loophole and a thick estate agent, managed to secure the freehold of a house of which the Dean and Chapter had intended to sell only a twenty-one-year lease. Unlike Bryant, Heath was not taken by Nazism. He had attended the 1937 Nuremberg Rally and was unimpressed: but then, he hadn't been the centre of attention. He was less fastidious about Mao's China, his 'consultancy' with that tyranny made him a fortune. Sadly the money bought him neither love nor even friends. He was to be found playing darts with squaddies in Salisbury pubs or eating enormous restaurant meals with his mute bodyguards. (He vainly assumed that he was worth assassinating.)

The North Canonry was bought by a man who had made a

pile in container shipping and who, when he died, left over £10 million.

An important wholesaler of deep-frying equipment was granted permission to build a house in the grounds of Leadenhall, a regrettable excrescence in officers'-mess-Georgian. The Close turned into a gated community of the very rich. Which is what, mutatis mutandis, it had been half a millennium earlier when tithes and the gelt from simony, indulgences and chantries allowed the clergy to live high on the hog, bloated as bankers.

The choristers in capes and caps processed as they always had through the autumn dusk thick with spores and damp air from the river.

SONGS: DIANA

August 1957. The school swimming pool was free to pupils' families throughout the summer holidays. Others paid a small fee. There were numerous Americans, the families of USAF pilots, marine liaison officers, soldiers and spooks who were able to buy the future at a PX. One of them had a battery-powered record player – tinny but enticing nonetheless. It played 45 rpm discs, still an exciting novelty in England. Among them were 'That'll Be The Day' by The Crickets (the name Buddy Holly was yet unknown) and the fifteen-year-old Paul Anka's 'Diana', which I instantly recognised to be *my* song: *Diana* was Diana Cullumbine. I begged my mother to buy it for me. She reluctantly got me the Embassy 78 rpm cover version by David Ross,[27] from Woolworths. Embassy was its own record label; Winfield was the clothes brand. Embassy records: 4/6d. Columbia 45s: 6/8d. The pastiche might be indistinguishable from the original but that wasn't the point. The song of my lost love across the sea was cheapened in this fake version, simply because it was a fake. I would not have given Diana a pinchbeck ring instead of gold. My love itself was compromised. I felt cheated, affronted, ashamed. My mother, too, was affronted – by my ingratitude. So I convinced myself it sounded better on the tinny portable than on my parents' radiogram, a sort of double coffin which had once all but electrocuted my mother. She received a shock from a wire which she picked up whilst cleaning behind it. The improperly earthed current raced through her body and tightened her hand so that she was stuck to it, unable to articulate the

27 Possibly a pseudonym of Ross MacManus, singer with the Joe Loss Orchestra and father of Elvis Costello.

muscles. She was wrenched away by her wartime lodger Mary Sutcliffe, who had just come into the house from the garden. A few seconds later Mary would not have heard her scream. She would have died. She suffered no injuries save bruising to her hand.

Those late summer late afternoons at the pool were an early rehearsal for the perpetual party of my teens. I got to know most of the people who lazed away long hours there. And if I didn't get to know them I found out who they were to assuage my snooping curiosity. I made sure they knew me: I was a turn, a fast and flashy swimmer, the fastest and flashiest in the school, a virtuoso of freestyle and beyond that of butterfly, the least functional, the most dandiacal, most boastful, most monstrous of strokes. Not the one you choose to swim to the bank when you come head to head with a pike. I abandoned competitive swimming in favour of teenage dissipation after I was beaten by the glistening man-mountain Brian Jenkin of Swindon Dolphin in a race of 100 yards (3 lengths), by 33.3 yards (one length); I was just making my last turn when he finished.

They, the people of those poolside summers, were: blonde Maggie, Liz, Flatfoot, whining Dunc, Jenny, the two American Lindas – the lithe one and the other one – the other one's mother and her plaid rug, the Wallis family from Brigmerston who squeezed into an Aston Martin DB3, dashing gent-farmer father (though he carried the germ of the fat gene), glamorous mother in a turquoise and black one-piece, three perfect children (did they remain thus? Ah, they were human beings). *They* were Ham, Richard, Brian and the flashy racing bike he fondled as though it were a sexual organ, the Sessions twins Aubrey and Arnold and their sister Ann, David Hayden, the future scientist and writer Martin Woodhouse, the shooting-brake Wolstans, the Whitaker-Bovill girl, proudly keen to display the bruise on her bottom where, she claimed, it had been pinched in Rome.

And then there were the Shemilts. They would arrive en masse in the late afternoon. Philip Shemilt was supple and outdoorsy.

What remained of his hair was dark, his skin was tanned and smooth. I don't remember how I knew that he lived on the northern side of the Close with his wife and several small daughters. I don't remember how I knew that he was a surgeon, inevitably a distinguished surgeon. I never spoke to any of them. They didn't invite social contact. The parents would take turns to teach the girls to swim. The family's closeness, trust and integrity were patent. At ease in their collective reticence, they were serenely oblivious to the splashing, high-spirited world beyond their towels and togs.

One evening my father asked me who had been at the pool. I mentioned the Shemilts. 'Shemilts?'

My father was not conscripted in 1939. As a representative of William Crawford & Son he worked in food distribution so was, to his shame, exempted. A nation at war needed its biscuits. He volunteered for the Auxiliary Fire Service. In that capacity he witnessed the destruction of Southampton in November and December 1940. He sought and obtained a waiver of his exemption, joined the Wiltshire Regiment, applied for a commission, was admitted to 165 OCTU Dunbar where he was bullied by a Sergeant-Major Mackmurdo and lost a front tooth. A fellow rookie scaling a cliff above him dropped a rifle whose butt struck his mouth. He was condemned to a lifetime of Steradent. He continued to a further OCTU at Oadby in suburban Leicester, a town for which he quickly developed a visceral loathing. In January 1942 he was seconded to the Indian Army and sailed from Liverpool to Karachi. Here is a photo of my parents, my paternal grandmother and my father's siblings. My father is in uniform. They are gathered to wish him farewell before he sails to India. My mother's smile is forced, as though the Virgin Witch Kitty had just inflicted on her one of the understated, unanswerable humiliations she specialised in. No doubt something snide about being widowed young.

His first posting was to Jhelum, south-east of Rawalpindi, where he worked in a department controlling convoys. He was subsequently at Kakul in North West Frontier Province, Jaipur in Rajasthan and at Meerut in Uttar Pradesh. The India he photographed was thick with local colour: dust roads, extravagant mosques and temples, camels, scrawny cattle, pack ponies, marshalling yards, collapsed bridges and forded rivers, wizened oldsters, bivouacs, distant mountains.

A year later he was seconded again, to the newly established Paiforce. He embarked at Bombay, disembarked at the ad hoc port of Umm Qasr. After a brief period at Kirkuk his three years in Iraq were spent near Basra. His photographs record brief furloughs in Damascus and Babylon (the lion walls, the processional way), duck shoots at Hammar Lake, his pet gazelle, bazaars, dhows, hockey matches, Nissen huts and a touchingly seedy tourist attraction called The Original Garden Of Eden. The richness and variety of India is mostly absent. The desert landscape is relentlessly grim. There was indigenous hostility to contend with. The Arab world was broadly sympathetic to the Axis powers. (The Nazis' successors are not the lost causists of the BNP, NPD and Vlaams Belang but the totalitarian Islamist post-Khomeini terror states.)

Long after the Anglo-Iraqi war of May 1941 desultory acts of sabotage continued: trains derailed, pipelines severed, British-owned plant and buildings subjected to arson attacks. Maintenance of security at the petrol depot he commanded was a persistent problem: the troops under his command, mostly Hindu, were met with hostility.

A naïve programme of appeasement (or sycophancy) towards Bedouin chiefs was decreed in the hope that they might control their tribes. This appeared to my father to derive from the military (and political) establishment's unreflective trust of Arabs, a trust founded in an endemic romanticism, a swooning admiration for horsemen and falconers and warriors. Chivalry and nobility were detected where there was only vengeful primitivism. The entire sentimental Arabist package, the tradition of the fawning British buggerocracy – Richard Burton, T. E. Lawrence, St John Philby, Glubb Pasha, Wilfred Thesiger and countless other harmful eccentrics – had become *la pensée unique* of the army's higher strata. It was also (not that its adherents acknowledged it) effete, homoerotic, misogynistic, irrational, anti-urban, Luddite and gullible.

Still, my father would surely have been less contemptuous of it had that same top brass, composed entirely of career soldiers, bothered to dissemble its distaste for the necessary evil of 'unprofessional' conscripts and volunteers who were left in no doubt that they were second-class soldiers no matter what rank they attained.

This divisiveness seems likely to have had a bearing on the outcome of the 1945 general election. It unquestionably had a decisive influence on my father's prejudices, for this strain of Arabism, like all strains of Arabism, was invariably complemented by a 'social' anti-Semitism, a coded anti-Semitism that slyly invited collusion, an anti-Semitism that was disguised in those years as a concern for the Middle East's stability in the light of Zionist colonisation. This snide malediction was all the more indecent given that the anti-Semitism of the Muslim majority was far from 'social'. It was physically malevolent: theft, looting, violence, murder. This excited a martial blind eye.

Not all the causes of philo-Semitism are honourable. My father initially favoured the Zionist cause not because of its probity, not because of its necessity, not because of the immane crimes committed against Jewry, but because he felt personally slighted by a military establishment whose approval he sought but which, even in the middle of a world war, had ample time for hierarchical gradations and nuanced ostracism. Having failed to detect anti-Semitism in Freiburg in 1938 he now sided with the excluded because he knew that sycophancy towards that establishment would merely incur its further despisal. His temperamental inclination was towards the optimism and physical bravery of the aspirant Israelis. The self-pity and mendacity of the Arabs he had to deal with infuriated him. He would be dismayed by Clement Attlee's government which – even as pogroms and expulsions were being effected throughout the Middle East and the Maghreb – supported the Arab League's attempt to destroy Israel in 1947–8. (The Arab armies included Bosnian Muslim veterans of the Handzar SS brigades.)

His philo-Semitism took some unusual forms. Years after the man was dead, my father would rail against Attlee's foreign secretary Ernest Bevin, whom he considered anti-Semitic, cruel and ignorant: he was right on all counts. He reproached himself for having voted Labour in 1945.

Israeli women soldiers armed with Uzis impressed and excited him: he hoped that some had been employed in Eichmann's capture. None was. He seemed to admire Jewish virtuosi – Rubinstein, Landowska, Menuhin, Kreisler – *because* they were Jewish. He bought me a record by Esther and Abi Ofarim. Late one night, after what was not yet called the watershed, he woke me and insisted that I watch a documentary about the liberation of Belsen. The first film about the camps to be transmitted on British television. Was this part of the Sidney Bernstein work that was not shown in its entirety till thirty years later lest

Germans be offended? How could the mounds of starved corpses belong to the decade I had been born in? How could the craters and the plague pits filled with the living dead? And the pitiful clowns in pyjamas, the bone faces, the bullnecked woman guards? This horror came surely from some distant age of apocalyptic wrath when god had sullied the earth in his cleansing fury.

This was the sight that had tipped Jerry Savage over the edge. I gaped numbly. Here was the war that we had previously been protected from by War Picture Library, Jack Hawkins and Richard Todd, the war which god's usurper had won, the racial war – for which the war we knew might merely have been a cover. The Shemilts were to be accorded the greatest courtesy and respect. My father made this plain to me.

His dictate was redundant, I was too timid a child to treat anyone otherwise. Till I was thirteen or fourteen I behaved as I was bidden; in my father's tiresomely repeated formulation, 'with all due decorum'. So the Shemilts got the full treatment. The parents may have thought that I was a bit touched, the little girls were perhaps frightened. I grinned rictal greetings at them, mouthed a genial 'afternoon', nodded in sympathy. I lurked in hope of an opportunity to save one of the girls from drowning but, annoyingly, none occurred. I concocted a plan to offer to carry home some of the bags they struggled to heave but was too shy to go through with it. I wanted *to help*, I wanted to signal to them that I had the most profound sympathy for what they and their people had suffered. How many people in their family had perished? Was their tightness as a defensive unit founded in loss? Was the parents' evident protectiveness due to terrible crimes committed against their kin? Did they fear contamination by the carefree milieu that established itself around the swimming pool? Did they discern the germ of licentiousness? Or were they, on the contrary, besieged by the Close's Anglican piety? There was a lot of it about, a surfeit. Why did they choose to live there, in a house dominated by one of Christendom's supreme monuments? Where did they worship?

Maybe a forty- or fifty-mile round trip was nothing for the devout. There was a synagogue in Southampton, in the old town. There were several synagogues in Bournemouth. There were even kosher hotels in Bournemouth, sites of exotic noodles and mysterious rites behind pines. Their dining rooms were, needless to say, not frequented by my mother's Aunt Nesta and her formerly Jewish subsequently Anglican husband Joe Janda who lived in the town. Nor, it transpired, were they frequented by the Shemilts.

The next summer beside the pool, sometime no doubt between the Kalin Twins' 'When' and Ricky Nelson's 'Poor Little Fool', the (absent) Shemilts' standoffishness was mentioned. I confidently ascribed it to their being the inheritors of centuries of pogroms and persecution. My audience included a vague acquaintance of my mother, Daniel Pettiward, an illustrator, actor, librettist, 'humorist' (contributed to *Punch*) and problem dresser with a taste for lace-up shirts as ruddy as an inner tube. He lived in the Close's northernmost house, darted hither and scurried thither, and was altogether too sensitive to be an artist. He gaped at me with incredulity. His neighbours the Shemilts were not Jews. God forbid! What did I mean by impugning them! The family name, he splutteringly insisted, was a good old English name, a staunch English yeoman name common in parts of the English Midlands. (The Potteries, specifically.)

I never told my father.

SONGS: JOHNNY REMEMBER ME

The afternoon of Saturday 26 August 1961. The Exeter bypass was at a standstill. Leo Lush was at the wheel of his Rover 3-litre. Beryl sat beside him. They grudgingly tuned into the Light Programme. I was in the back between Chris and Angela.

'When the mist's a-rising and the rain's a-falling and the wind's a-blowing cold across the moor . . .' Few pop songs send a shiver down my spine as this one of ghostly lost love does. Maybe it's the B-feature eeriness; to teenage ears it supplied the plangent angst we long for at that age, and it located hammy melancholia in that week's Dartmoor dusks. More likely it's because I've spent a lifetime failing to dissociate the song from the news report which followed it. It detailed a murder, rape and assault in Bedfordshire, at Deadman's Hill. The crimes had been committed on the night of 22–23 August yet this bulletin announced it as though it had not previously been made public. Had there been a police embargo? The horrible events were, anyway, previously unknown to everyone in the car.

I have never heard that song without recalling them and the lay-by and Valerie Storie and the delusional Alphon and the psychopathic Hanratty and the industry of pious indignation that burgeoned around the presumption of his innocence, an innocence which is still insisted upon by dotard DNA-deniers whose faith survives all known fact. As faith does: that's the problem with faith.

Thirty-five years after he had recorded 'Johnny Remember Me' I was introduced to John Leyton in the bar of Meridiana, a pretty South Kensington restaurant which he then owned. A minute's small talk. Then I said: 'Do y'know – whenever I hear "Johnny Remember Me" I think of James Hanratty.' He looked at me with speechless astonishment, clearly thought I was mad, or insulting, or both. Before I could elaborate he fled down some stairs. Thus I was denied the opportunity to ask him whether he reckoned that Joe Meek had ever fucked Joe Orton. The two died violently within months of each other in 1967. For many years previously they had been the Holloway and Islington's top cottagers. It seems inconceivable that they had not conjoined somewhere between Nag's Head and Angel. Had it been with anonymity or with knowledge of who the other was?

SONGS: SINGING THE BLUES

Peggy Worrin drove a left-hand-drive Studebaker, drove it with her left hand, her cigarette hand, whilst she turned to talk to us in the back. Its kinship with Ice-Cream Rigiani's sleek gleaming Loewy Studebaker was that of marque alone. Hers was of the mid-1940s at latest, bulbous, lumbering, putty-colour, cold – one of its windows failed to shut wholly, a sheet of celluloid was taped over the gap to little effect. It slewed through Bulford Camp's slushscape of muddy thawing puddled roads, half-built garrison houses, future utility and sewer trenches, tarpaulins still fretted with snow, stacks of bricks and tiles, pipes, scaffolding, icicles detumescing in windowless apertures.

David Worrin and I were friends because our parents were friends. Even though David's younger brother was called Jonathan it amused both sets of parents to allude to the friendship between our biblical namesakes. That David was a shepherd who killed Goliath of Gath with a sling, beheaded him, then murdered two hundred of his fellow Philistines and cut off their foreskins to prove to Jonathan's treacherous father Saul that he would make a worthy son-in-law: an unusual form of proof.

He became a king. In old age, after a lifetime's regal gangsterism, slaughter, warfare, pillage, deception and remorse, David turned, as biblical characters and light entertainers will, to paedophilia and *warmed himself* with virgins. Jonathan, the passive partner, worshipped David.

Had I known any of this I'd have resented being flippantly cast as an idolater, as the one who looks up. But I knew none of it because my mother had assured me that the old testament was risible tosh. And so it is. So, of course, are all 'holy' books. But risible tosh can be persuasive. If god can allow his only son to die on the abattoir hill of Golgotha then he surely sanctions crucifixion: thus Cary Grant's illegitimate half-brother Eric Leach, better known as Foreskin Eric, was merely doing god's will when he nailed Joseph de Haviland (né Ramirez), an unemployed Hungarian illusionist from Ramsgate, to a cross on Hampstead Heath in 1968. If god can be a genocidal warrior why, then, cannot man who is made in god's image be a genocidal warrior too? To a certain cast of mind god's acts legitimise gulags and gas ovens.

I was thinking more about hot chocolate and buttered crumpets than mass death when we got to the Worrins' house, newly built to the same design as every other house in the newly metalled road which would be separated from the pavements by strips of lawn, just now strips of earth pitted with little puddles which grass seed floated on. The army camps on the southern and eastern edges of Salisbury Plain were uniformly neat and ordered, embodiments of routine. Even when unfinished their plans were appealingly legible. There was nothing out of place, nothing which didn't fit: the church, the fire station, the parade of shops, the messes, the barracks, the houses graded by size according to the rank of soldier who occupied them.

There was an obviousness which appealed to the infantile taste for easy comprehension: no nuance, no ambiguity. The camps conformed to the illustrations of towns in pedagogic children's books in a way that few civilian towns did. They might have been composed of Minibrix buildings inflated to life size. I was unable to see in the ubiquitous neo-Georgianism the aesthetic blight which, according to my mother, was the inevitable mark of armed forces' settlements. It was evident that one camp was more or less indistinguishable from the next. I did not understand that this was deliberate, that these places were essays in determinism, in conditioning the will of the individual by site and example. The road names honoured top brass: Shrapnel, Alanbrooke, Templer, Godley, Haig. Soldiers, wartime friends of my father, posted with their families to Bulford, Tidworth,

Durrington and Larkhill, often knew no civvies other than my parents whose society offered some respite from military insularity; the camps were places apart.

All military quarters provided only temporary accommodation. And military families lived as though they were camping within their house. Some of these families trashed their billets, turned them into tips that anticipated crack dens. My parents' friend Len Gill was Southern Command's land agent before he was promoted to the even less enviable post of BAOR's land agent. He recounted with grim gusto countless tales of the domestic sordor achieved by even the highest ranks, especially by the highest ranks. I was fascinated and repulsed by the experience of some people who took over a letting and discovered that what looked like a heavy grey rubber mat beneath the oven was in fact a two-inch-deep deposit of cooking grease.

The Worrins' house was hardly furnished, meagrely carpeted, sparsely curtained. It looked as though they were in the process of moving in or moving out. Their perennially provisional life did not depress them. They were amiable, merry and talented: as my parents constantly reminded me, Jonathan, a year my junior, had learnt to blow his nose whilst I still snivelled lavishly and sprouted a seagreen moustache. Major Worrin was extrovert, hearty, back-slapping, uncomplaining, unreflective and aptly nicknamed Tigger. I was disappointed when they moved to far-distant Harrogate where he was seconded to the Army Apprentices School.

I was even more disappointed when Tigger reappeared some four years later, shortly after my tenth birthday. An early Saturday evening in February, coal fire in the sitting room, hot buttered toast and Patum Peperium, the maroon velvet curtain to my father's den pulled shut for snugness. Though unexpected he was jovially welcomed. I was initially delighted to see him. Then I squatted on a leather pouffe to watch an early edition of *Six-Five Special*, the first pop music show on British television. Its titles comprised a steam engine hauling the supposedly eponymous train and a corny song whose chorus was 'over the points, over the points' repeated four times. The presenters Pete Murray and Jo Douglas were embarrassing: even a ten-year-old winced at the cataract of self-conscious hep-cat drivel. Freddie Mills was goofily troubling. Much of the skiffle and trad jazz was dreary. Tommy Steele wasn't. He was exciting and cheeky. He came on at the end of the show to sing 'Singing the Blues', then my favourite song: it has displaced 'Mountain Greenery', which I had heard at the Rep's panto where the principal boy had been dressed in velvet of a green that I took to be mountain green. But I could hardly hear 'Singing the Blues' for Tigger's whisky'd ranting about how this common little yob, been in the Merchant Navy, the *Merchant* Navy, had been spared National Service simply so he could sing his common little songs which would destroy the fabric of the nation and confirm the ruddy Communist bloc's conviction of western decadence.

Those who had been through the war had known fear and horrors and the proximity of mortality. They had looked the four last things in the face. They had every right to behave as they did and to expect more of their pampered children, every right to despise the minoritarian tyrannies of PC, anti-racism, the compensation culture, the euphemistic society etc. They knew eschatology at first hand rather than as a theological concept.

This was my first taste of what would soon be trumpeted as 'the generation gap': good timing, no doubt, for 'Singing the Blues' was the first pop song that appealed to me. I had not yet heard Elvis Presley, Charlie Gracie, Buddy Holly. I doubt that I'd even heard of them. Before Tommy Steele there had been Lynn's copy of 'The Ballad of High Noon' by Frankie Laine. My father had a few Inkspots records and a couple by Bing Crosby but rarely played them. With the exception of 'St James Infirmary', my mother's extensive collection of Louis Armstrong was also largely mute. Uncle Hank would sometimes put 'Big Rock Candy Mountain', presumably by Burl Ives, on the curiously assembled turntable in Evesham's dining-room cupboard. And I loved to be frightened by Henry Hall's 'Teddy Bears' Picnic'.

Comedians and comic actors were accorded a sort of respect: Al Read, Ted Ray, Charlie Drake, Benny Hill, Ted Lune, Bill Maynard, Eric Sykes, Hylda Baker, Alfie Bass, Michael Medwin, Bob Monkhouse (even though he was on the smooth side), Jimmy Edwards, Dick Bentley, June Whitfield, Tony Hancock, Sid James, Hugh Paddick, Kenneth Williams, Kenneth Horne, Hattie Jacques, George Cole with Percy Edwards as Psyche The Dog in *A Life of Bliss* and, in later years, Stanley Baxter, Peter Cook, Dudley Moore, Marty Feldman, Dick Emery, Les Dawson.

Most popular music was dismissed and mocked. Edmund Hockridge and Donald Peers excited a special scorn and were deprecated as 'full fruit' – I agreed, though I had no idea why that expression, so far as I know peculiar to my father, should signify a particular kind of treacly light operatic baritone. I still have no idea.

Musicals and light orchestral music were abhorred. *Rose-Marie* and *South Pacific*, Mantovani, Cyril Stapleton, Eric 'Little Pig' Robinson, Jack Payne, Shirley Abicair, Eve Boswell, Malcolm Vaughan, The Mudlarks, Dennis Lotis, The Dallas Boys, Salisbury's own Rosemary Squires, the unfortunate Dorothy Squires, The Stargazers, Dickie Valentine. My parents considered them all trivial beyond contempt. Light entertainers and song and dancemen too: Bruce Forsyth, Dickie Henderson, Norman Vaughan. The Range Rider's sidekick, the grinning All-American Boy Dick West and the bonhomous children's telly presenter Ross Salmon, who used to address 'chaps and chapesses', caused my father to wonder why we have to share a planet with such people. I shared my parents' contempt. I absorbed their taste.

That compact would soon be shredded by former truckers with DAs, leather boys on the lam from slums, delinquent hair-dressers, the slide guitar of smalltown Lotharios.

And Tigger, confronted by the unstoppable tide of teen, would turn into Eeyore. I didn't see him again after that evening in 1957 but my parents kept in touch. They would meet up infrequently. I would receive reports of Tigger's raging at the world, of his fury that Jonathan was now a long-haired lefty. My parents' attitude to my foibles was, on the contrary, sanguine, expressed most forcibly in the advice that 'you'll probably grow out of it' – whatever *it* was.

STEWART? STUART? JOHN?

My mother's boyfriend of her early twenties. A fellow student or maybe teacher at University College, Southampton: he is gowned in formal group photographs with her. I only learnt of his existence from a photo I found after her death. I asked her sister Mary who he was.

Stuart/Stewart – almost certainly.

But on the verso in some he is John in soft pencil.

Not John. Mary was certain that she had never had a boyfriend called John before she met my father.

In 1932 they were in Southsea High Street, a sojourn in a different town captured by a street photographer. He wears a thin moustache, a full head of gleaming Marcel'd hair, waisted jacket, Oxford bags – a bit late in the day for those, surely. Her expression is that of a woman in love. Whatever happened to him? Whatever happened to gleaming Marcel'd hair?

At Mary's funeral their crabby cousin from Bournemouth, grudge-bearing Dorothy Bolton (née Janda), whom I'd never previously met, told me, accusatorily, that as a child she had resented that on several occasions she had had to give up her bed to my mother and her boyfriend who played in a jazz band. Was this Stewart/Stuart or John moonlighting with a cornet? Or another lover? The cousin couldn't remember his name.

'Stuart?'

She shrugged and hit the tea.

'John?'

She bit a biscuit.

She had borne this rancour for getting on seventy years. She had a lot to get off her chest. She had married late in life, another of these embittered virgins no doubt. She exuded spite, bile, moralistic superiority. I shrugged: I was not my dead mother's keeper before I was born. The old bitch contorted her biscuity mouth. I was relieved never to have met her before. Indeed I had not been aware of her sanctimonious existence. She was the daughter of Nesta Hogg, my grandfather's sister, and her husband Joe Janda, a tailor who claimed to be Christian rather than Jewish and despite his surname to be Viennese rather than Czech. Vienna enjoyed a certain cachet in Britain in the earlier twentieth century, indeed still enjoyed it long after it rolled over to let Hitler fondle it. There was, after all, a ladies' hairdresser in Salisbury called Hans of Vienna; this was a crimper who hedged his bets, he was also Hans of Bond Street.

The Jandas' other child was a son, Dennis, a sometime Bournemouth school teacher whom I have never met. I had heard of him, but only because of his sexual demeanour. His first marriage was annulled due to non-consummation. And so was his second marriage – which was rather overdoing it. This was a matter of comical wonder to my parents. Third time lucky, Dennis married a woman called Phyllis. They produced a son, Howard, another Bournemouth school teacher, whom I have of course never met.

SUBTERRANEAN

The distant past is always with us. Around Salisbury it is inescapable. The extent of the inhabited past is greater than anywhere else in Europe. It stretches over horizon upon horizon.

This is where British archaeology was born in the seventeenth century, out of an intellectual curiosity about English antiquity prompted by the multiple interventions in the landscape. A taste for the past is not elemental – it has to be learnt. As a child growing up in the midst of this ancientness I was persistently encouraged to awe, to humility, to pride in the precious patrimony that surrounded me. For a long time I was unable to summon those properties. I just didn't get it. I failed in what was presented to me as a duty.

Then, when I was eight, an elderly gardener's hand was pierced by a rose thorn. He contracted tetanus. He died. Lockjaw. The inquest fascinated me. The thorn was rumoured to be a vector of tetanus because of the bodies buried millennia ago beneath the garden in Breamore where the deadly rose grew. The very earth was contaminated by chemical ghosts. The past was present. The dead were with us still, they were active from the grave, they were adding to their number, recruiting with poisons seeping from their long decomposition.

I began to get it. The loose notion of the past was illumined by specificity, physicality. For all its wretchedness and ill fortune the old man's death was touched by mystery from deep strata. I didn't know that, given the multiplicity of their hosts, tetanus spores were ubiquitous. So this rumoured diagnosis might be scientifically dubious. But even had I known I'd have been unwilling to discount the satisfying and simple tale. Faith, or wishfulness, would have trumped fact. That, as I say, is what faith does.

Above Breamore near the tawny groves of Great Yews and beside the gallops there is a dense clump of blackthorn. Beneath the bushes are just discernible a building's ruinous foundations. I pored over a large-scale OS map. The house which had stood here was called Vanity. The name made me shiver. I thought of Milady de Winter, of venom and plots, of damask hangings, dark carvings, vast curtains swelling like a man-o'-war's foresails. Why was such a house isolated on the high downs with clouds and skylarks when all the others were sheltered in valleys or declivities? These downs west of the Avon valley above Breamore form the edge of Cranborne Chase. Here is the Mizmaze, a turf labyrinth whose purpose may have been no more than decorative, though it is of course routinely connected to pagan rites: where isn't? Its vaguely 'Celtic' pattern resembles that of an infuriating game in a glass-topped box whose end was to coax a tiny ballbearing between ridges to a slot in the centre. I could not master it. I railed at my clumsiness. This is an area dense with barrows: Knaps Barrow, Grans Barrow, the Giant's Grave, the Duck's Nest. There are field systems, strip lynchets, tumuli, castle keeps. Fortresses moulded from flinty chalky earth are announced by clumps of beeches whose roots are witches' claws: Castle Ditches, Soldier's Ring, Clearbury Ring. Here are Bokerley Dyke and Grim's Ditch. Grim is a name of the devil: the walls and the trench between them will repulse him. These sites were forever being excavated. Vessels, blades, tools, lumps of rust and shards of leather, cloth, beads, arrowheads, tiles, pipes, bones, rings, cooking utensils, bracelets, seeds and tesserae were exhumed with bounteous abandon.

The majority of excavations were undertaken by the Ministry of Works or supposedly responsible archaeological faculties and societies. Nonetheless over certain digs there still hung a hint of the chase, a suspicion of pillage. The earth was violated as it had been by early antiquaries and would be again by hick chancers armed with metal detectors – that is, by indiscriminate collectors, looters of the past who sought trophies as though participating in a subterranean lottery. The Roman villa at Rockbourne was intermittently excavated over two decades by Morley Hewitt, a Fordingbridge estate agent, a well-intentioned amateur with sparse knowledge of then current field-archaeological practices. During the war he had bought the land after a tip-off from a man whose rabbiting ferret had uncovered tiles and oyster shells. It was his fiefdom to uncover as he willed. When he began excavations in the 1950s the practices of scientific archaeology proselytised by R. G. Collingwood as long ago as the 1920s were still in the future for want of an appropriate technology. But Morley Hewitt's dig lacked even the rigour applied by General Augustus Pitt-Rivers in the 1880s. Hewitt's helpers were enthusiastic tyros: schoolchildren, students, farm workers, families on outings, ramblers. Procedures were lax, finds were haphazardly recorded. Nonetheless objects that had been occluded for over a thousand years were brought to light even if the particular stratum from which they were dredged was ignored, so debasing their value as data.

One deliriously happy afternoon in August 1964 I climbed with some friends to the top of the monument erected to a member of the Eyre Coote family of West Park in the early c19. West Park House itself had yet to be demolished. Twenty miles south, the Isle of Wight and the dazzling Channel were visible. And all around the Roman villa swarmed an inchoate formic army, putting on a fine show of endeavour and sweat.

When Hampshire County Council adopted the villa in the late 1970s its archaeological department backfilled parts of the site in the name of preservation. It covered it beneath turf. Why? To appease the shades of Roman colonists? Out of respect for a past – a temporal abstraction, after all – which is incapable of acknowledging or reciprocating that respect?

Antiquarianism pillage is hardly scholarly and far from scientific, but its perpetrators were not culpable of a misanthropic relativism which grants rights to ancient amphorae and entitlements to yokes' remnants. Nor did they conceive of history in terms of movements, big ideas and sweeping theses. Their empiricism militated against generalisation. The further scientific-archaeological method has abandoned antiquarianism's delinquency, the more emphasis it has laid on understanding context through the gathering of information rather than through the coarse acquisition of objects: indeed the objects may often remain in situ, like fish thrown back in the river, like tagged birds which will never know an aviary. It was, however, that coarse acquisition which fascinated me in the museums I frequented as a child.

The Pitt-Rivers Museum at Farnham was in a Pitt-Rivers's village, deep in the thousands of Pitt-Rivers Acres, an hour or so from Salisbury on my metallic carmine and cream Raleigh Space Rider (note the American tan saddle and friable caramel plastic handlebar grips). A stitch-inducing slog there past the deep dry valley which I had identified as the Valley of the Shadow of Death. A thrilling return with a southwesterly at one's back and mewing buzzards circling overhead. Farnham is a small and remote village. The museum occupied a dour former schoolhouse built for gypsy children whose truancy soon rendered it redundant. It was doubtless their descendants who camped on the Old Shaftesbury Drove near Dogdean. The school was distinguished from countless others only by its multitude of insipidly Tudorish extensions. On Sundays Pitt-Rivers would send charabancs and carriages to Salisbury, Shaftesbury and Blandford to fetch the populace so that it might recreate itself at the alluring pleasure gardens called the Larmer Tree Grounds and inspect his ethnological and archaeological collections rather than attend church services. This was a pedagogic, improving programme: every exhibit was meticulously described and the pleasure gardens were instructionally decorated with pavilions in exotic architectural styles. Those with the means to do so could stay at the Museum Hotel, built expressly to that end rather than as a public house. It may during the General's day have been teetotal. The Larmer Tree Grounds certainly were. By the time I discovered the museum it was decrepit, ill kempt, ill frequented. Its heyday was long gone. Indeed I never saw another visitor. Seventy years previously a thousand people had come here each month. Nearly all those witnesses to the distant past were now dead.

So too was its singular sometime curator Trelawney Dayrell Reed. The rooms were harshly skylit. Many of the painted objects, drawings, manuscripts and fabrics were faded from an excess of sunlight. The ambient brightness was unnerving. There were impressive dunes of dust in the cabinets. Paleness abounded. The rooms were almost monochromatic, approximately bleached putty. Were there shrunken heads and craniometrical drawings and stuffed monkeys? Inventories of the long since dispersed collections include these and countless other items of ethnographic bric-a-brac. I have no memory of anything other than the issue of the chalk surrounds, of my soil. My soil. *Mine* . . . which I came in early adolescence to realise was *not mine*, it was another lie, it was not part of me, it was not connected to my blood, whatever that meant.

This pernicious patrimony was determined by chance, by my parents having made their home in Salisbury because that was where my father had been posted by William Crawford & Sons Ltd – biscuits determine destiny. Even had they come from 'Salisbury families', incuriously immobile vertical groupings stretching back generations, I would still not have owned *roots*. Roots are illusory chains suturing man and mineral. It's the easiest thing in the world to cast them off: we are not vegetables. My appetite for ancient artefacts was not conditional on an ersatz ancestral bond with stone-age mumblers or ragged beaker folk or woaden berserkers rupturing a deer's chest to feast on the still-beating heart. (I had no more taste then for venison than I have now.) I prided myself, rather, on appreciating artefacts with a reasoned objectivity and an obedient understanding of history's rigid taxonomy, of periods and ages – including prehistory which implied that history began at a definitive point before which it had presumably been in utero.

Salisbury and South Wiltshire Museum was in St Ann Street,

the southernmost street of the grid. It had been founded in the mid-c19 to house the predominantly mediaeval objects retrieved from the grid's canals (i.e. open sewers) when they were replaced by subterranean ones. The museum had long ago amalgamated with the Blackmore Museum, named not for the Dorset vale but for a lawyer, adventurer and eventual suicide who had acquired many of the aboriginal objects excavated in Ohio by Squier and Davis and rejected by the Smithsonian. The collections were eclectic, even haphazard. A taxidermised great bustard, shot between Shrewton and Berwick St James on the hostile Plain in the mid-nineteenth century, was among England's last. There were detailed scale models of the cathedral (maybe ivory) and of Stonehenge, sculptural capitals from Clarendon, heavy ornate keys (sure signals of status), glazed jugs and so on.

The most eyecatching exhibits were Hob Nob and the Giant, who gave his name to Gigant Street a few blocks away. He was minatory, blackbearded, implacable, a Caliban robed in red and twice the height of a tall man. Hob Nob was a long-necked animal or fowl, possibly a dragon. They belonged to a mediaeval tailors' guild. They processed through feast day carnivals when Hob Nob would clear the way by jocularly attacking members of the crowd. Jocularly? Both creatures incited a particular terror. Further, they were associated with the morris, a further source of terror. Those ale-breathed beardies with silly hats and clacking sticks and bells around their ruggerbugger calves were far from quaint. My mother delighted in pointing out the bogusness of what passed for folkloric custom. Thus I knew that morris sides were a late Victorian creation, the clumsily terpsichorean analogue of a Voysey house or a Gimson settle. That did not prevent these lumbering clodhoppers promising antic misrule and Merry English violence.

The raucous gaudy of the Giant and Hob Nob seemed incompatible with the donnish archaeologist and numismatist who was the museum's curator. Hugh de S. Shortt (known, not without mockery, as 'Hugh de S') was a fastidious presence on such telly programmes as *The Brains Trust* and *Animal, Vegetable, Mineral?*, whose star was the beguiling vaudevillian Mortimer Wheeler. Shortt haunted his museum with the fugitive air of the White Rabbit. He had scurried into middle age before he married the widow of a man who had been eaten by a crocodile. They lived in a wing of a pretty castellated Gothick house at Britford. Its name, The Moat, was apt given the frequency with which it was flooded.

The past's imminence was signalled not merely by tumuli and the contents of glass cabinets. Were a social history of c20 English archaeology to be composed its loci need never extend much beyond a thirty-mile radius of Salisbury. The conduits to the past, its decryptors – the seers who read the earth's yield and heeded the dead's pleas to be remembered – were close by, almost neighbours. They had all spent time here, many lived here:

Avebury. **Alexander Keiller** (1889–1955), Dundee marmalade magnate, excavated Windmill Hill and West Kennet Long Barrow. He lived at Avebury Manor and restored or recreated or created the stone circle there. He financed *Wessex from the Air*, which he produced in collaboration with O. G. S. Crawford. The most revealing photographs were made at dawn and dusk, the 'lynchet hours'. In the early Thirties he proposed constructing, at his own cost, a subterranean visitor centre at Stonehenge.

Coombe Bisset. **Tancred Borenius** (1885–1948), quondam art historian, quondam Finn, founder of *Apollo*, consultant to Sotheby's. Like many of his contemporaries he came to archaeology from other disciplines. He directed the excavation of the twelfth-century Clarendon Palace a couple of miles east of Salisbury. He began this project in 1933. It was initially abandoned at the outbreak of war, reprised and abandoned again when he died. Whereupon the palace's remains were once more overgrown with brambles. Rangers Lodge Farm, whose buildings stood beside the road to the ruins, was desolate and sinister, surely a location in a B-feature – all barns stuffed with swag, and stolen lorries, and aspirant Stanley Bakers.

Gorley. **Heywood Sumner** (1853–1940) was a sgraffitist, water-colourist, calligrapher, textile designer etc. In the earliest years of the c20 he built a house for himself and his family at Gorley on the western edge of the New Forest, less than a mile from the Avon. Like most artists associated with the arts and crafts he was prone to whimsy and twee archaism. Yet there is beauty in much of his work, not least in *Cuckoo Hill: The Book of Gorley*. After he moved there his life was increasingly dominated by archaeology. He joined the digging hordes. His illumined map of 'Ancient Sites in the New Forest, Cranborne Chase and Bournemouth District' is an exquisite thing. In this instance he mercifully desisted from his occasional practice of spelling it Chace. I was aware of the house from my earliest years. We'd pass it on the way to Ogdens, my favourite place on earth, where I'd attempt to dam Huckle Brook, paddle, catch minnows, seek birds' eggs in the furse. Beside the prevailing mangey thatched cottages, disintegrating cob cottages, shacks, shanties and rural slums – the genuinely vernacular Forest buildings – Cuckoo Hill was grandly incongruous and surprisingly stern, as though Sumner, a decorative artist rather than an architect, lacked the capability to translate to three dimensions his douce sensibility. It was on a slope. High above it on the Forest's very escarpment stood three twisted pines which according to local lore had been planted as a warning: they represented men hanged in the civil war or hanged as smugglers or hanged as highwaymen. When I was at the age to believe I duly believed it. In the early Sixties, more than two decades after Sumner's death, the house was owned by a soldier, a barely credible cartoon of a bristling artillery colonel. He fulminated against the ignorance of those who dared to live in the Forest and, not being *true Forest people*, failed to understand commoners' rights (pasture, mast, estovers etc.). He fulminated against mechanised agriculture (always a bad sign). He fulminated against the moral decline he detected in his daughters' generation. He glared menacingly at their friends. He discerned dishonourable intentions in teenaged boys. He engaged a French au pair to look after his young son. He left his wife for her. His wife killed herself. Cuckoo Hill became a care home.

Nursling. **O. G. S. Crawford** (1886–1957), photographer, gullible fellow traveller, founder of *Antiquity*, pioneer of aerial archaeology, lived on the periphery of Southampton, where he was employed at the headquarters of the Ordnance Survey – where I yearned to work. Among the sites he discovered from the sky was Little Woodbury, between the former Alderbury Union Workhouse and the future Odstock Hospital. He financed its excavation by the German Jewish refugee Gerhard Bersu who was subsequently interned.

Rockbourne. **Stuart Piggott** (1910–1996), who lived in that village till his marriage broke up, described his contemporaries as making 'a conscious and concerted effort to professionalise prehistory for its own good'. As a schoolboy he had taught himself to draw by imitating Heywood Sumner. He was employed by Keiller at Avebury. He worked at Stonehenge, Woodbury and Wayland's Smithy. For much of his life he was exiled from Wiltshire in Edinburgh academe. He collected the work of a generation of archaeologically and geologically preoccupied artists: Paul Nash, John Piper, Graham Sutherland.

West Parley. **Trelawney Dayrell Reed** (1886–1958) delighted me. He wore a cloak, owned a Rolls-Royce, listened to gramophone records so loud that conversation was impossible. He was dandiacal, fedora'd, mocking, mad, thin as a stick. He had been tried for attempted murder. He had written books. He had a cane and a temper. He was a disputatious charmer, a contrite boor, an earnest dilettante, a self-proclaimed mountebank, an industrious vagabond, a scrounger who affected aristocratic airs and lived far beyond others' means. My parents first encountered him in the late Thirties as one of Augustus John's intimates. In the middle of the war he took to calling on my mother, whom he would regale with monologues dense with mordant wit, garrulously ignoble gossip and bitchy mimicry, though everyone he guyed inherited his stammer. He was by then in his late fifties.

Just as my great uncle John in distant Sandycove had his nattily uniformed 'chauffeur valet', the grossly mute Frank, so did Reed, despite his indigence, have a 'major-domo' who would sit silently as his benefactor performed a doubtless familiar repertoire. It was in imitation of Reed that Peter Lucas affected red socks. Lucas drew the line at suits which my mother said *would frighten the horses*. He was a self-taught archaeologist, a muralist, a rancorous historian, a Wessex supremacist, the author of a bizarrely fantastical account of immediately post-Roman England and of a survey of shove-ha'penny's development. His modest fame (or notoriety) had, however, nothing to do with his eclectic scholarship.

It rested on:

a) An event of Good Friday 15 April 1927. His house at West Parley, then a village, now subsumed by northern Bournemouth, was close to Ensbury Park, that town's racecourse which in the 1920s was increasingly used for air shows. Having failed by numerous legitimate means to quash such displays he fired a twelve-bore at a Blackburn Bluebird piloted by Squadron Leader Walter 'Scruffy' Longton. The aircraft's wings were damaged, the pilot was untouched. Described as a 'gentleman farmer aged about 38' (the farm was barely a smallholding, he was forty-one), Reed was tried at Dorchester Assizes for attempted murder. Not guilty – despite the judge's advice to the jury. A few days after the trial, on Monday 6 June 1927, 'Scruffy' Longton, one of the earliest stunt pilots ('crazy flyers'), was killed during Ensbury Park's Whitsun meeting. The air displays moved to Christchurch.

b) A few years later Trelawney Dayrell Reed sold up and moved to Farnham, where he had been appointed curator of the Pitt-Rivers Museum and press officer of the green, bucolic-fascist Wessex Agricultural Defence Association (Chairman: George Pitt-Rivers, grandson of the General).

He and his major-domo lived in a Pitt-Rivers estate cottage. For a while they had a jig-dancing bog-sprite of an Irish lodger, William Joyce, past deputy leader of the British Union of Fascists and future Lord Haw-Haw, hanged at Wandsworth Prison in January 1946. When he appeared in Cranborne Chase in the late Thirties he had been dismissed by Oswald Mosley and had founded the short-lived National Socialist League. As it gradually became known that the former lodger and the notorious propagandist were the same man, his host was tainted by association, his already sulphurous reputation grew.

I remember Trelawney Dayrell Reed, I remember him well. I never met him. He was a figure of familial myth and maternal fairy tale. He belonged to that infinitely mysterious life my parents led before I existed. All I know of him is from their disparate accounts of long ago and from Augustus John's striking portrait made even longer ago, probably in the mid-1920s. He is not yet grey or scrawny, alcohol has not yet worked its malevolent magic. My mother was flattered to be entertained by him. They would sometimes drink in The Rose and Crown where Reed satisfied a Bedlam-sniffing appetite by observing then sparring with mine drunken host (and my parents' landlord) Stiffy Edwards. My father grudgingly conceded that Reed was a scholarly countryman, a mine of botanical and geological information, a consummate decipherer of footprints and droppings. That was as far as it went.

YURI

In 1964 all the nice people were still as poor as they had been in the 1945 of Muriel Spark's 1963 novel *The Girls of Slender Means*.

My parents had sent their academically inclined only son to a bucolic, defiantly non-academic, dim, backward, muscular Christian bootcamp whose purpose was apparently to make gentlemen of the sons of Somerset farmers and knock Newbolt into Devon's garagists of tomorrow. There was a better grammar school where we lived, Bishop Wordsworth's. William Golding still taught there, almost a decade after *Lord of the Flies*; Derek Warner and Gus Barnes were, locally, famously inspirational teachers. My mother believed in grammar schools as democratic instruments of improvement. She subscribed to The Black Papers on Education and execrated Shirley Williams. I had passed the eleven plus. My essay was on Sir Nigel Gresley. Since the age of seven my mother had made me sit Moray House intelligence tests every few weeks. I thoroughly enjoyed them so found the

exam beguilingly easy. The reason why I was sent away to a boarding school was never vouchsafed to me.

Most likely they didn't want me around (most school holidays I was sent to stay with Uncle Wangle and Auntie Ann or went on an 'exchange', often one-way, to France). A striving for social cachet was not really a habit of my parents. And whether social cachet attached to having a son at King's College, Taunton was, and remains, moot. The whole regrettable business may have originated in my mother's rich uncle's offer to stump up the greater part of the fees. My frequent demands to be taken out of the wretched dump were rebuked as displays of ingratitude.

John Baird was my maternal grandmother's younger brother. He had been a chartered accountant, a partner in Deloitte Plender Griffiths. He retired in his mid-forties in the mid-1930s. He had made his fortune gambling on the stock exchange during the depression. At the time of my parents' marriage in May 1939 he was living in Langford Place, St John's Wood, in a sinister, malevolent neo-Gothic cottage which looks in pain, an ideal home for a dominatrix.

Soon after war was declared he moved to Dublin with his bulgy-muscled, aggressively silent 'chauffeur-valet' Frank, whom he had met at a boxing club for deprived boys. Every couple of years John designed a new uniform of increasingly Ruritanian dash for Frank. They lived in a Regency house at Sandycove, close by the Martello tower. I doubt that he read *Ulysses*: he may not even have been aware of Joyce's existence. Great Uncle John read little but the city pages. He and Frank visited England most summers in an immaculately maintained prewar Rolls-Royce, black and grey with spare wheel covers protruding from the wings.

Togs Must Be Worn. That's the notice at the entrance to Sandycove Men's Bathing Association round the corner from his house. He used to watch appreciatively when as a small child I swam untogged in the Nadder and in the sea at Chewton Bunny. He was less appreciative when I got self-consciousness and trunks.

Thoroughly unappreciative when I walked out of school, though he chided me only gently. Mute Frank scowled.

My parents despaired. The prospect of having living with them a teenager whose only aptitude, once he had abandoned competitive swimming, was for sullen shirking was too much to bear. Whose idea was it to send me to a crammer? I forget. But the idea was enticing. And Great Uncle John was somehow enthused. And me, I could escape the old, martial, churchy provinces to London: which had not yet been designated swinging – but that American anointment came, of course, after the event. There was something going on. Something new, something long-haired and Cuban-heeled. I could grow my hair, I could walk tall in Cuban heels, wear a black PVC mac, dance in clubs, meet fast girls, chain-smoke Kents and Gitanes, take speed – and retake exams.

But where was I to live?

At a fancy dress party in a roadhouse between Fordingbridge and Ringwood called the As You Like It, my parents, yet unmarried, had, in the late Thirties, met Augustus John. They were introduced by Peter Lucas, a painter who was their contemporary and one of John's many young acolytes around that fringe of the New Forest. My father was outdoorsy, an unambitious biscuit company rep, fanatical only about chalkstream fly-fishing.

Save for music he had no interest in art: and that interest probably derived from Schubert having had the predictive good sense to write 'The Trout' for him. Despite this or because – surely because – John took a shine to him and they struck up an improbable casual bibulous friendship which endured till John died in 1961.

April 1964. Mike B (recently expelled from Stowe for masturbating on socks that didn't belong to him) and I are hitching to Bournemouth. A (white) forty-year-old evangelical with a beamer and abundant crinkly hair on leave from his 'mission' in Ghana picks us up in his open-top Morris Minor.

Despite smoking moodily Mike and I fail to pick up girls in the cafés and bowling alley where we loiter.

Hitch home late afternoon. On Holdenhurst Road we are, weirdly, espied by our Ghanaian friend. He's clearly pissed. But not totally badered, not speechschlurred. So we climb in. At St Leonard's, a decrepit shack colony north of Bournemouth, he insists we go for a drink in a grim bungalow pub: Mike and I have 'shorts' – he is pleased to treat us. He enthusiastically gets in another round. We pass the graceful Georgian bridge at Ellingham, the ancient church tower across meadows that are still fulldyke, mad Colonel Crowe's cottage and the now tatty As You Like It. The evangelist's next stop was a riverside hotel at Fordingbridge. I had sufficient memories of drunken Christian chaplains not to want to hang about with this increasingly chummy godly sponge whose intentions might prove dishonourable and whose ability to drive would soon be impaired. I nudged Mike.

We walked past dour brick villas and fruitholdings gone to seed and a thatched restaurant. Outside it on offensively ginger gravel was parked its thatched van, a cause of joy to Daniel Richmond, who had once driven me here to show me it and hoot with laughter. We had almost reached the bridge over the disused railway at Burgate when Yuri came into my life.

There was a noise behind us, a motor in decline, it passed us, just, then stuttered, stopped, groaning.

Yuri White – big slab head, straight hair, barrel body – turned astride his sick Vespa and bellowed at Mike B: 'Christ, you're the fellow [I shall never forget that 'fellow'] that wanked on what's his name's socks.'

Mike B grinned.

We trudged along beside Yuri as he pushed the motor-scooter. Where the rail track and the river run beside ruinous watercress beds he turned through an aperture in a high hedge. Here was Yew Tree Cottage, cramped and tiny, his parents' weekend house. His grandmother lived nearby. He was less than a year older than I was, but his sophistication was obviously immense: bell-bottom jeans and horizontal striped 'Breton' T-shirt; his self-proclaimed diet was R&B and girls; he lived in London where all the girls were sexually obliging. Unlike the sisters we all knew who lived just across the river.

Yuri found some filthy wine. Fastidiously, I took no more than a sip.

A couple of days later Yuri arrived on his mended scooter at my parents' house. My father liked him. His wretched son was taciturn, offhand, bored, self-conscious, self-preoccupied and a reader. Yuri was exuberant, lusty, outgoing, unreflective.

My father never found in him the neurosis and despair which would come to define Yuri for me: but, then, we fashion them as we want them. He found instead an appreciative audience for his fishing lore and the stupendously filthy wine he made from his Seyval vines – an annual few hundred bottles of emetic, fit only for distillation. He found, too, Augustus John's grandson, the elder son – born in Moscow, hence his given name – of the painter's youngest daughter Vivien and her husband, the haematologist John White, whom Augustus had derided as 'the hospital orderly' and 'the medical attendant'.

Yuri turned up over and again that spring and summer of '64. He'd Vespa into Salisbury even when I was away suffering my last term in Taunton. My mother was a generous cook used to catering for people I had picked up. He was a good fit with my parents. Late one afternoon, lying on the scorched lawn beside the river, I looked up from my book to watch him, bottle in hand, and my father, side by side on a bench formed from a broken willow trunk, leaning towards each other rocking with laughter, man to man in some shared intimacy.

He was not alone in seeking other people's families. Though it is perhaps a trait more developed in only children.

In those days before a second home was normal there were provincial people and there were London people. Those who were both were exotics. The sheer worldliness of such siblings as Kate and Carola, Chris and Gay, of Julian . . .

I routinely sought out contemporaries whose family had a London base. And here, reciprocally, in Yuri's, I had found one. I would rent a room from his parents. All the nice people rented.

Vivien White wore a homemade 'geometric' bob. John White wore his very black hair *en brosse*, as much an oddity then in England as now: it lent him the air of a military policeman who had been up to no good in the cellars of Oran.

They lived in Holland Park. A century previously it had been one of London's grandest inner suburbs. Twenty years later it would become so again. In 1964 its long desuetude was in its dotage: not that anyone knew. Like most of London's core – Islington, Camden Town, Bloomsbury, World's End etc. – it had suffered from the bourgeois flight to the outer suburbs throughout the first half of the twentieth century, that hardly chronicled diaspora which abandoned Georgian order and Victorian pomp to the dispossessed, to exploited immigrants, to slum landlords – and to bohemia. There was yet little sign of 'gentrification' and, indeed, that word was uncoined. Holland Park and the adjacent Ladbroke Estate were all crazed paint and encrusted soot. The Hanging Gardens of Northern Kensington (Christopher Gibbs's coinage) were goosegrass and nettles. The Clean Air Acts of a decade before were effective: 1960s smog allowed you to see five yards ahead rather than the three of the 1950s. Smog never swirled the way studio-rendered peasoupers did. It was still and thick, like stone that one might pass through. There was, however, movement in the air: sooty stucco peelings flew like freeform bats.

Most of Pottery Lane was an anthology of wrecked, burnt-out and, at best, semi-ruinous two-storey cottages – a mews hoping for a grand terrace to which it might attach itself. Seal House was, is, at its northern end, and quite different. It adhered to no building line. It gaped down the lane, an imperious punctuation mark built on a different scale, a late Georgian oddity, flat-fronted, double-fronted, tall, one room deep, exclusively south-lit, occupying a space occasioned by a kink in the lane, with a wedge of garden ahead of it. Vivien and John had bought it in the late Forties for, presumably, a song: in 1964 friends of theirs bought a house in the neighbouring, Portland Road, four storeys and basement for £2.2. Thousand, that is. The complexion of Britain was different when there was no such thing as 'the house price differential' between, say, undesirable central London and desirable Salisbury.

That would change that very autumn when Harold Wilson attained power. That most underappreciated of prime ministers achieved three things:

He acted on Walter James's vision of the Open University. He resisted LBJ's increasingly truculent requests for troops rather than for words in support of his no-win war. (A conscripted old Fettesian might have died there.) He effected the centralisation of Britain.

The politicisation of newness was on its way.

To walk into Seal House was to walk into a chaotic museum of a world new to me, but far from a new world. Metropolitan neophilia was hugely absent here. Where were the man-made materials and glossy gadgets – those fresh balms? Where were the tokens of the mythic city of the future, the playground of thoughtful hairdressers and getaway people? Elsewhere, evidently.

The newness in Seal House was the newness of the New English Art Club and its contemporaries, the newness of more than half a century before. I had never heard of Matthew Smith before I stepped on the frame of one of his paintings negligently propped against a crazed wainscot. Nor of Gwen John, who was then largely forgotten, buried beneath the edifice of her brother's still miraculously intact reputation. Although acquainted with Rodin I had never expected to handle his maquettes. There were sheaves of prints, rolled-up canvases, cairns of precious doodles. The walls were all but invisible behind the works hung on them. Monographs and recherché art magazines formed teetering piles. Augustus John was everywhere. His omnipotent shade made his having been dead for three years an irrelevance. He oversaw Vivien from the grave. She felt it her inhibiting obligation to second-guess a corpse.

There was a drawing by Henry Lamb, a fine painter whose blond son Valentine had been the ganymede of all Salisbury girls a few years previously. Henry Lamb's widow Pansy (née Pakenham), en route from Coombe Bissett to the Vatican, had moved to Blenheim Crescent: at a party there I met shaky relics of Bloomsbury who, to my astonishment, were gratified that a mere child should be interested in them.

I studied in a desultory way. I strolled four days a week down streets of multiply occupied former mansions and seedily genteel terraces to the 'tutorial college' less than a mile away. I was flattered when, out of the early evening smog on Holland Park Avenue, a man's voice asked me if I knew a nearby Turkish bath, sonny: he had obviously taken me for a Londoner. Which didn't happen at the Café des Artists where a Mod, even more sullenly pouting than I was, marked your hand when you entered with ink that showed under ultraviolet light – the idea being that you could come and go. I went. A girl whom I attempted to talk to jokily called me 'Bumpkin'. It still hurt. I had thitherto been unaware of the accent I had acquired in Taunton. Why had no one told me? Why had my parents, normally so punctilious in matters of speech and usage, not grimaced in shame? Had they not noticed? I resolved to speak posh.

And to hang out at The London Cavern, Blaise's, The Cromwellian. Oh, the humiliations . . .

My hair wasn't right. My clothes from The Modern Shop, Catherine Street, Salisbury turned out – despite the assurance of the owner Mr Wakeham, a fifty-year-old former newsagent from Eastleigh – to be *so last month*: my John Langford twin-tab, giraffe-collared shirt with French cuffs was crushed raspberry. That autumn mid-grey was the colour. My Anello and Davide Cuban heels didn't make up for that chromatic solecism. Further, I had served no apprenticeship in long cool silences and it showed.

My half-provincial, half-metropolitan friends were different when in London – sharper, more assured, familiar with arcane cafés, richer. They knew the form. Their parents' friends designed film sets and owned important bistros. The long nocturnal walks to their flats and to the clubs which daunted me became more attractive than the destinations. Thus they became increasingly circuitous. I didn't want to arrive. Frequently I had no chance of arriving because I was lost in the smog and reliant on the tube map which I had yet to realise was diagrammatic. It would be years before I read *The City of Dreadful Night*. Yet here was that very maze where terror lurked in milky pools of light cast through grubby curtains, in alley shadows, in craterous bombsites where flaccid buddleia sprouted, in walls of brick and seeping mortar, in the teeming slums of Little Napoli (© Colin MacInnes) where the ten-year-old urchins (© Roger Mayne) were more wised up than I was: I don't know how I learnt that Vince was called Vince. He used to sit up in his hoodless, tyreless pram, eye me and shout: 'Cunt!' Westbourne Grove was clamorous. The broad avenues of Maida Vale were always deserted. Not everyone had a phone. St Paul's was black with soot and smuts. When it was cleaned its magnificence was scrubbed away too; André Malraux has much to answer for.

A couple of times I dropped by a schoolfriend's flat in Observatory Gardens near the Victorian water tower on Campden Hill. He wasn't there. At a party on 21 November 1964 I learned that he had been killed the previous Friday, the 13th, when a furniture pantechnicon was blown over on top of his father's car on the Hog's Back. It was years before I dared venture back to that square of *oeil-de-boeuf* windows and heftily French rustication. I guess that my superstitious avoidance suggests that I was marking out my own London, a city of permanently absent friends and architectonic solaces.

It was a city, too, that was mediated by Seal House. The interior was like an interior by Sickert or Tonks. I knew this because I spent hours among the paintings and reproductions.

It did not occur to me that the house was oddly anachronistic, that it was unmarked by the fashions of post-war Britain, that the Whites' taste belonged to an era before they were born. Painting was generically francophile, generically post-impressionist, generically splodgy: it was some years before I had the confidence to admit to myself that I prefer the cold northern precision of Fouquet and Schad to enthusiastic impasto.

In the world of Seal House artists were arty, paintstained, carelessly dressed (in bright colours). Augustus's widow, the sainted Dodo, was still a make-believe gypsy of sixty years before. Her son Romilly, a priestly man, would sit for hours in quietist contemplation. There was no end to the Johns. Was the thickset man Edwin? There were Johns with Augustus's profile, beanpole Johns, sober Johns. They constituted more than a diffuse family, they made up a tribe with its own lore and traditions. Vivien's elder sister Poppet, much less cowed by her parents than Vivien, drank and smoked and laughed with appealing abandon.

One day she arrived with the most beautiful young woman I had ever seen, her stepdaughter, the starlet Talitha Pol. I stared, conspicuously amazed. She was, however, entirely atypical of the exotically shabby galere which regularly assembled at the house then moved down the road to the Prince of Wales. William Morris, founder of the Free University of London (a shed beyond the North Circular, and the first of several dodgily utopian ventures to bear that name), was a grown-up beatnik. He had filthy clothes, a lopsided beard, barley-sugar fingers, a worse scooter than Yuri's and a ginger girlfriend whose myopia forced her to wear glass bricks on her wan face. He also had a revolver with which he threatened a friend of mine who wouldn't sleep with him. Happily the great educator passed out and she ran away with a Spanish basketball pro.

The night before I left the crammer (and Seal House) Vivien gave a party for me – and herself – in the pub. It was a generous gesture which cannot but have rankled with John White, a man of fabulous meanness. It was also a curious gesture, for even the youngest of the guests were at least twenty years older than I was. But I was now a garrulous expert on Gilman, Ginner, Gore. I could sing for my supper. They had been my age in the war or through the privations of the late Forties. And it was this world that they carried with them – and whose memory and fascinations they had passed on to me, an intangible keepsake. They sort of made me their contemporary.

Two years later I returned to London, to RADA. I had learnt enough, mostly in France, to take part in the rites of the Cult of Youth – regrettably mandatory, and not to be confused with the immemorial rites of youth.

With some cause Vivien White was more edgily preoccupied than ever and John White more sullen than ever.

And Yuri had made a shift, the inevitable shift, from carefree to careless. He had a daughter. He was also a junky. Heroin was fairly rare in those days. But Yuri had always sought to go further, faster, deeper. He packed as many car crashes, scrapes, accidents, fights, trips, binges and blackouts into twenty-three years as most people fail to achieve in several lifetimes. He had no brakes. He was both supra-hedonist and an enthusiast for oblivion – the latter prompted by his loathing of his father. Had he not died when he did he'd probably have turned patricide.

Talitha Pol, a RADA student seven years before me, was now Mrs John Paul Getty. She and Yuri died within months of each other: overdose.

Now newness's time had arrived, at last.

LIST OF ILLUSTRATIONS

P. vi–vii: Parents at Lulworth Cove, autumn 1959.

P. 2: Author, 1959.

P. 15: Paternal grandfather, *c.*1917.

P. 53: Uncle Eric outside his garage, Cambridge Road, Portswood, Southampton, 1946.

P. 54: Auntie Mary outside her parents' house, 58 Shakespeare Avenue, Portswood, Southampton, *c.*1922.

P. 56: Mother, *c.*1919.

P. 59: Author, between Uncle Wangle and Auntie Ann's caravan and the Elsan. Walkford Woods, Highcliffe, 1955.

P. 79: Ken James painting beside the Avon in what would become his garden, Watersmeet Road, East Harnham, September 1960.

P. 93: The author and parents outside 55 Harnham Road, East Harnham, 1950. The face at the window is The First German Girl, Christine.

P. 106: Rowing on the Nadder with Posty, 1958.

P. 138: Holmwood School, on Choristers' Green, Salisbury Cathedral Close, September 1953. Left to right (standing): Janet –, –, Priscilla –, author, Howard Dodson, Caroline Colville, Janet Wheelwright, Christopher Lush; (kneeling): Elizabeth Morgan, Janet Sanger, Hilary Sinclair, Jennifer Laing, Susan Allenby, Elizabeth Drummond.

Harnham Road Group, at the gates to the Rose and Crown car park, April 1953. Left to right (standing): – Dean, author, Roger Davies, Susan Hapgood, Douglas Sewell, Graham Dean; (squatting): Paul Dean, —.

P. 143: Kalu, 1960.

P. 150: Roger Davies and the author, 1955.

P. 180: Mother, Mary Sutcliffe and Dorothea Craven, Birks Bridge, Duddon Valley, Furness, 1943.

P. 204: The garden at Watersmeet Road, East Harnham: the confluence of the Nadder and, further away, the Avon.

P. 229: The author and parents, St Malo, 1955.

P. 271: Father vaulting over a fence at Offenham near Evesham, c.1932. The building is the Fish and Anchor. The distant hill is where I believed the world ended.

P. 277: Left to right: Father, Uncle Hank, Auntie Kitty, Uncle Wangle. Foreground: maternal grandmother, Auntie Ann.

P. 287: Author with 38lb salmon taken at Ibsley near Fordingbridge, March 1952.

P. 288: Daniel Richmond, July 1965. (Photo courtesy LAT Photographic, with additional thanks to Mark Forster.)

P. 292: Author with Mother, Port Merion, August 1962.

P. 305 Paiforce Christmas Card, 1945.

P. 331: Author, 1964.

All photographs courtesy of the author, except where noted.